Always Resisting

Always Resisting

*Choosing Prison
Over Vietnam and Awakening
to American Racism*

Eric Newhall

McFarland & Company, Inc., Publishers
Jefferson, North Carolina

"(There'll Be Bluebirds Over) The White Cliffs of Dover" by Walter Kent and Nat Burton is used by permission of Walter Kent Music and Reservoir Media Music on behalf of Shapiro, Bernstein & Co., Inc.

Copyright © by Walter Kent Music (ASCAP) All Rights Reserved. Reprinted by Permission. Courtesy of Reservoir Media Music on behalf of Shapiro Bernstein & Co., Inc.

Note: All photos and illustrations not accompanied by rights and permissions information are used under the Fair Use doctrine of U.S. copyright law, which permits the limited use of copyrighted materials for purposes of scholarship, criticism, and commentary.

Author's statement: This memoir is a work of nonfiction based on real people and actual events. The names of some characters have been changed to protect their privacy and that of their families.

LIBRARY OF CONGRESS CATALOGING-IN-PUBLICATION DATA

Names: Newhall, Eric, 1945– author.
Title: Always resisting : choosing prison over Vietnam and awakening to American racism / Eric Newhall.
Other titles: Choosing prison over Vietnam and awakening to American racism
Description: Jefferson, North Carolina : McFarland & Company, Inc., Publishers, 2024 | Includes bibliographical references and index.
Identifiers: LCCN 2024030447 | ISBN 9781476694030 (print) ∞
ISBN 9781476653549 (ebook)
Subjects: LCSH: Newhall, Eric, 1945– | Conscientious objectors—United States—Biography. | Prisoners—United States—Biography. | College teachers—United States—Biography. | Vietnam War, 1961–1975—Conscientious objectors—United States. | Racism—United States.
Classification: LCC DS559.8.C63 N49 2024 | DDC 959.704/31 [B]—dc23/eng/20240809
LC record available at https://lccn.loc.gov/2024030447

BRITISH LIBRARY CATALOGUING DATA ARE AVAILABLE

ISBN (print) 978-1-4766-9403-0
ISBN (ebook) 978-1-4766-5354-9

© 2024 Eric Newhall. All rights reserved

No part of this book may be reproduced or transmitted in any form or by any means, electronic or mechanical, including photocopying or recording, or by any information storage and retrieval system, without permission in writing from the publisher.

Front cover images: *inset* Eric Newhall in his early years on the faculty at Occidental College, circa 1975. Photograph: Joe Friezer. © Occidental College. Courtesy Special Collections and College Archives, Mary Norton Clapp Library, Occidental College. *Background* © eyal granith/MIA Studio/Shutterstock.

Printed in the United States of America

McFarland & Company, Inc., Publishers
Box 611, Jefferson, North Carolina 28640
www.mcfarlandpub.com

"For Jacki"

Table of Contents

Acknowledgments   ix

Preface   1

Chapter 1. An Examined Life   5

Chapter 2. County Jail   35

Chapter 3. Fish Tank   46

Chapter 4. Mainline   73

Chapter 5. The Hole   149

Epilogue   189

Suggestions for Further Reading   213

Index   215

Acknowledgments

I want to acknowledge the people who stood by me during the decades I was working on *Always Resisting: Choosing Prison Over Vietnam and Awakening to American Racism*, and to thank them for their support and assistance:

My parents, for teaching me that the unexamined life is not worth living.

All the men who were in the Hole at Lompoc during August of 1969.

My colleagues and friends on the Occidental College Faculty, David Axeen, Norman Cohen, and Mike McAleenan, for reading early sections of this memoir long before anyone should have been asked to read any of it.

My writing coach and editor for hire, Mark Dery, for helping me trim down the "loose baggy monster" and for guiding me through the publication process.

My friend, Daryl Ogden, for conversations about writing and life that helped to produce a more hopeful and empathic book.

Dwight Morrill, my "partner in crime," for his friendship in the joint and ever since.

Dr. Patricia Gurin, family mentor and friend, for her wisdom and advice.

Dr. Lewis Merklin, the lone psychiatrist at Lompoc in 1969, for his support-group for draft resisters and for his recognition that prisons are "anti-therapeutic environments" and failed institutions.

My sister, Cynthia Newhall, for multiple phone conversations from Mississippi about race relations.

Youlonda and David Copeland-Morgan for their friendship, vision, and contributions to diversity at multiple institutions of higher education.

My friend, Jesus Trevino, an accomplished writer, who read my manuscript and urged me to persevere.

Logan Weidman, my son-in-law, for technical assistance above and beyond the call of duty.

Gary Mitchem, my editor at McFarland, whose advice and counsel helped move my manuscript through the final steps to completion.

Andrea Minkoff, my daughter, for her careful editing and proofreading.

Amanda Rodriguez-Newhall, my daughter, for being the inspiration—and motivation—that drove me to finish the book.

And, most of all, thank you to my life partner, Jacki Rodriguez—for everything.

Preface

This memoir is about one of those "hidden episodes of the past" Howard Zinn had in mind when he spoke of those moments "when, even if in brief flashes, people showed their ability to resist, to join together, and occasionally to win." The book is set, for the most part, inside Lompoc Federal Correctional Institution, where I was incarcerated for refusing to participate in the Vietnam War. *Always Resisting: Choosing Prison Over Vietnam and Awakening to American Racism* is about ordinary people resisting racism and violence, the conditions that prevailed in the prison at that time.

I arrived at Lompoc on April 28, 1968. I can remember the exact moment when things began to change for the better. During the last week in May, about a month after I'd arrived, my friend Dwight Morrill (also sentenced for refusing induction into the U.S. military) and I went out to the yard after breakfast to play basketball. On one of the two concrete courts, a full-court game between Native American inmates was in full swing. The other court was divided, as usual, between two segregated half-court games—White players at one end, Black players at the other.

Dwight and I joined the White players and played two games. At that point, the other players, mostly bikers and low riders, drifted off to other parts of the yard. Dwight and I were just getting warmed up and felt like playing some more, so we sat down on the grass to watch the Black game, hoping we'd be asked to play.

After about twenty minutes, two of the eight Black players dropped out of the game, saying they had to go to work in the kitchen. The remaining players scanned the area to find replacements so the four-on-four game could continue. A man nicknamed Crow, the best player on the court, asked several of the Black spectators if they wanted to play, but got no takers. Then he looked in our direction and said something to his friends. They laughed, and Crow sauntered over to where Dwight and I were sitting.

"You boys want to play some ball?" he asked us.

We heard his taunting use of "boys," but ignored it. We both wanted to play some ball with players who knew how to play.

"We thought you'd never ask," said Dwight.

"Let's run," I said.

Everything that happened at Lompoc later that summer began then and there on that ugly concrete basketball court when we came together to break the color line. In fact, the solidarity I forged for the first time in my life with Black, Latino, and Native American men my age, as well as White men whose social and economic backgrounds were worlds away from mine—played a significant role in shaping who I am today—as a professor, a spouse, a father, and as a citizen who believes in social justice.

Always Resisting traces my political awakening, and my efforts to understand and respond to mass incarceration, racism, and the political right's never-ending attempts to defer the real democracy promised by our Constitution. In the pages that follow, I trace my political evolution from my youth in an all–White neighborhood in the Portland, Oregon, of the 1950s and early 1960s; through my undergraduate experience at Occidental College in Los Angeles (from 1963 to 1967); my prison sentence; the powerful impact that my time behind bars had on both my 44-year teaching career and my 34-year marriage to Jacki Rodriguez, professor emeritus of psychology and Latino/a studies at Occidental College, and proud Chicana, born and raised in East L.A.

My experience in prison is the heart of this memoir. For the first time in my life, I had long, serious conversations with young Black and Latino men my age. For the first time, I experienced life in the United States, not from my privileged position in the White middle class, but from the perspective of oppressed groups. My time at Lompoc Federal Correctional Institution gave me a relatively brief but enlightening glimpse into what the novelist Toni Morrison refers to as the lives of "throwaway people."

My experience in prison had an unexpectedly positive impact on the rest of my life. When I think about Lompoc today, I feel hopeful, because I saw ordinary people speak truth to power, resist the prison culture of racism and violence, and experience a solidarity so strong that it changed the consciousness of everyone who was part of it. What I learned in prison helped me immeasurably in my life as a college professor, teaching American literature to diverse groups of students at Occidental College.

The final section of *Always Resisting* serves as a sobering counterpoint to the hope engendered by my time at Lompoc and reminds us of all the work that remains to be done. In the book's Epilogue, I discover that racism takes many forms and can be found even in outwardly progressive families like the one I was raised in. Decades after my release and in the last chapter of a long career as a professor, I come face to face with racism in the form of unconscious bias in my family of origin and in myself. This is a shocking discovery for a man to make late in life, and like many White Americans, I'm still attempting to make sense of it.

The social problems I discuss in this memoir are even more pressing today than they were for my generation 50 years ago because they have been exacerbated by climate change, which will require national and global cooperation if we're to solve the serious, potentially calamitous, threat it poses to humanity. Significant change never comes easily. As I've been telling my students for years, if you want a just society, your life will be a permanent struggle. This memoir is my attempt to pass along, to anyone concerned about the future of democracy, some of the valuable lessons I learned about resistance when I was young.

If history is to be creative, to anticipate a possible future without denying the past, it should, I believe, emphasize new possibilities by disclosing those hidden episodes of the past when, even if in brief flashes, people showed their ability to resist, to join together, occasionally to win. I am supposing, or perhaps only hoping, that our future may be found in the past's fugitive moments of compassion rather than its solid centuries of warfare.—Howard Zinn

The past is never dead. It's not even past.—William Faulkner

Chapter 1

An Examined Life

With the benefit of hindsight, I can see that my path to prison began, imperceptibly, when I was ten years old, in 1955, the year our family moved from Washington, Pennsylvania, to Portland, Oregon. My father, who taught philosophy at Washington and Jefferson College, had been offered a position in the Philosophy Department at Portland State College.

Looking back, those early years in Portland seem almost Edenic—*prelapsarian*, as literary critics like to say. Before the fall. At the time, I thought I lived in a perfect neighborhood. There was no crime. Neighbors knew neighbors. If I got lost or hurt, someone would notify my parents. My two sisters, the two younger brothers who'd arrived since we put down roots in Portland, and I explored the nearby woods, the fresh smell of Douglas fir all around us. Roses of every variety bloomed in front yards up and down our street. Every weekday, my father drove fifteen minutes to work at Portland State, at that time the newest school in the Oregon State system of higher education. My mother was a homemaker devoted to caring for five children until the youngest, Mark, entered the fourth grade, at which point she went "back to work." The Newhall family lived a version of the American Dream.

Today I can see what I couldn't see as a boy. There was little, if any, discussion of race in southwest Portland during the 1950s and early 1960s, because there was virtually no racial diversity. We lived culturally insulated and racially segregated lives. The state of Oregon has an extremely racist history, but that history was never discussed at my elementary school or, for that matter, my high school. Even today, Portland, Oregon, is one of the whitest cities in the United States among cities with a population of 500,000 or more.* There were no Black students at my elementary school or high school—not one. There were virtually no Latinos in all of Portland, and very few Asians. Most of the city's small population of

---

*Alana Semuels, "The Racist History of Portland, the Whitest City in America," *The Atlantic*, July 22, 2016.

CHIEF KLUXERS TELL LAW ENFORCEMENT OFFICERS JUST WHAT MYSTIC ORGANIZATION PROPOSES TO DO IN CITY OF PORTLAND

Ku Klux Klan leaders meeting with Captain of Police John T. Moore, Chief of Police L.V. Jenkins, District Attorney W. H. Evans, U.S. District Attorney Lester W. Humphreys, Mayor George L. Baker, and others, Portland, Oregon, August 1, 1921, as reported in the August 2, 1921, edition of the *Portland Telegram*. "The photograph indicates how comfortable KKK leaders were in the public spotlight during the early 1920's," notes The Oregon History Project website, "and how indulged they were by many civic governments." One of the Klansmen brazenly declared that the Klan felt free to administer lynch-mob justice because "some crimes are not punishable under existing laws, but the criminals should be punished." The OHP adds, "In a room full of enforcers of the law, the two Klan members spoke freely, without fear of prosecution." *Public domain; original archived at the Oregon Historical Research Library.*

African-Americans lived across the Willamette River in northeast Portland in a district called Albina. Although I didn't realize it at the time, Black Portlanders viewed our White-picket Eden on a hill as a closed White enclave. Our neighborhood wasn't *segregated* in the strict sense. It wasn't illegal for Blacks and Latinos to live in southwest Portland in those days, but they weren't welcomed either. The unwritten laws that enforced the whiteness of our part of town were *separation* and *exclusion*.

There were two Portlands when I lived there—a White Portland and a Black Portland with which my family and I had very little contact. My neighborhood was whiter than Melville's whale, and eventually that fact would prove to be a serious problem for all of us, Black and White alike.

The pivotal event in my early political development took place when I was fourteen and a first-year student at Woodrow Wilson High School.

Chapter 1. An Examined Life

Newhall family home for three generations (1956–2023), Portland, Oregon.
Courtesy Josephine Lura Newhall; used by permission.

I got up one Saturday morning near the end of February, ate a quick bowl of oatmeal, and was getting ready to meet several of my friends up the street to play some basketball at an outdoor hoop. It was cold outside, and the ground was wet, but if you grew up in Portland and loved basketball as I did, you played anyway. I can remember practicing my jump shot by myself at an outdoor basket for hours at a time when the ground was wet and the temperature near freezing.

"Hold your horses," my father called from the kitchen as I was bolting out the front door. "Why don't you come with me this morning?" he said casually. I could tell from the tone of his voice that something was up. "You can play basketball with those guys anytime." He'd already made up his mind: I was going with him. "Blame it on me if you want," he said. "Tell your friends I gave you no choice. Get your jacket. It might rain."

We drove along Terwilliger Boulevard in our aging Packard, into downtown Portland. To the east Mount Hood stood glistening white in the pale winter sun against the clear blue of the Oregon sky. We parked on Fifth Avenue, across the street from Woolworth's Department Store. We walked over to a line of about twenty people who were carrying signs and moving slowly up and down the sidewalk in front of the entrance to the store. Gathered near the picketers was a small crowd of people, some of whom were shouting hostile comments at the marchers: "Nigger lovers." "Communist trash." "Traitors." "Go back to Russia where you belong." The picketers simply kept walking, not bothering to respond in any way to the taunts showered on them. I remember wishing I were playing basketball with my friends.

My father picked up two signs from a pile on the sidewalk and handed one to me. It read "Freedom and Equality" in large black letters. My father's sign said simply, "Justice." We stepped into the picket line and started to walk back and forth in front of Woolworth's. The threatening mob grew larger, the angry voices louder. All but two of the picketers were White. I remember an elderly African-American man and woman walking together in the picket line that day. They didn't say anything, at least nothing that I could hear, but they were both still walking when my father and I left.

"Dad," I whispered urgently, "You said this was going to be interesting." Walking back and forth in front of Woolworth's Department Store was not going to help me realize my dream of playing shooting guard for the Boston Celtics. The Trailblazers had not come to Portland yet. My friends and I all wore low-cut black Converse All Star basketball shoes and rooted for Bill Russell, K.C. Jones, and the Boston Celtics.

"Keep your eyes and ears open," said my father. "We'll talk over lunch."

After we'd been walking for about two and a half hours, a wizened little old man suddenly ran up to the picket line and stopped in front of my father. His eyes were blood-shot, he needed a shave, and he smelled. I noticed that he had an egg-sized rock in his hand and wondered what he planned to do with it. He launched into a diatribe against my father, asking him, "Are you a card-carrying member of the Communist Party? How can you bring your own kid into something like this?" Cool under pressure, my father kept walking, giving no indication whatsoever that he was even aware of the man's presence.

We walked the picket line until noon, then handed in our signs to the man who seemed to be in charge and went to lunch at a nearby hamburger joint called the Carnival. It served charbroiled burgers and the best chocolate milkshakes in town—thick and creamy, almost like soft-serve ice cream.

"Well," said my father after we'd gotten our burgers, "What do you think?"

"I think I should have played basketball. Why did you want me to see this today?" I said. "It was pretty boring."

My father told me about the sit-ins earlier that month in North Carolina, when four Black students sat down at the Woolworth's lunch counter in Greensboro and asked to be served. The young men were shoved to the ground, squirted with ketchup and mustard, and beaten by a mob of angry White men. Their names were Ezell Blair, Jr., Franklin McCain, Joe McNeil, and David Richmond—names I didn't know then but know today because for the past forty years I've taught a seminar about the social movements of the 1960s.

"They're brave young men," my father said. "They deserve our support. That's why we're here. What we participated in today is called a 'sympathy picket.'" The Woolworth's in Portland served Black customers in 1960, but the Southern branches of the national chain were segregated. "We were picketing the Portland branch," my father explained, "to pressure the national chain to desegregate their southern stores."

"Will we make a difference?" I asked. "Will they change down South? Will they serve Negroes?"

"I don't know," he said. "I *do* know that we won't make any difference if we do nothing. There's power in the sound of marching feet. People tend to listen when they're losing money."

That Saturday morning in February of 1960 was the beginning of my political awakening—and the first small step along the path that would lead me to prison. After marching in the sympathy picket, I gradually started to pay attention to news stories about the civil rights movement. I remember seeing pictures of college students at other lunch counters as the sit-in movement spread rapidly across the South. It struck me that the students were about twenty years old, only five years older than I was. They were involved with serious issues, running significant risks; I was still playing games in the street with my friends. I wasn't instantly politicized after walking in the picket line that morning with my father, but my racial awareness was expanded. Before that day I didn't really see race or think about it; I was isolated in a sea of whiteness—White family, White church, White friends, White teachers, White classmates, White curriculum. After walking on the picket line that morning with my father, I became aware that there was a complicated world beyond the borders of my own comfortable neighborhood. I slowly began to see more clearly, more critically, noticing things I'd never noticed before.

Television played a crucial role in my awakening to the world beyond our neighborhood. Once I saw young people my own age being clubbed and swept down the streets by water cannon and frail, silver-haired, Black grandmothers set upon by vicious, snarling police dogs, I couldn't get free of the images. This was happening in our country. *My* country. Things had to change, I thought. I needed to do more than sit on the sidelines watching television.

§

In 1962, my junior year in high school, I was required to take a full year of American history. At the start of spring semester our teacher, a bright young Harvard grad in his mid-thirties, assigned us a research paper. We were to select an episode in American history since 1945 and write a fifteen-page paper about it. I struggled to come up with a topic. Nothing really sparked my interest.

"What's happening in your history class these days?" my mother asked me one evening at dinner.

"Nothing," I mumbled around a mouthful of baked potato. Like most teenagers, I turned monosyllabic when questioned about my school day.

"Come on," my mother said, never deterred. "You have to be studying something."

Published in 1958, *Stride Toward Freedom* is Martin Luther King, Jr.'s account of the 1955–1956 Montgomery bus boycott, an early milestone in the civil rights movement.

"America since World War II," I said unenthusiastically. "We have to write a paper about some episode in American history since World War II."

"What about a topic that deals with the civil rights movement?" my mother suggested. "Remember when your father took you down to Woolworth's a couple of years ago? What about the bus boycott in Montgomery, Alabama?" She went upstairs and came back with a book titled *Stride Toward Freedom* by Martin Luther King, Jr. "Try this," she said, handing it to me.

History had never seemed the slightest bit interesting to me before. It was just a long chain of dusty dates, places, old men, and events that didn't seem to relate to my life in any meaningful way.

I read *Stride Toward Freedom* in one day. What I found most engaging about the bus boycott in Montgomery, Alabama, was that it took place during my own lifetime—the boycott began in 1955 and ended in 1956—and its impact spread to Portland, Oregon. I could see the injustice in people having to move to the back of the bus simply because of the color of their skin. I still didn't know a single Black or Latino person. But reading about the boycott made it clear to me that change was urgently needed and that it could be brought about through non-violent means. And I could see the power in a mass movement. Learning about the bus boycott taught me that ordinary people can create change if they're united and act as one.

§

I graduated from Woodrow Wilson High School in June of 1963. I spent the summer working with two friends in the shipyards up in Vancouver, Washington, earning money to help pay my tuition at Occidental College, the small liberal arts school in Los Angeles that I planned to attend in the fall. I did well academically in high school, particularly in my humanities courses. I lettered in four sports and was named Most Valuable Player on our basketball team. I was self-conscious and uncomfortable in social situations because of a nervous tic that caused involuntary eye blinking. This self-consciousness about how I appeared to others, particularly young women I was attracted to, was a problem I carried with me to college.

The March on Washington took place that same year on August 28, a few weeks before I left Portland for Los Angeles, college bound. The March culminated in Martin Luther King's "I Have a Dream" speech—the high-water mark of the civil rights movement. Two hundred and fifty thousand people of all races, religions, and socio-economic backgrounds experienced a powerful and transformative sense of community; for many who were present that day, the impact of the march would last a lifetime. Watching it together on television, my family absorbed the spirit of the event.

§

I began college in September of 1963, about a month after Dr. King's famous speech. I felt socially out of place at Occidental, a continuation of my difficulties in high school. At Wilson High School I'd been socially inept and painfully self-conscious. I didn't know how to dance. I didn't go to the Senior Prom. Unsurprisingly, I was lonely much of the time at Occidental too; I spent a great deal of my time struggling with the heavy reading assignments for my classes. What social life I had consisted mostly of playing pickup basketball in the gym.

There is one day during my first year at Occidental I'll never forget: November 22, a date everyone my age remembers. The day John Kennedy was shot. I was waiting for someone to unlock the door to the room where my "Introduction to Philosophy" class was held when a classmate came running down the hall, tears streaming down his face. "The President's been shot, the President's been shot," he shouted, gasping for air. "My God, the President's been shot."

At first, I thought this was a bad joke he was playing on us. Then I saw his tears—tears of shock, pain, and grief. And it hit me with full force: President Kennedy had been shot and no one in that hallway knew how serious his condition was. Stunned, we walked numbly to the quad at the center of campus to see if anyone had additional information. A few minutes later, at 11 a.m. California time, President Kennedy was pronounced dead. Word spread quickly on campus—and around the world.

Until that day, I had always taken it for granted that assassinations of this sort took place in authoritarian dictatorships in underdeveloped parts of the world. Before November 22, 1963, it was simply unthinkable to me that the President of the United States could be shot and killed. Up to that moment, I'd lived, unwittingly, in an insulated bubble of social and political innocence. I'd never been touched directly by the political violence that plagued much of the rest of the world.

Many college students of my generation, particularly White students from the suburbs, had come of age behind a protective veil of innocence; President Kennedy's assassination tore that veil away. It was the beginning of a painful process of loss and disillusionment ("this isn't who we are") that was to continue to the end of the decade and, arguably, to the present day ("get your knee off my neck").

My time as an undergraduate was divided between my academic studies as an English major, my social life (what there was of it), and my political awakening and growth. At Occidental College in the mid–60s, there wasn't a great deal of overlap between these spheres, particularly for those of us who chose to major in English, a monastic pursuit that probably helped to prepare me to spend time in a cell when I arrived at Lompoc FCI (Federal Correctional Institution). The faculty was all White except for an Asian man, who taught in the Department of Philosophy and Religion, and all male except for eight women, most of them young and untenured. As an English major, I was never required to read a single work by an

Chapter 1. An Examined Life

author of color. No Frederick Douglass, nothing from the Harlem Renaissance, no Zora Neale Hurston, no Langston Hughes, no Richard Wright, no Ralph Ellison, no Gwendolyn Brooks, no James Baldwin.

The student body was nearly as White as the faculty. It included a handful of Latinos, a few more African-Americans, fifty or so Asian-Americans, and about ten non–White international students from around the globe. The Occidental I attended from 1963 through 1967 lagged behind schools like UC Berkeley and the University of Michigan with regard to the level of political activism on campus. It was a relatively conservative institution and, despite its location in Los Angeles, only marginally more diverse than the high school I had attended in Portland. The social climate had begun to simmer during the mid-sixties when I was an undergraduate, but it had not yet come to a full boil.

Throughout my sophomore year, the war in Vietnam was increasingly in the news. One of my history professors, an immigrant from Germany via Argentina, delivered a tirade in class one day about "American imperialism around the world," arguing that our presence in Vietnam was evidence of what he called "our national arrogance." No professor had ever talked this way in my English classes. In fact, I don't remember any of my English professors ever *mentioning* the war in Vietnam. At age nineteen, I was by no means a flag waver, but the tone of my professor's angry diatribe struck me as arrogant. Like most college students at that time, I knew little about international issues or foreign policy. Asia seemed far away and not particularly relevant to my life. Like most Americans in those days, I believed in "leaving foreign policy to the experts."

After my professor's outburst, I went straight to the library, looking for information about the small nation of Vietnam—and some ammunition to refute my professor's remarks, which struck me then as smug and self-righteous. The intensity of his anger, a level of outrage I hadn't seen in any of my other professors, made me question his objectivity. Some part of me still believed that America was a "city upon a hill," a beacon of democracy spreading our enlightened values wherever we went.

I found little in the library about Vietnam, but, to my surprise, what I found corroborated my professor's views. The United States had, in fact, supported the French colonial presence in Vietnam from 1945 until 1954, when the Vietnamese defeated the French at a place called Dien Bien Phu. After the French were defeated, Vietnam was temporarily divided into two halves—North Vietnam and South Vietnam. Elections were supposed to have taken place in 1956 to reunify the country, but for reasons I couldn't understand at the time, these elections never happened. One article by Bernard B. Fall, a war correspondent and expert on Indochina (as it was then called), wasn't flattering to our government or our leaders, but I read it with a skeptical eye. At that point I was what critical theorists now refer to as "a resisting reader."

I'd been following news about the civil rights movement with increasing interest since my father took me to the picket at Woolworth's. Now, I began to think about American foreign policy as well, particularly our increasing involvement in Vietnam. It was hard not to think about Vietnam from 1965 on, because news about the war was constant, and there was significant disagreement about how well it was going. Lyndon Johnson had campaigned in 1964 as the peace candidate who, as he put it, "would not send American boys to fight a war that Vietnamese boys should fight." He portrayed his ultra-conservative opponent, Barry Goldwater, as an anti-communist extremist who would use nuclear weapons at the slightest provocation.

During the summer of 1964, Congress passed the controversial "Gulf of Tonkin Resolution," which enabled President Johnson to wage war against Vietnam without an official declaration of war. In the final months of '64 he began to increase the number of American "advisers" in Vietnam substantially. President Kennedy had sent more than 15,000 "advisers" to Vietnam; by 1965 there were so many American boots on the ground that President Johnson could no longer plausibly refer to them as "advisers," so he started calling them what they were: ground troops.

§

As I entered my senior year at Occidental, it slowly dawned on me that I could be drafted to fight in the Vietnam War. Until that fall of 1966, the war had seemed real enough, but it had also seemed distant. As the fall quarter moved along, however, the war showed no signs of ending soon. If you believed the generals who testified before Congress and spoke to the media, the prognosis was good. The body counts always ran in our favor, there was always "light at the end of the tunnel," the enemy was becoming "increasingly discouraged by our superior firepower." Yet we rarely heard directly from the other side. Most of our soldiers in the field were nineteen or twenty years old. They knew next to nothing about Vietnam before going there to kill or be killed, and they certainly had no idea what most of the Vietnamese people thought about Americans bombing their country in the name of spreading democracy and drawing the line against the spread of communism. It's no wonder I struggled to understand the acrimonious national debate about our foreign policy in Southeast Asia.

The issue of the Vietnam War came to a head for me during my senior year, in the spring of 1967. As my final quarter as an undergraduate moved along, I found it more and more difficult to concentrate on my classes. The news media showered us with stories about the war and about civil unrest here at home that was rooted in racial injustice. I was twenty-one years old, and it bothered me that American soldiers, many younger than I was, were being killed in droves. Some of them were drafted right out of high school. Others enlisted, full of idealism, responding to President Kennedy's famous call to "ask not what your country can do for you but what you can do for your country." "Always remember," my father told us, "there are conscientious soldiers just as there are conscientious objectors to war." That's part of what made the war in Vietnam the most divisive American conflict since the Civil War. On both sides of the cultural divide, rational and essentially decent people believed deeply that the other side was not only wrong, but criminally wrong.

For the first time in my life, I failed to complete all of the work my professors assigned. I wanted to graduate at the end of the spring quarter with my class, but amid the chaos around me, I found it impossible to analyze metrical variations in Shakespearean sonnets. I would sit down at my dorm-room desk to write an assigned paper, and my mind would wander off to images of violence in Vietnam or in American streets: Newark, Detroit, Oakland.

Pressure was building on young men my age to confront the Vietnam question on a personal level. By the spring of 1967, I was reading and watching news of the war intently. At school I read the *Los Angeles Times*, some of the political journals in our library, and watched the nightly coverage of our first televised war. At home in Portland, during school breaks, I read *Liberation*, the *I.F. Stone Newsletter*, and *Ramparts Magazine*, progressive journals my parents subscribed to, all of which were strongly opposed to the war. I read that we now had over half a million troops on the ground in Vietnam and that over 13,000 of our soldiers had died, to say nothing of the Vietnamese dead. Earlier in the year, Muhammad Ali had been stripped of his heavyweight boxing title for resisting the draft. William Fulbright, the chair of the Senate Foreign Relations Committee, was holding hearings about the Vietnam War. In addition, both of Oregon's senators, Wayne Morse, and Mark Hatfield, opposed the war.

It bothered me immensely that Bertrand Russell and Jean-Paul Sartre, two of my intellectual heroes, were critical of America's involvement in Southeast Asia. I found this confusing, and wondered if my country was on the right side of history. *Which side should we be on? Why did we side with France, a colonial power—rather than supporting Vietnamese independence at the end of World War II? Didn't the United States begin in revolution against the British? If an anti-colonial revolution was right for us, why wasn't it right for the Vietnamese?* I began to wonder whose interests were being served by our presence in Vietnam—and whose needs were being ignored, and whose rights trampled on—in what we were told was America's crusade to spread democracy.

Martin Luther King was scheduled to visit Occidental College on May 5, 1967, about a month before our commencement. I was eager to hear him speak. During my last term I'd begun to think seriously about refusing induction if I received a draft notice. At the same time, I felt intimidated by the implications of such a decision and the potential consequences of opposing my own government's policy, especially during wartime. I'd read about young men at Stanford, Berkeley, and Michigan burning their draft cards, but nothing like that was yet happening at Occidental.

I was looking forward to Dr. King's visit in May. I thought that hearing him might help me to figure out what I should do to resolve the most important personal question I'd ever confronted. Everyone knew that Dr. King was a pacifist and that he opposed all wars on principle, but prior to 1967 he had carefully avoided any specific criticism of President Johnson's foreign policy. Johnson had, arguably, been more supportive of civil rights than any president in American history. It was Johnson, after all, who had pushed the Civil Rights Act of 1964 and the Voting Rights Act of 1965 through an ambivalent Congress. It was Johnson's apparent soundness on domestic policy that made me uneasy about resisting his decision to intervene in Southeast Asia. He was a New Dealer and protégé of FDR whose vision of a "Great Society" was rooted in his own experiences growing up poor in west Texas. I was looking forward to Dr. King's visit in May because I had some specific questions that I hoped to be able to ask him about the relationship between our foreign policy and the anti-poverty programs President Johnson hoped to put in place.

As it turned out, most of my questions were answered before Dr. King arrived in Los Angeles. On April 4 of that year he delivered a historic speech at the Riverside Church in New York entitled "Beyond Vietnam: A Time to Break Silence." He told his listeners that his conscience would no longer allow him to remain silent about the Vietnam War. Dr. King read the opening line of a recent statement by the Executive Committee of Clergy and Laymen: "A time comes when silence is betrayal." For him, that time had come, he said. Although Dr. King had expressed his opposition to the war before in general terms, this was the first time he directly attacked the Johnson administration's foreign policy in specific detail, and it was the first time he had spoken publicly about a connection between the civil rights movement and the war in Vietnam.

I saw clips of this speech on the evening news the day Dr. King delivered it and read the entire text in the next day's *Los Angeles Times*. I pored over it intently, taking in every word. As I read, many of my doubts about what I should do if I received a draft notice evaporated. Although I remained concerned about what the future might hold for me, I remember feeling an inner calm. From this point on, I had a growing sense of clarity about what I *should* do if I were called to fight in Vietnam.

Still, this emerging conviction didn't entirely dispel my uncertainty and anxiety. I knew that if I acted on my new sense of what I "ought" to do, I would be at odds with most of the people I knew in Portland, most of my classmates at Occidental, and most of my professors in the English Department. Dr. King accused our government of being "the greatest purveyor of violence in the world today." He saw the war as the enemy of the poor and believed that if we were at war In Vietnam, we would not be able to afford to wage a war on poverty here at home. In addition, he believed that we were on the wrong side of an anti-colonial struggle in Vietnam. The Vietnamese had driven out the French only to have the United States replace the French as Western invaders of their country. We were denying the people of Vietnam the right to self-determination, he argued, because we didn't like the ideology of their leader, Ho Chi Minh.

Students in my classes today feel much more comfortable with the Martin Luther King who led the Montgomery Bus Boycott than they do with the anti-war leader who spoke out so powerfully and persuasively against Lyndon Johnson's foreign policy. I point out to them that the same man did both. The older Martin Luther King was able to see the connection between our costly intervention in Vietnam and our failure to alleviate the suffering of the poor in the United States. He was able, before he was assassinated, to see through the rhetoric of political leaders of *both* parties to the inhumanity of what we were doing in Southeast Asia.

For the next four weeks, I waited impatiently for Dr. King to arrive at Occidental. I was on edge. I had difficulty sleeping. Time dragged. I was sure I'd be drafted right after I graduated in June. I knew that if I refused induction, I'd wind up in prison. Going to class was painful. The thought of going to prison, the rising anger in African American communities around the country, and the building intensity of the anti-war movement made it impossible for me to focus on my academic work.

The self I knew from my Portland days still had traditional goals and wanted to be successful in the gray-flannel-suit sense: good grades, graduate school, career as a college professor, live a comfortable life in the suburbs somewhere as my parents had done. But my increasingly alienated and politicized self was growing in strength. This part of me thought more about civil rights and the war in Vietnam than about classes and pursuing a career. This part of me thought that having a felony on my record was less objectionable than killing people who simply sought independence from foreign powers, people who refused to submit to the colonial yoke. This part of me was beginning to question the value of the education I was

Martin Luther King, Jr. with Occidental College President Richard Gilman, Occidental College, April 1967. *Photo: Joe Friezer. © Occidental College. Courtesy Special Collections and College Archives, Mary Norton Clapp Library, Occidental College.*

receiving and the moral position of Occidental College and higher education in general; I wondered whether we were truly being educated or simply being prepared to become faceless cogs in "the system."

I was starting to become a resister.

On May 5, 1967—Cinco de Mayo—Dr. King came to Occidental College. Our main auditorium, Thorne Hall, was filled for his speech. The atmosphere in the auditorium crackled with nervous energy. It was standing room only, and additional arrangements were made to set up loudspeakers outdoors so that people who didn't get a seat inside could at least listen to the talk.

That morning Dr. King drew heavily on the speech he had given the month before in New York at the Riverside Church, but he also made some pointed references to Watts and the uprising that had taken place there during the summer of 1965. "If we want peace at home and abroad," he said, "we need to work for social justice. If you want peace, work for justice." At the end of his address, the crowd erupted, giving Dr. King a standing ovation.

Then, he took questions from the audience. A conservative classmate, the head of the Young Republicans, walked over to one of the microphones that had been set up in the aisles. "How was it," he asked, that Dr. King was "speaking out so emphatically about American foreign policy when all of his political experience to date was in the more limited area of civil rights?" I've never forgotten Dr. King's answer. He said that his experience had taught him that there's a connection between our foreign and domestic policies. He'd seen the war on poverty get off to a promising start under President Johnson's leadership only to have funding and energy diverted to the Vietnam War. "We can't have guns *and* butter," he said. "I have to speak out against the war because the war is undermining the civil rights movement and the War on Poverty here at home. I am not linking the two movements. I'm simply pointing out that, in fact, they are linked."

A young woman walked to one of the microphones and asked Dr. King if he believed that it was possible to eliminate racial prejudice by passing legislation like the Civil Rights Act. "Passing legislation cannot root out racial prejudice that is deeply embedded in the hearts and minds of many of our citizens," replied Dr. King. "That process is going to take years, perhaps a good many years. However, I think it is important to distinguish between *prejudice* and *discrimination*. Prejudice is an *attitude*, and discrimination is an *action*. I would ask you to pass legislation today that makes it illegal to beat me over the head for demanding my legal rights. Make it illegal to discriminate against people because of the color of their skin while we continue to work to root out prejudices that have deep historical roots. Perhaps if our children are raised in an environment in which discrimination is illegal, it will move us forward into a new era in which racial prejudice does not exist."

Dr. King's speech raised my sagging morale and helped to confirm my growing conviction that I should not participate in the American war effort in Vietnam. The war, unjust in itself, drained people and resources from the struggle against racial and economic justice in this country. To fight racism and poverty, I had to resist the war.

After Dr. King's visit, the rest of spring quarter and commencement seemed anti-climactic. Academically, I was just going through the motions. The English Department at Occidental in 1967 was proficient but, for the most part, politically disengaged. I can see now that the mid-sixties, when I was an undergraduate, were a transition period from the early to the late years of the decade, which would become synonymous, in hindsight, with campus radicalism, the counterculture, drugs, and the Black Power movement. Protest against the war was beginning to simmer in 1967, but it took a while to reach the boiling point. As a result, those of us who were thinking about refusing induction or applying for conscientious objector status were more isolated from each other than would be the case by the end of the decade. I was aware of only one classmate who was thinking of refusing induction or going to Canada, and he was criticized by his parents for "going away to college and becoming a pinko."

I don't remember much about my graduation other than a conversation I had with my parents after all the formal ceremonies were over. We spent the evening talking at the nearby Comfort Inn where my family was staying, with the television on in the background to keep my younger siblings occupied. Eventually, after everyone else had gone to bed, my father poured three glasses of red wine and I sat down to have a serious conversation with my parents.

"Well, what's next?" my father asked. "What's the next phase?" This was the sort of question my father liked to ask all his children. It was one of the ways he encouraged us to "live the examined life."

"I'm not sure, Dad," I said. I've applied to do graduate work in literary studies at UCLA, next year, and I'm waiting to hear back from them. But I'm also expecting to hear from my draft board any time after I graduate. "I really feel sort of strange right now. It's odd. Until recently I've worked hard in all my classes, but I don't feel as though I've really learned very much. In fact, I feel sort of ignorant."

He chuckled. "Socrates would see that as a hopeful sign."

"How is that hopeful? It feels pretty disconcerting."

"Socrates said that a wise man knows how much he doesn't know. Only a fool thinks he knows it all. At least you understand that your knowledge has some limits and that there's a lot more to learn. That puts you ahead of most people."

"Where did he say that?"

"Plato's *Apology*. Try reading it."

"I'll do that."

We sipped our wine in silence for a few minutes. Then I decided I owed my parents a more complete answer to my father's question about what was next for me. "Based on what I'm reading in the newspapers and watching on television, I think I'm going to be drafted this summer, and if I am, I think I'm going to refuse induction. I don't think we should be interfering in Vietnam when we have serious problems in our own country."

"So that's what's on your mind," my father said. "I could tell that something was bothering you."

"I've done a lot of reading, I've listened carefully to the news on television, and I've followed the political debate in Congress," I said. "I think I understand the arguments on both sides of the question. The bottom line, for me, is that the arguments against the war are far more convincing than the argument that we need to stop the spread of communism in Southeast Asia."

"As you know, your mother and I agree with you completely about the war," my father said. "The question I have is about the most effective way to make yourself unavailable to the war effort. Have you thought any more about applying for conscientious objector status?"

"I've thought about it a lot," I said, "but that's just not me. I'm a non-violent person, but I'm not a pacifist. If I'm drafted, I'm going to refuse induction. I'm just going to say 'no.'"

"Do you know what that means?" he said.

"It means a fine of up to $10,000 and a prison term of up to five years," I said. "I've looked into this. In the South, the sentences are closer to the maximum. In the Bay Area they're running around eighteen months. I've followed a few trials in the Portland area, and the average sentence up there seems to be about twenty-four months."

"I'd urge you to consider applying for CO status, anyway," my father said. My father was a pacifist who had internalized the values of Mahatma Gandhi and Martin Luther King. In contrast, I'm a non-violent person who is capable of violence if pushed too far or if I think a particular situation leaves me no other viable option.

"Your father's right," my mother said. "I don't like the idea of your spending time in prison."

"I'll keep thinking about it," I said, "but any way I slice it I come out as a 'selective objector.' The government's view is that individuals can't pick and choose their wars, and I understand their point. To be classified as a CO, I have to claim to object to all wars. I'm not sure what I would have done during World War II or what I might do in some future war. I'm only being asked to fight in one war, and that's the one I object to."

My father looked at me for a while. Then, he put his hand on my shoulder. I remember this clearly, because in general he wasn't emotionally demonstrative. Despite his progressive politics, my father was, in many other respects, a man of his generation.

"I want you to know that whatever you decide to do about this, you have your mother's and my complete support."

"Our complete support, no matter what you decide," my mother echoed.

§

After graduation, I went home to Portland for the summer and waited to see if I would hear from my Draft Board. Down in San Francisco people my age were creating a counterculture, a community of mutual support, but in Portland the summer of '67 didn't feel much like "the Summer of Love"; I felt alienated, alone, unsettled. I had received a student deferment for four years while I was an undergraduate, but that ended when I graduated. I still clung to the faint hope that the war would be over before I received a draft notice, but it showed no signs of ending soon, despite the optimistic predictions from generals and constant assurances from politicians that we had just "turned a corner in Vietnam."

§

As things turned out, I was accepted at UCLA in literary studies for the academic year 1967–1968. I did not hear from my draft board before classes began in the fall, so I rented a small apartment in Venice and started graduate school. I enjoyed my classes that first year at UCLA, but my single most powerful memory came during the spring quarter, on April 4, 1968, and had nothing to do with academics.

Late in the afternoon I was driving along Venice Boulevard, heading back to my apartment, when a report came over the car radio. Martin Luther King, Jr., had been shot and killed in Memphis, Tennessee. The news hit me like a vicious blow to the solar plexus. I remember pulling my car over to the curb to catch my breath and collect my thoughts. Dr. King was a voice of peace, reason, and compassion in a country gone mad with war, racism, and violence. It can be dangerous to be prematurely right. Dr. King had a beautiful vision of an inclusive democracy, what he called the "beloved community," but he'd preached his vision before most of his fellow citizens were ready for it. He paid the ultimate price for sharing a vision that others weren't yet prepared to embrace, for seeing too far, too soon. The loss of Martin Luther King was a blow from which our country has never fully recovered.

After classes ended for the year in June, I went home to Portland for the summer. I wanted to return to graduate school in the fall, but the war was not going well, and more and more young men were being drafted and sent to fight in Vietnam. The summer dragged along. I had the strange sensation of dangling in an existential vacuum. I felt disconnected from everything and everyone except my immediate family. The rest of the world moved ahead with business as usual, indifferent to my thoughts, concerns, and as time went on, my increasing anxiety about the uncertain future.

In the first week of August, I came home from painting a house in

Northeast Washington, D.C., on fire during riots following the assassination of civil rights leader Martin Luther King, Jr., April 5, 1968. *Used by permission of Underwood Archives, Inc./Alamy Stock Photo.*

nearby Lake Oswego and found a letter waiting for me at my place at the dinner table. It was from my draft board. It ordered me to report to the Portland Induction Center at 7 a.m. on August 26, 1968.

§

There wasn't a cloud in the sky that morning, unusual for Portland at any time of year. If it had been a scene in a novel, the literature student in me would've flagged that cloudless sky as a textbook example of situational irony. The Induction Center was on Third Street, only fifteen minutes or so from our house. I parked, fed some quarters into the parking meter, and walked into the Center.

The young men to be inducted that morning were assembled in Room 101 B. Twenty rows of chairs, twenty chairs per row, nearly all of them occupied. The buzz of quiet conversation filled the room. At about 7:15 a man dressed in military khakis walked into the room carrying copies of a one-page form that he passed out. The questions asked for basic information—name, address, telephone number, and so on. The last question was, *"Do you intend to accept induction into the Armed Services today?"* They wanted to know how many troublemakers they had on their hands in this group of about four hundred men.

The officer in charge collected our forms and carried them into an adjoining room, where other khaki-clad men skimmed and sorted them. The officer came back into the room.

"Men," he said, "When I call your name, follow the blue line down the hallway and up the stairs to Room 203." He began to read names in alphabetical order. He read rapidly until there were only four of us left in the room. "You boys follow me," he barked, scowling at us. I remember thinking to myself, *"Who are you calling 'boy?'"*

He led us to a smaller room down the hall where older men in military uniforms ordered us to sit down on metal folding chairs.

"You boys are making a big mistake," said the man in charge. "Do you all understand the significance of what you're doing?" *I know what I'm doing,* I thought to myself. *Do you understand the significance of what you're doing? Have you even thought about the significance of what you're doing?*

We all nodded that we did.

"All right," he said. "Let's do the drill. You boys stand on that white line over there and listen to what I'm going to read you."

The four of us walked over to the line and listened while the man read a formal statement. It concluded by asking us to accept induction into the Armed Forces of the United States by taking one step forward. *I would prefer not to*, I thought to myself. No one moved. Up to that point I had spoken out against the war, written letters against it, participated in small demonstrations and anti-war marches in Portland, but I hadn't yet done anything illegal. This was the moment I parted ways with most of my fellow Americans and officially became a resister.

"This decision is going to haunt all of you for the rest of your lives," the man in charge said to us. "The country is calling for your support, and the four of you are refusing to answer the call. Think of how ashamed your parents must feel." *My parents might surprise you*, I thought.

At this point, two men dressed in black suits entered the room, and the three military men returned to their offices.

"Gentlemen," said one of the dark-suited men. "We are with the Federal Bureau of Investigation, and we have a few questions to ask you. It won't take more than 10 minutes. Then you will be free to go about your business."

Jesus, I thought. *I'm about to be interviewed by the FBI. The motherfucking FBI.* My palms were suddenly sweaty.

"We'll start with you," said the agent in charge, pointing his finger at me. "Please come up to this table." His manner was cool and detached, unlike that of the military man earlier who was obviously irritated with us.

I did as I was told. The agent asked me a series of questions, focusing on my membership in political organizations, my thoughts about the United States, and my loyalty to the country. I told the two agents that I was a loyal citizen of the United States but that I had become convinced over time that the war in Vietnam was immoral and that it was doing great damage to the United States as well as to Vietnam. That was it. I was free to leave, said the agent in charge.

As I walked back to my car, I felt strangely different, renewed by the events of the morning. I felt more fully alive, more engaged with the world than I'd ever felt before. Some of the artificial veneer of my daily life had been stripped away, and my true relationship to the state and my fellow citizens was revealed to me with crystal clarity. The state was telling me that if I carried out its orders, I would retain my good standing and reputation, but if I did not do as I was told, I would lose favor and be stigmatized and punished.

It's as though a great wall was erected between my fellow citizens and me that morning, and that wall has never really come down in all the years since. I don't think I'm the only one who feels this way. The bitter disagreement about civil rights and the Vietnam War will haunt my generation until all of us are gone and it won't be over even then because, again, the past is never really past. For my generation, the disagreement about the Vietnam War and the struggle for racial equality have never really ended. The open wound has closed, but for many of us, the scars remain.

§

As I drove home along Terwilliger Boulevard, I savored the view. I'd taken this drive literally thousands of times before, but this time I looked at it with fresh eyes. Mount Hood in the distance, the trees on both sides of the road, the rose gardens in Laurelhurst Park down at the foot of Terwilliger, the Carnival on the right hand side of the road just before I turned left up the hill: the familiar landmarks of a million childhood memories seemed vaguely alien, all of sudden, in some way I couldn't quite put my finger on; that trip to the Induction Center had changed me—and my relationship to the world I knew.

I was still feeling more than a little shaken at being interviewed by the FBI. I knew those guys have a lot of power, that they can play rough, and that I was just one little insignificant citizen. On the other hand, my head was clear. I felt lighter, as though a burden had been removed from my back. I knew why I was doing what I was doing. For the first time in my life, I'd had a taste of what it feels like to be liberated. I'd read that word in books countless times, but this was the first time I'd ever actually *felt* what it meant. My consciousness changed that morning—permanently.

§

Life went along for the most part just as it had during the earlier part of the summer. I continued to earn some money painting houses. I also began to attend potluck dinners at a Unitarian church that had taken a public stand against the Vietnam War. These dinners were an attempt to build resistance to the war as well as to support young men such as myself who had made the decision to refuse induction. The Unitarians were part of what came to be called "the Portland Resistance."

I first met Bigfoot at one of these dinners. I was seated at a table in the large basement of the Unitarian Church, eating lasagna, when he walked in. I knew immediately who he was, because he'd been described to me by a friend of my parents who knew both of us. Bigfoot, or Foots, as he would come to be known at Lompoc (real name: Dwight Morrill), was about 6'5", weighed a very solid two hundred and twenty-five pounds and did indeed have Yeti-sized feet. He had long, dark brown hair pulled back in a ponytail and a full beard. He wore Levi's, a blue work shirt, and a denim jacket—the unofficial uniform of the counterculture. After he'd loaded up his plate from the potluck dishes people had brought—lasagna, tuna casserole, macaroni and cheese, homemade wheat bread, and a large cucumber salad—he took a seat at my table.

We immediately began to share thoughts and compare experiences: how we came to oppose the war, why we decided to refuse induction rather than escaping to Canada, going underground, or applying for CO status.

Chapter 1. An Examined Life

Dwight Morrill during his senior year of high school in Ashland, Oregon, 1966. *Courtesy Dwight Morrill; used by permission.*

Dwight's father was a minister in the Brethren Church who had died when Dwight was five years old. Their mother, a registered nurse in Ashland, Oregon, had raised Dwight, his older brother, Hank, and his older sister, Edie. Dwight and I shared a comfortable middle-class upbringing, and we had both grown up in households filled with books and serious conversations about ideas. I had just graduated from Occidental when we met, and Dwight had just finished his sophomore year at Whitworth College up in Spokane, Washington.

After the dinner ended, we walked a few blocks to a coffee shop, where we talked until 2:00 in the morning. Neither of us knew anyone else who was going through what we were; we found it reassuring to compare notes with another draft resister. Dwight's mother and sister were initially very upset about his decision to refuse induction, he said, but they had gradually come around to his way of thinking. Now, he had the full support of his mother and sister, but his older brother, who worked for one of the major oil companies, was angry with him for disgracing the family name.

I told him that my parents worried about me and still wished I'd filled out the CO form so I could do civilian service outside prison, but that they agreed with my view of the war—or, rather, I agreed with their view of the war, since most of my core values could be traced back to my parents and how I was raised.

A few minutes after 2:00 a.m. we both remembered that we had to get up and go to work the next morning. We shook hands, exchanged phone numbers, and agreed to stay in touch in the days ahead. I remember thinking that I'd just met someone who would remain a lifelong friend, regardless of what happened in the next few years.

§

It felt strange to be back home in Portland in familiar surroundings, a college graduate living in my old bedroom in my parents' house and waiting for the government's next move. I was in limbo, unmoored from the social structures that had defined my life up to that point. I continued to paint houses to earn spending money, and, with the permission of several instructors, I audited some English courses at Portland State in case I eventually returned to graduate school. I heard nothing from the government about what they planned to do with me for five months until the arrival of a letter in early February of 1969 informing me that I had been indicted and that the date set for my arraignment was March 18, 1969. Clearly, the government had not forgotten about me.

Although my family would have been considered middle class in those days, we couldn't afford a lawyer. I was assigned a court-appointed attorney named Hardy Myers, a soft-spoken, intelligent man in his late thirties or early forties when I met with him. He asked me some questions, trying to get a sense of what my situation looked like from a legal perspective. After a while he paused and looked at me. "Mr. Newhall," he said, "your position is untenable from a legal point of view. You're suggesting that the law you violated is illegitimate and that because of that you're not guilty. No judge will accept that argument."

"I think the government's position is morally untenable," I replied. "If I'm in a legally untenable position it's only because the government has forced me into that position. I'm going to plead 'not guilty,' and I want to tell the judge exactly what I think of the war and the people who are running it."

Hardy Myers shook his head slowly and said, "Mr. Newhall, I'm not really sure what I can do for you."

He was a decent man who was just trying to do his job; I simply didn't fit neatly into any of the standard legal categories.

On October 15, 1969, hundreds of Oregon State University students marched from the quad to Central Park. Their protest, staged in solidarity with student anti-war activists across the nation, was part of Vietnam Moratorium Day. *Photo: John L. Robbins. © Oregon State University; used by permission of the Oregon State University Special Collections and Archives Research Center, Corvallis, Oregon.*

"Mr. Myers," I said to him, "I'm not interested in trying to beat this charge on some sort of technicality. I want to speak directly to my government—the government's representatives, at least—and tell them what

I think about the war. I want to represent myself." *Legal technicalities are beside the point*, I thought. *The point is to speak out in some small way against policies I consider to be destructive and deeply immoral.*

"Mr. Newhall," said Myers, with what seemed to be a mixture of sympathy and frustration, "Have you ever heard the old expression, 'the man who defends himself has a fool for a client?'"

§

On March 18, 1969, I was formally arraigned in the Federal Court in downtown Portland. The judge's last name was Belloni; the prosecutor was Tommy (not "Thomas") Hawk. It was hard not to hear those names as ill omens. Judge Belloni, a thoughtful man in his late fifties or early sixties with black hair and black-framed glasses to match, set April 7, 1969, as the date for my trial. He didn't appear particularly hostile toward me because of my political views. Just the opposite: his demeanor was concerned, even avuncular. He was just another guy doing his job in unusual circumstances for which nothing in his life on the bench so far had fully prepared him.

It turned out that Dwight and I had both been assigned to Judge Belloni's court and that our trials had been scheduled to take place on the same day—April 7. In fact, they were both scheduled to take place in the morning of that day.

I spent the next few weeks in a profoundly unsettled state of mind, getting ready for my trial. I've always tended to procrastinate, and despite the gravity of the situation, I delayed writing the statement I planned to deliver in court. Upstairs, in my old bedroom, I worked at the same wooden desk I'd used in high school. I wrote out a detailed outline of what I wanted to say on a sheet of lined yellow paper and started typing after breakfast on Sunday morning, April 6. I finished typing the last paragraph, re-read my statement one last time, and went to bed around 2 a.m. Monday morning.

My father cancelled all his classes on April 7, 1969—according to my mother it was only the third time he had cancelled any class in over twenty years of teaching. I remember driving down Terwilliger Boulevard to the Federal Courthouse. My father and mother were sitting in the front, my dad at the wheel; my brother Matt, my sister Helen, and I were in the back seat. I was a little nervous and having my family around me made me feel better. I was going up against the FBI and the federal government. I believed I was right in my resistance to the war, but I couldn't help feeling intimidated by the tremendous power aligned against me.

The five of us walked into the courtroom together. The prosecutor was already seated at the table on the left, so I sat down by myself at the table on the right. My parents and siblings sat together in the front row of the gallery. After a few minutes I saw Dwight Morrill walk in along with his mother and his sister, Edie.

At 10 a.m. sharp, Judge Belloni entered the courtroom, and the bailiff asked us to rise. Judge Belloni told us to be seated and asked the clerk to call the first case. The first case was "The United States of America vs. Eric Luther Newhall." Judge Belloni turned to me and asked me how I intended to plead. "Not guilty," I said. The prosecutor, Tommy Hawk, called only one witness—one of the military officers who'd been present on the day I refused induction. The officer testified that I had, in fact, refused to step forward on August 26, 1968, when ordered to do so. That was the prosecution's entire case.

I had the surreal feeling that I was an actor in a play or a TV show, *Perry Mason,* or something like that. I had refused to obey the law; case closed. On the other hand, I'd decided to make it clear that I was a serious person who had thought long and hard about the Vietnam War before I refused induction, not someone who broke the law capriciously. Gandhi, whom I'd been reading in the months leading up to my trial, is clear on this point. He believed that if you plan to commit civil disobedience to put pressure on a particular law, it is important to obey all other laws. Several of my friends in the peace movement thought this was a silly position because, they argued, the whole system was corrupt to the core. For my part, I still think King and Gandhi were right. I still believe in a system of laws written by duly elected officials.

In my sports coat, white shirt, olive slacks, and tie, I even looked the part of an upstanding, law-abiding citizen. Dwight, in contrast, was every Middle American's idea of a hippie draft resister in his blue work shirt, Levi's, beard, and peace medallion.

When I rose to speak in my defense, I read my statement—four single-spaced pages, hammered out on my father's battered, Smith Corona portable typewriter. "I am being charged by my country, not with causing injury to other people, but with refusing to do so," I told the court. "I am being charged with refusing to murder Vietnamese people. I am being charged with refusing to bomb and napalm Vietnamese villages. I am being charged with believing that the United States has better things to offer other countries than death. I am being charged with refusing to violate every important belief that I hold. A person's liberty should be taken from him only when he commits a crime. Mine is being taken from me because I refuse to commit acts that by any decent human standards must be considered criminal. I have broken an immoral law, and it is only because I have done so that I can plead not guilty with a clear conscience. I

The Courts: New Problems Over The "SSS"

By James Magmer

Eric Newhall—A new-type resister

Dwight Morrill

Eric Newhall and Dwight Morrill at the time of their trials for refusing induction into the armed forces. "A graduate of Occidental College, Los Angeles, with a major in English, Newhall is typical of the new kind of young man who is becoming common and prominent in the draft resistance movement in Oregon," notes the article, which ran in the March 23, 1969, issue of *Northwest Magazine*. "He was calm, polite, articulate, sure of himself and displayed an uncommon knowledge (for a layman) of the Selective Service law and of the formal and sometimes stilted court jargon and procedures." The reporter goes on to quote Dwight Morrill, whose trial followed Newhall's: "I believe it is no longer necessary for us to use violence to solve problems." Newhall was 23 at the time of his trial, Morrill 20. (*Note*: The "SSS" referred to in the headline is the Selective Service System, the government agency that oversees military conscription—colloquially, "the draft"). © 1969, Oregonian Publishing Co. Images provided by NewsBank/Readex.

call what we are doing in Vietnam murder, and as a loyal American citizen I cannot participate in it.

"While attending college in California I heard Dr. Benjamin Spock

Chapter 1. An Examined Life

speak about Vietnam. He reminded us of the following statement by President Eisenhower: 'If we were to have an election in Vietnam, 80% of the country would vote for Ho Chi Minh.' Do we favor free elections, or do we favor only those elections whose results we approve? Why are we supporting a government that has sentenced the second-place peace candidate, Truong Dinh Dzu, to five years of hard labor for advocating a coalition government as a possible means to peace? Why are we supporting a government that is non-democratic and that suppresses freedom of speech?

"The casualties and inhumanity in Vietnam are only part of the reason I have chosen to become a 'criminal.' Because we are spending thirty-five billion dollars per year in Vietnam, we are sadly neglecting the problems of our own country. As Martin Luther King argued, we must give higher priority to building houses and cities than to destroying them, and we must give higher priority to achieving peace than we do to body counts. We must wage war on poverty and human misery rather than producing them. The war is destroying Vietnam physically, but it is destroying this country spiritually and morally. We must not allow ourselves to become merely another in the long line of military machines that have come and gone again, adding little of importance to human experience.

"These are the reasons I give to the people of the United States for my actions which they consider to be criminal. I have been forced to choose between doing what is legal and doing what is right. I have chosen to act as this country required German war criminals to act at Nuremberg. I have gone outside the law of this country in an attempt to stop it from committing crimes. I have broken the law, but I have done nothing wrong. Having done nothing wrong, I am not guilty. Since I am not guilty, I believe that I should be acquitted."

When I finished reading my statement there was a small burst of applause from the gallery. Judge Belloni quickly called for order, then made a few comments of his own, comments that for a seemingly staid judge, charged with impartially upholding the laws of the land, struck me as more than a little unusual at the time. He indicated that the issues raised by the Vietnam War also troubled him. He urged me to reconsider applying for status as a Conscientious Objector. Then he set the date for sentencing for the following week, same time, same place.

§

Dwight and I were sentenced on the same day, the following week. Before sentencing, Judge Belloni made some remarks of his own. I didn't realize it at the time, but some of what he said was actually quite extraordinary. I remember being surprised to hear a Judge say that he felt he was

Killing time at the Multnomah County Jail at Rocky Butte in Portland, Oregon, May 31, 1957. *Photo: Al Monner. Photo courtesy Oregon Historical Society Library. © 1969, Oregonian Publishing Co. Images provided by NewsBank/Readex.*

"in a bind." I also remember biting my tongue and thinking to myself, *how do you think I feel, your Honor?* Having expressed his apparent discomfort with the role he was playing, Judge Belloni sentenced me to twenty-four months in a federal prison. When I looked behind me, I saw my mother trying to hold back tears. My father was his typical stoic self, at least outwardly. "Analyze the nature of the pain," he used to tell us when we got bumped or bruised. "Analyze the nature of the pain. Read Epictetus."

Judge Belloni sentenced Dwight to two years as well. He gave us time to "get our affairs in order," instructed us to turn ourselves in to the federal marshals on April 16, 1969, then announced that we were "released on our own recognizance." I heard nothing hostile or vindictive in the Judge's tone as he delivered our sentences. On the contrary, he struck me as someone who felt compelled to perform an unpleasant chore.

Chapter 2

County Jail

On April 16 my parents drove me down to the Federal Building and dropped me off. I took the elevator up to the federal marshals' office. As the door to the office closed behind me, I had a strong sense that a chapter of my life had just come to an end. I walked up to the counter to turn myself in. A stocky man seated at one of the desks came up to the counter. His tie clip was an American flag, and he wore a pin on his white shirt that read, "Have a nice day." By all appearances, he saw no irony in that smiley-face catch phrase.

"What can I do for you today?"

"I'm here to turn myself in."

"I've been reading about you in the newspaper. Some of us were wondering if you'd show up today or run off to Canada or something."

"If I were going to go to Canada, I'd have left a long time ago."

He fingerprinted me, just as I'd seen it done hundreds of times in detective shows. A large portrait of Richard Nixon loomed above me on the wall. Judging by his smile, he appeared to approve of the proceedings. "So, you're the hot-shot college boy. You thought you were pretty smart, defending yourself in court and all. I'll bet you're not feeling so smart right now. I'm not sure you're ready for prison."

"I said what I wanted to say."

"College boy wise ass," he said with a scowl. "With that attitude, you're going to do some real hard time. Let's get your picture. You're really dressed for success today, aren't you?"

He was right about that. I'd chosen my oldest, most tattered clothes for the occasion. I knew that the government would give me a uniform to wear in prison, but I wasn't sure what would happen to my own clothes, so I wore some worn-out black Converse All Stars, a pair of faded Levi's, and an old shirt that I painted houses in. The prison system was the enforcement wing of the political system, and I was determined to give them as little of myself as I could during the next two years; that included my clothing. On that first day, I gave them some paint-covered rags. A little over two weeks later, after Dwight and I had both been transported down to Lompoc, my parents received a brown paper package containing the clothes, shoes included, that I'd been wearing when I turned myself in. It was like receiving my remains, my mother told me, after I got out.

"We're going to put you in a holding cell until we can get you transported out to county jail," the marshal said. His tone dripped with contempt.

The holding cell was at the back of the marshals' office, behind a heavy, gray, metal door. There were five or six metal folding chairs in the cell and one prisoner. I walked over to one of the chairs and sat down. My new cellmate was looking me up and down. He was less than six feet tall—about 5' 10" I'd guess—and as wiry thin as I was in those days. He appeared to be about fifty years old with close-cut, receding, gray hair. He was wearing Levi's, a white t-shirt, black shoes, white socks. He looked like a caricature of a convict from a fifties jailhouse movie.

"I hear you won't defend your country," he said, with a hard stare. "The bulls told me all about you and your buddy."

"I'll defend the U.S. if we're attacked," I said, "but I don't want any part of what we're doing in Vietnam. What we're doing there won't make the U.S. any safer."

The old convict glared at me and shook his head. "You and your buddy are going to do some real hard time," he said. "I don't really give a fuck about you one way or the other, but a lot of guys in the joint hate people like you. The vets don't like your kind. To them, you're on a level with child molesters."

So now it's started, I thought to myself. *Here we go. Ten minutes in custody and it starts.* What the old convict said came as no surprise. I'd made a point of reading about life in prison, so I had some sense of what I was getting into. I'd also spoken with several friends of my parents, who gave me some useful advice. Among other things, they'd advised me to "do your own time" and "not to get too friendly with people too soon"—not a problem, in this case.

The old convict and I sat there in silence for about half an hour, at which point the door into the holding cell opened again and Dwight walked in. At this point I heard the old convict mutter something to himself. It sounded like "shit, not another one," but I couldn't hear him clearly enough to be sure. He glared contemptuously at both of us, and then repeated, for Dwight's benefit, his earlier soliloquy. "Draft dodgers. You guys are right on the same level with child molesters. You're going to do some real hard time."

"What do draft resisters have in common with child molesters?" Dwight asked the old convict calmly.

"I'll tell you what they have in common," our cellmate snarled. "Neither one of them has the balls to make it with a real woman. That's what they have in common."

Dwight and I looked at each other and said nothing.

We chatted for about an hour, at which point the marshal opened the door. "Newhall and Morrill, we're going to transport you out to County Jail. Put your hands together in front of you, through these two bars." The marshal cuffed us, then put leg irons on us and linked us together with a waist chain. "Follow me," he said.

Down the hallway, onto an elevator to the basement parking lot, into a van that already contained 10 other prisoners. Moving awkwardly because of the leg irons, Dwight and I took the last two seats in the rear. Two marshals sat up in the front next to the driver.

I didn't know it at the time, but Rocky Butte Jail in Multnomah County was built in the early years of the twentieth century. In 1946 it was condemned as "unfit for human habitation," but it continued to do a brisk business well into the 1970s. By the time I got there in April of 1969, the exterior brick walls were cracked in numerous places and splotched by large patches of moss. As I soon learned, conditions on the inside of the jail were every bit as bad as its decrepit exterior.

The drive from downtown Portland out to Rocky Butte took about twenty-five minutes. When we arrived, we were shepherded from the van into the bottom floor of the jail, where we followed a series of signs to a room labeled "Admittance."

In the Admittance Room the federal marshals turned us over to a tall, gray-haired guard whose nametag identified him as Mr. Wilson. Boss Wilson told us to strip down to our underwear and socks and to hold on to our shoes. In single file we walked across the room to a counter where an old man with a black patch over one eye handed each of us a pair of blue denim pants, a blue work shirt, and a pair of white tube sox. Two men in our group were assigned to a section of the jail referred to as "B Unit," a block of individual cells where prisoners who had a history of serious violence or psychological problems were housed. The rest of us were assigned to "the bull pen," a large room that resembled a military barracks except for the rusty bars and stale air.

Boss Wilson and two other guards escorted us up two flights of stairs and then directed us toward a metal gate that opened into the bullpen. Two guards sat at wooden desks just outside the gate, talking and listening to country western music on a radio. One of them unlocked the metal gate, motioned us inside, and then locked the gate behind us.

The air in the bullpen was simply foul. The room contained sixty bunk beds, most of which seemed to be occupied, top and bottom. Over a hundred men in cramped quarters with little or no ventilation, sweating, coughing, farting, defecating, and occasionally vomiting produced a truly suffocating stench. I retched a little as I entered the bullpen. I tried to appear calm, as though I'd been here before.

The ten of us walked down the rows of bunks like late arrivals to a movie theater, looking for empty seats. Dwight and I found two empty beds in the back of the bullpen, both top bunks. Most convicts preferred the bottom bunks, I learned. Every night, somebody would fall out of a top bunk as he thrashed around in his sleep trying to escape his personal demons. He'd hit the floor with a loud thump that was immediately followed by shouts and curses.

I lay there listening to the sounds of the bullpen. Up toward the front of the unit, several clusters of men sat around card tables. At one table, several Black inmates were playing a spirited game of dominoes, slapping their tiles down on the table when they played and shouting comments and friendly taunts at their opponents. At several other tables, men were playing poker, using matches and small pieces of torn paper for chips. I'd been warned against playing poker in prison. "You don't want to get into debt to anyone in prison," I'd had been told by one of my parents' friends.

After about an hour of lying on my bunk listening to the sounds of the jail, I needed to use the bathroom. I swung myself down to the floor and stepped to the back of the pen where I found a row of ten toilets and an equal number of urinals. The toilets were out in the open—no closed stalls. I could see immediately that there is next to no privacy in prisons and jails. No privacy and very little autonomy. Nearly every action is observed, and every choice controlled by those in power. This is good training for life in prison, but poor preparation for life on the streets.

Walking back to my bunk, I noticed a book lying on the floor. It didn't seem to belong to anyone, so I picked it up. I was pleasantly surprised to discover that it was a copy of Ralph Ellison's *Invisible Man,* a novel I'd heard a lot about but hadn't read. I looked around to be sure that it didn't belong to someone else. No one seemed to own it, so I took it back to my bunk and read for the rest of the afternoon. Dwight, who was always more gregarious and open than I was, had wandered up to the front of the bullpen and was talking with several other prisoners. I wasn't unfriendly, even in those days, but compared to Dwight I tended to be more bookish and more of a loner.

At 5:30 a loud bell rang, and people began to get up from wherever they were and move to the front of the bullpen. "Chow time," I heard one of the guards call out. "Time for chow."

I got into line with Dwight so that I would have someone I knew to talk with over dinner.

"This should be interesting," he said. "I wonder what's for dinner."

"More of the same slop," said a short, bald man behind us.

We marched in single file out of the bullpen, into the corridor, and all the way to the far end of the building, where we entered a large room labeled "Dining Hall." We sat down in order, eight men to a table. This was a surprise. I'd been expecting a cafeteria line; instead, my first meal in jail turned out to be a sit-down dinner.

As soon as we were seated, six blue-clad prisoners who worked in the kitchen fanned out, carrying bread and butter to each table. Everyone grabbed his share, two slices of bread.

"Leave some of that butter for me, you motherfucker," I heard someone say two tables over.

"Fuck you, too," came the reply. My own table was relatively genteel in comparison, all sharing and cooperation. I had just started in on my bread and butter when the servers returned, this time with metal platters of meat that, judging from the odor, seemed to be liver—*very* well-done liver. Calf or pig, I couldn't tell. As we passed the liver around our table, the servers returned again, this time with trays of vegetables—canned corn, boiled potatoes, sliced tomatoes.

"Eric," Dwight said to me, gesturing to a man seated on the other side of the table, "this is Dale Hartman." Hartman was one of the three prisoners I had seen Dwight talking to earlier in the bullpen.

"Where are you guys headed?" he asked us.

"They're sending us to a prison called Lompoc, down near Santa Barbara," I said.

"Right on," said Hartman. "That's where I'm going. It's good to know a few people before you get to the joint. Fewer people try to mess with you if they know you have friends."

Hartman was a shade less than six feet, with pale blue eyes that constantly darted back and forth and dirty blond hair that looked as though it hadn't been washed in a while. He was also carrying forty to fifty extra pounds, most of it in rolls of fat around his stomach. Watching him devour the food in front of him made it clear where the weight came from. He emptied his metal tray quickly and looked up and down the table for more. "Bread here," he sang out. The plate of bread made its way down the table; Hartman took two slices, folded them in half, and mopped up the gravy from his tray. When he was done, he leaned back and smacked his lips. "It's not like home, but it's not bad," he said.

"Shit," exclaimed the man seated to Hartman's right. "I wouldn't feed this crap to my dog." I ate a little of everything, thinking to myself that under the circumstances it made sense to keep my strength up.

At this point a bell rang, signaling the end of dinner. We all stood and walked out of the Dining Hall, once again in single file. Back in the Bullpen Hartman pulled out a deck of cards from beneath the mattress on his bunk. "Do you guys play hearts?" he asked.

"I do," I said. I liked hearts because of the strategy involved. Dwight, on the other hand, had no feel for card games whatsoever. When the call came for lights out, Hartman was a few points ahead of me and both of us were way ahead of Dwight.

"Not bad for a rookie," said Hartman to Dwight. "We'll have to play some more tomorrow."

I didn't sleep much that first night at Rocky Butte. I was very much on edge because of what I had heard and read about prisons and jails. I didn't want some sexual predator creeping up on me while I was sleeping. Then, too, one hundred men crowded together in a single room make a lot of noise in their sleep. People snored and tossed and turned in their bunks. Some of the men talked in their sleep or moaned. In the bottom bunk next to me a Latino who appeared to be about my age kept calling out in his sleep for "Maria." I wondered if Maria were his wife, girlfriend, sister, or daughter. Clearly, he was far from home and missing Maria so much that he sought her in his dreams.

§

I woke up with a start when the lights came on the next morning. It took me a moment to remember where I was. Day two in the slammer. *Only seven hundred and some more to go*, I thought to myself. *Just take it one day at a time. Stay alert.*

Hartman came over. "Grab your stuff and follow me," he said. "Two bunks are going to open up by mine. Make your move now, otherwise you'll get stuck back here doing hard time next to the shitter. You got to move up front where you can do some easy time. That's the American way." He chuckled.

Dwight and I swept up our personal items and scrambled toward the front of the Bull Pen, following Hartman. That's how the system worked at Rocky Butte. Newcomers took the empty bunks that were left in the back of the Bull Pen and gradually worked their way up to the front where the air was a bit better, and you could listen to whatever music the guards happened to play on the radio. Most prisoners charged with felonies stayed in the county jail for between ten and twenty days. At that point they were either found innocent in court and released or found guilty and transferred to the prison where they would serve out whatever sentence had been imposed on them at their trial. Hartman, who seemed to have spent some time behind bars, explained the system to Dwight and me. "If you're sentenced to a year or less, you do your time in county jail," he said. "Anything more than that and they send you to a penitentiary. That's why you sometimes hear about someone being sentenced to 'a year and a day.' That extra day sends you to the penitentiary to do your time instead of staying in county jail."

My stay in the county jail lasted ten days, and the days passed slowly. Breakfast, lunch, and dinner at the same time each day. One hour's exercise, once a week, in a small courtyard outside the jail. Dwight, Hartman, and I walked the circumference of the yard, talking the whole hour. I spent the time between meals reading *Invisible Man,* playing hearts, or just talking.

"County Jail is some hard time," Hartman said with conviction. "In the joint things aren't so uptight. There's more room to move around. You're assigned a job and you work from 8 a.m. until 4 p.m. with time out for lunch. After dinner, your time is your own until lights out. On weekends you don't work unless you're assigned to the kitchen or the chow hall. During free time most guys go out to the yard and shoot the shit with their friends. I want to get down to Lompoc and get me a job in the kitchen and learn how to be a short-order cook."

"What other kinds of jobs do they have?" I asked him. "I don't know how to cook anything."

"You ought to get yourself a job as a clerk," he said. "Those jobs are some of the best jobs in the joint. You could do some easy time."

"How do you get a job as a clerk?"

"You won't have any trouble. You graduated from college, didn't you? I read that article about you and Dwight in the paper last week."

"Yes, I did. I graduated last June."

"The hacks are always looking for guys who can type and spell to work in their offices. Put the word out that you're looking to be a clerk. Somebody will have something for you."

"How do I put the word out?"

"Hell, they'll find you. They need guys like you to help them run the joint. Guys who can type letters, fill out forms, and keep their files straight. You'll see how it goes. Without us, the hacks' jobs would be a lot harder. You help them with their job, and you get to do some easy time. Everybody wins."

I thought about what Hartman was telling me. If I played my cards right, I thought, I could find a prison job that would be pretty easy. I might even be able to get some reading done. Doing some reading in prison to fill in the gaps in my preparation for graduate school sounded like a good idea. And the federal government could pay for my room and board while I prepared. Brer Rabbit would be proud of me; Lompoc could be my briar patch.

My parents came to visit me on Sunday, at the end of my first week in jail. We spoke over telephones through a thick, plate glass window, just the way I'd seen it on television. My mother was trying so hard to lift my spirits that it was painful. My parents updated me on each of my four siblings and how things were going at home. I told them about my daily routine in the county jail. The hour went by rapidly. We said good-bye, touching hands against the glass, and I returned to the bullpen. I knew that the next time I would see my parents would be at Lompoc.

Three days later I was reading on my bunk after dinner when one of the guards shouted my name. After ten days in jail, I knew the drill. When a guard called your name, you reported to the front of the bullpen to see what was up. Sometimes you had a special visit on a weekday. Sometimes you had mail. This time the guard had news for me: I would leave for Lompoc Federal Prison the next morning with two federal marshals. He told me to put any belongings I had into my pillowcase and be ready to go right after breakfast.

I could feel my heart pounding as I walked back to my bunk. This was it. The next phase. I was being transferred to the joint.

"What was that about?" Dwight asked.

"I'm being transferred to Lompoc tomorrow morning," I said. "I'm guessing that means you won't be far behind."

"Ten days," said Hartman. "That's pretty standard. I've been here over two weeks now. I'd sure like to get out of this motherfucking County Jail and get to where I'm going." He took a bite out of an Oreo cookie as he said this.

"Hey," I said. "Where'd you get that cookie?"

"From the Commissary," he said. "Once a week you can buy stuff from the Commissary. It's a little store. You have to have money on the books, though, to buy anything." He opened the door of the small metal locker next to his bunk and I was surprised to see packages of cookies and crackers, a row of candy bars, and packs of cigarettes.

"If you have cash on the books, you can get by," he said. "I'd do real hard time without the stuff I get from the Commissary."

Just then, the guard up front called Hartman's name.

"Hot damn," he said. "Maybe I'm shipping out too."

That turned out to be the case. Hartman and I and one other prisoner were to be shipped out the next morning. I was hoping Dwight would be the third, but someone up the chain of command had decided that Dwight and I should be transported on different days. A few minutes later the guard called for someone named Martin Winters. A short, surly looking inmate with tattoos all over his arms and neck swaggered slowly to the front of the Bull Pen. Winters would be our traveling companion the next day.

Chapter 2. County Jail

§

I bolted up early the next morning before the wake-up call. I was eager to leave the stench of Rocky Butte behind and the long hours of soul-killing boredom. After breakfast Hartman and I said good-bye to Dwight, who seemed despondent that he wasn't leaving with us.

"Be sure to save me a cell," he said. "I'll catch up with you as soon as I can."

Our empty bunks had been claimed before we were even out the door that led downstairs to the garage. We were handcuffed, again, and linked to each other with leg irons and a waist chain. "Standard procedure," said one of the two marshals. "We know you boys aren't going to run off, but the regulations say we have to put on the leg irons and waist chain." The marshals both conformed to the image I had of cops in the '60s: military-style crew cuts, bull-necked, thick around the middle. They looked like former high school football players who'd seen better days. Both wore wedding rings. I wondered about what their wives were like. What their goals in life were. What they most feared.

They loaded us into the back seat of a new model Pontiac, and we rolled out of Rocky Butte. As we drove toward the freeway that would take us south, I searched the streets for someone I knew, hoping to see a friend out jogging in the early morning rain. I wanted to flash the peace sign to a friendly face as I left my hometown, but there was no one I recognized. We turned onto Interstate 5, and then we were flying south toward Lompoc.

Winters seemed sullen and agitated, so we left him alone. Hartman and I talked quietly about our families and what our lives had been like, growing up. He was impressed that my father was a college professor and that my mother was a college graduate who planned to go "back to work" as soon as my youngest brother turned eight. "Man," he said. "I didn't have anything like that. My dad dropped out of high school after his junior year. He moved around from job to job. Most of the time he worked moving furniture, until he hurt his back. He used to get drunk and beat my brother and me. He really thumped on us. A few times he hit my mother, too. He'd always be sorry the next day, but that didn't make up for it."

I was shocked when he said this. At that time, I didn't know anyone whose father beat his wife and children. I'd read about abusive parents and observed scenes of domestic violence on TV or in movies, but I'd never encountered it in real life. I had many conversations like this while I was in prison, conversations with people I would never have encountered at the nearly all–White, middle-class high school I attended or my relatively insular college.

"Does your father still do that?" I asked awkwardly, not knowing what else to say.

"Hell no," Hartman said. "He's long gone. I don't ever see him anymore. When I was ten, he beat my mother so badly that she wound up in the hospital with a fractured eye socket. She didn't want to press charges, but they charged my dad anyway and convicted him. I never saw him again after he went to state prison back in Kentucky. My mom still lives back there. The first thing I'm going to do when I get out is to go back there and see her. After that I'm going out to dinner at a place called Smokey Joe's Rib House. The best ribs I ever tasted." Hartman was always thinking about food, whether past meals or meals to come or meals he planned to cook when he landed that job in the kitchen at Lompoc.

We stopped in Red Bluff at the end of the first day and stayed overnight in the Tehama County Jail. The marshals picked us up at 7:30 a.m. the next morning and drove hard all that day, stopping only for lunch and bathroom breaks. They wanted to deposit us at Lompoc as early as possible so they could continue south to Los Angeles in time for dinner and whatever else they'd planned for that evening. I wondered what my weekend was going to be like. At Rocky Butte I'd talked with several men about life in prison and how to deal with it. They all stressed a few basic principles: "Don't carry yourself like a target. Do your own time. And if anybody messes with you during the first few days you're inside, hit him in the mouth as hard as you can, immediately. Make it clear you're not a target. Make it clear you're a man." I wondered if I really would hit someone in the face as hard as I could. I'd only been in two fights in my life, and they were more like youthful scuffles than serious knockdown drag-outs. *I guess time will tell*, I thought.

To get to Lompoc Federal Prison you leave the main highway and drive through twenty miles of undeveloped ranchland. The road you take is a dead end. The last mile before arriving at the prison cuts through a large field of flowers—tulips, I think they were. The contrast between the colorful richness of nature and the ugly brutality of the prison seemed sadly ironic to me at the time. Next to the flower field stands a large, glistening Air Force missile, white against the clear blue coastal sky. A giant phallic symbol, its suggestive ambiguity worthy of Herman Melville or maybe Thomas Pynchon. A mocking welcome to prison for anyone opposed to the war.

We all have images etched in our minds, images we can't shake. My first clear sight of Lompoc never leaves me. I carry it with me every day. It's been over fifty years now, but I remember driving through the colorful flower fields and pulling up to the prison with gut-clenching clarity. The three gun-towers peering down at the complex. The double chain link

Chapter 2. County Jail 45

U.S. Penitentiary Lompoc, Lompoc, California. Photo: Federal Bureau of Prisons. Public Domain. *Source: Wikimedia Commons.*

fence topped with razor wire, glittering in the sunlight. The prison itself, built almost entirely of concrete—heavy, brutal, gray. The cellblocks protruding at right angles from one long central corridor like the tentacles of a monstrous octopus or the legs of a giant centipede.

"Holy shit," Hartman muttered to himself. "Look at that motherfucker." Winters just stared. He hadn't uttered a single word the entire trip. The prison looked cold, merciless, and foreboding. I couldn't imagine living inside it for two years. I felt as low and despairing as I'd ever felt in my life.

"Here we are, boys," one of the marshals announced cheerily. "Your home away from home."

We got out of the car, awkwardly because of the shackles, and passed through several gates that the marshals unlocked, then locked behind us. We shuffled along, passing, finally, through the prison's main entrance. We stopped when we came to a door labeled "Admission Center." We were going inside.

Chapter 3

Fish Tank

Once we were inside the Admission Center, the marshals removed our handcuffs and leg irons and told us to take a seat on a gray, wooden bench against the far wall. One of them handed what I assumed were our files to a guard seated at a desk in the middle of the room; then both marshals disappeared through the door to begin their weekend. They were my last tangible link to the familiar world outside the prison. I felt my former life and identity slipping away, a disorienting sensation. I was now officially a federal prisoner. I felt very much alone.

There were three guards in the Admission Center. "Strip down, boys," one of them said. "Let's get rid of those county jail blues." His nametag read "Mr. Gridley"; his tie clasp announced, "I Love Lompoc." He strolled back to his desk while we stripped down to our underwear and waited for further instructions. He made a show of thumbing intently through our files. After a long while, he walked back to us, scowling. "Didn't you boys hear what I said?" he growled. "I told you to strip down. *Everything*. We don't want you bringing no lice or God knows what else with you into the Institution."

I noticed in the months that followed that the guards never referred to the prison as "the prison." It was always "the FCI" (Federal Correctional Institution) or "the Institution." The prisoners never referred to it as "the prison" either. It was always "the joint," "the slammer," "the can," "the big house." I've always been interested in language and its power not just to *describe* but also to *shape* what we see. With the passage of time, prison slang began to slip into my way of expressing myself. I didn't consciously adopt prison jargon; it just seemed to seep, gradually, into my speech without my realizing it. That's how it works in the joint; people change without even realizing it.

We took off our underwear and sat quietly on the bench. Guards came and went. Hartman began to fidget. "It's the same thing every joint I've ever been in," he said. "You show up and they have to show you who's in charge. They strip you down and try to break you down. And they tell us they're trying to rehabilitate us. It's bullshit."

"Stop your fuckin' sniveling," hissed Winters. It was the first time he'd spoken in at least two days. "Why don't you just shut the fuck up and do your time?"

"There's no need to cuss, dude," said Hartman, who seemed almost hurt by Winters' sudden outburst. "I'm just saying there's no good reason for them to leave us sitting here like this. Sitting here being stared at by all these assholes isn't going to rehabilitate me."

We kept our eyes glued to the concrete floor until guard Gridley returned. "Follow me, boys," he said. We followed him through a door that led to an open shower room equipped to accommodate ten convicts at a time. He handed us each a bar of coarse brown soap. "Shower down," he ordered. "Wash your hair, too." We did as we were told. It felt good to take a shower after ten days without one. I hadn't taken a shower in the county jail because of what I'd heard about shower rooms in jail. I let the warm water run over me until Gridley said, "that's enough." He handed each of us a washcloth. "Put these over your eyes while I hose you down."

He sprayed us all over with some sort of chemical solution designed to kill lice and vermin. "Wash off again," he ordered. We did as we were told. "Dry off with those towels," said Gridley, pointing to some towels hanging from hooks on the shower wall. Again, we did as we were told.

"Follow me," he said. We followed him across the bare concrete floor to a counter that opened into a large supply room. "Get these three fish set up, Thomas," Gridley said to the blade-thin, khaki-clad inmate who worked behind the counter.

Inmate Thomas asked each of us what size pants and shirts we wore; then he walked up and down several long aisles of clothing, searching for items that would fit. He handed each of us three long-sleeved khaki shirts, four white t-shirts, three pairs of khaki pants, four pairs of white tube sox, and four pairs of white boxer shorts. The three of us quickly dressed in the clothing we had been given.

"The legs are too long on these pants," Hartman complained. "They look like shit."

"If you don't like 'em, why don't you just go on down to Macy's and exchange 'em," Thomas said curtly.

I had the opposite problem. My pant legs were too short; the high-water khakis made me look like a high school nerd from the nineteen-fifties. *I would have looked better if I'd joined the army*, I thought. "Look at us," said Hartman. "One way or another, they get you into a uniform."

Inmate Thomas gave us each a pair of plain black leather shoes and a brown paper bag containing toiletries: toothpaste, toothbrush, a plastic comb, a bar of soap, and a safety razor with a blade so narrow it couldn't possibly be used as a weapon. Then we returned to our place on the bench.

Boss Gridley shuffled papers at his desk, eyeballing us every few minutes. After a long while, he said, "Let's get you boys down to the fish tank. They'll assign you to a bunk, then you can probably make it to the mess hall in time for dinner before they shut down." The "fish tank," Hartman told me, was what they called A & O, the Admission and Orientation unit. "All the fish, the new inmates, stay in A & O for thirty days of observation before they are moved out into the general population," he said. "They want to observe you for a while and evaluate your behavior. The hacks want to see if you're violent or a troublemaker, that sort of thing."

As we walked down the main corridor of the prison to A & O, several surly inmates flashed us menacing looks and occasional taunts.

"I get the pretty one," one muscular guy said to his friends.

"Hey, fish," said a heavily pockmarked inmate. "I got some silk panties for you. Drop by my bunk tonight."

Verbal harassment is a rite of passage for most new arrivals at state and federal prisons. Viewed as fresh meat, new arrivals come under close scrutiny by inmates who are already out in the general population. I looked straight ahead and just kept on walking. Winters, on the other hand, fired back. "Fuck you, you punk ass piece of shit," he snapped over his shoulder. "You bring *your* sorry ass by my bunk tonight."

When we finally reached A & O, the guard in charge, Boss Schwartz, led us down a row of occupied beds to the far end of the room. "Let's find some bunks for you boys," he said. The fish tank was a large, barracks-like room; the entrance was flanked by big picture windows that looked out onto the central corridor. The unit contained four rows of twenty beds each, a metal locker to go with each bed, and not much else. Inmates who'd already been moved into the general population constantly circulated past the windows, peering in, sizing up each batch of new arrivals, looking for any sign of weakness.

"These three should do it," said Boss Schwartz, pointing to three empty beds. "Put your personal belongings in the locker next to your bed. Be quick about it, and we'll get you down to the chow hall before dinner gets cold."

I put a few letters from my family and the copy of *Invisible Man* into my locker. To my right, barred windows looked out onto the prison yard, a large open area that consisted of an oval-shaped dirt track, two concrete basketball courts, two tennis courts, a volleyball court, a weight-lifting area, and a large grassy patch inside the oval of the track where small groups of men sat talking or strumming guitars. I looked up and down the aisle at my fellow fish. Most of them were lying on their bunks listening to music on headphones, reading, or writing letters to friends or family. Just then Boss Schwartz called out, "You three new fish, come on up here, now. We need to get you down to the chow hall."

Dinner consisted of lukewarm lasagna, coleslaw, cooked carrots, and a chocolate chip cookie. Hartman griped about the quality of the food, although I noticed that he cleaned his plate in record time. Winters ate in stony silence. There was a tension in his manner that suggested a seething anger, just beneath the surface, that he was struggling to control. When we were done, we followed Boss Schwartz back to A and O.

I thought about going out into the yard to see what was going on, but I decided to wait until morning. No need to rush things. I had plenty of time to learn about the place that was to be my home for the next two years. Looking back, I think of Lompoc as my equivalent to Ishmael's time aboard the *Pequod*. We both experienced "higher education" about the world.

I lay down on my bunk and plugged in the earphones I found in my locker. I discovered that the earphones were connected to four radio stations. One played country western music, another played jazz and blues, a third played rock and popular music, and the fourth was a religious station that carried religious programming twenty-four hours a day.

As I was listening to music on my earphones, I saw a very young-looking inmate from down the aisle approach Winters' bunk and say something to him. I saw Winters yell something in response. He leaped off his bunk and began to shout. I took off my earphones so I could hear what was going on.

"What did you say your name is?" Winters snapped.

"Brown. I'm Billy Brown," stammered the young man, clearly rattled by the hostility of Winters' tone.

"Well, Billy, where I'm from is none of your fucking business," snarled Winters. "Didn't they give you a number when you drove up to this here joint?"

"Yes, they did," Billy, said softly. "My number is five-one-two—"

Winters cut him off. "Shut the fuck up," he barked. Up and down the aisle, heads turned, wondering what was up. "I don't give a damn what your number is. Do me a favor: you do your number and I'll do mine. Stay the fuck away from me. We don't have a goddamned thing to talk about." Brown, who had turned a deep red during Winters' outburst, retreated slowly back down the aisle to his bunk, embarrassed and humiliated. Winters watched him go, shaking his head disgustedly. "Punk ass motherfucker," he muttered.

"That guy Brown needs to learn the ropes quick, or the wolves in here will eat him alive," said Hartman, under his breath. "You just don't do that. Do your own number and don't fuck with someone else's.

Don't ask anyone what their beef is—what they're in for, where they're from."

As I'd learned at Rocky Butte, that's one of the fundamental rules of prison life. "Do your own time." It's a major violation of prison etiquette to ask about someone else's background—where they're from, their upbringing, and especially the offense that brought them to prison. These are all taboo topics. If someone wants to divulge personal information, he'll do so voluntarily, as a sign of trust.

I took a long look around the room at my fellow fish. They came in all shapes and sizes: large, small, fat, thin. Several big, buff men looked as though they'd spent plenty of time working out with weights. These guys worried me because a couple of them looked mean. Ethnically and racially, the group seemed like a cross-section of the United States: Blacks, Latinos, Asians, Native Americans, Whites.

A & O at Lompoc was only the second room I'd ever been in that contained as many people of color as Whites. (The first was the Bullpen at county jail in Portland.) That says a lot, I think. I'd lived in the United States for twenty-two years, and it wasn't until I spent time behind bars that I'd ever been in a room containing as many people of color as there were Whites. For me, Lompoc turned out to be appropriately named. It was a sort of "borderland" (Gloria Anzaldua) in which people from different sides of the color line and the class divide came into direct contact with each other. For the first time, I saw and experienced the United States from the position of the marginalized, not the privileged. I lay back on my bunk and contemplated my fellow fish, reading *Invisible Man* and waiting for my first day in the joint to come to an end.

§

The next morning in the mess hall, I noticed that the tables were segregated by race: Black tables, White tables, Latino tables, Native American tables. During the sixties, there was a lot of talk about emphasizing the rehabilitation of prisoners rather than retribution and punishment. I heard this rhetoric the whole time I was at Lompoc. All the caseworkers and some of the guards would tell us about how they were there to help us get our lives back on track. The caseworkers used to refer to the new plastic tables and chairs in the mess hall as "conversational groupings."

My first conversational grouping included only Hartman. I noticed that Winters, rather than sitting with us, chose to sit at a table next to ours with two inmates he seemed to know from his previous stay at Lompoc.

"This is a bullshit breakfast," said Hartman after a spoonful or two of his oatmeal. "No eggs, no bacon."

Chapter 3. Fish Tank

"Well, damn," said Winters, "You should go ask for your money back." For once, he broke character and laughed.

Hartman glared at Winters but kept shoveling in his food. Just then, one of the guards approached Winters' table. His nametag identified him as "Mr. Redburn." He appeared to be in his late thirties, his gravelly voice the rasp of a heavy smoker.

"I told you when you left, you'd be back, Winters," he said. "You just don't have what it takes to stay out of here."

Winters shot the guard a piercing look but said nothing. He kept eating, as though Redburn didn't even exist.

"Cat got your tongue, Winters?" said the guard, his voice dripping with sarcasm. "How long were you out on the streets? Three months? Four, at most? They ought to lock you up and throw away the key."

"How about you, Boss?" Winters shot back. "You were here when I left, and you're still here now. You're doing time right along with us. Ever think about that?" Winters' tablemates nodded their heads in agreement but said nothing.

Boss Redburn glared at Winters, then turned on his heel and strode away.

"Friend of yours?" said Hartman.

"That motherfucker is going to get his someday," said Winters.

A short, brown-haired inmate wearing wire-rimmed glasses approached our table and, to our surprise, greeted us. "Hey fellas," he said in a friendly tone. "I'm John Surratt. I see you guys just got in from Portland late yesterday. You must be Eric Newhall," he said to me. "And you must be Dale Hartman. I saw your pictures in your files when they came in a couple of days ago."

We must have looked surprised—and a bit wary.

"Oh," said Surratt. "Sorry. I should have told you. I work in the main administrative office as a clerk. My job is to do most of the filing for the hacks that work there. That lets me keep track of who comes and goes. I like to contact all the hippies when they drive up."

Hartman and I looked at each other. "I don't think I'd call myself a hippie," I said.

"Me either," said Hartman.

"That's not exactly what I mean," said Surratt. "In here people divide up into different groups, and most of the time they hang out with their group. It's not a good idea to be isolated. White guys divide into low riders or hippies. Low riders tend to be bikers, gang members, guys who like to work on cars and bikes. Hippies are mostly in for dope or the draft. The Blacks, Mexicans, and Indians hang out with their own groups in different parts of the yard. Come looking for me out in the yard after dinner. I'll introduce you to some of the guys."

"Sounds good," said Hartman.

"See you then," I said.

"Damn," said Hartman as Surratt walked away. "I guess I'm going to be a hippie."

"You sure as hell aren't no biker," said Winters, who had been listening to Surratt. I thought I saw the faintest hint of a smile flicker across his face. For some reason, Winters seemed to be in a better mood, more relaxed than he'd been on the drive south with the marshals when he literally didn't speak for two days.

Surratt made his way back to the table where he'd been sitting with his friends. Over Hartman's shoulder on the other side of the chow hall, I saw Billy Brown, the kid Winters had yelled at the day before. He was engaged in a conversation with two hard-looking inmates. I learned later that Billy Brown was in his second year at San Francisco State when he was busted for selling marijuana. One of the tough guys put his arm around Brown's neck and pulled him closer, as if he were going to embrace him. Billy threw his arm off violently, rejecting the other man's advances. Hartman and I both watched as Billy leapt up and left the dining hall, his breakfast untouched. The two wolves watched Billy walk away and laughed.

"That sort of shit happens all the time in the joint, particularly when you first drive up," said Hartman. "People get tested to see how they'll react. That dude needs to defend his manhood, or he's going to wind up as somebody's punk. He'll do some hard time if he doesn't wise up real quick. This ain't no peace movement in here."

I spent the rest of the morning reading *Invisible Man*. I loved that novel. I still remember the thrill of reading it for the first time. I'm sure it had something to do with the circumstances. Life in prison is so grey and sterile most of the time that the world of a novel can seem more vibrant and alive than the real world. In Ellison's narrative, the nameless protagonist starts out innocent and gradually realizes that everyone has some sort of plan for him, but they never include him in the planning process. As Ellison sees it, his narrator can't be free until he shakes loose from the schemers and power brokers and charts his own course. At the time, I read the novel as an Emersonian coming-of-age story about the need to chart an independent path through life. All these years later, I still love *Invisible Man* and teach it every chance I get, but I see it differently now than I did when I first read it at Lompoc.

At 11:15 we filed down the corridor to the chow hall for lunch. Winters, Hartman, and I sat down at the same table, but Hartman and I did most of the talking. Winters seemed less and less sullen as time went on, but I could tell he was angry about something beyond the mere fact of being incarcerated. I looked around the chow hall for Surratt, the man who'd

Chapter 3. Fish Tank

introduced himself to us over breakfast, but couldn't see any sign of him.

I was beginning to get a feel for the daily rhythm of the prison. After lunch most of the fish filed back to A and O for the rest of the afternoon; a few decided to see what was happening out in the yard. I spent an uneventful afternoon reading on my bunk, listening to music, writing a letter to my parents, and sizing up the other men around me. At 4:30 p.m. a loud, jarring buzzer went off, and through the windows I could see men filing across the yard, returning to whatever unit they were housed in. The reason for this became clear a few minutes later. "Count time," Boss Schwartz shouted. "Inmates on your bunks." Count, I learned, was taken three times each day, once at noon, once before dinner at 4:30 p.m., and one more time at 9:30 before lights out at 10:30.

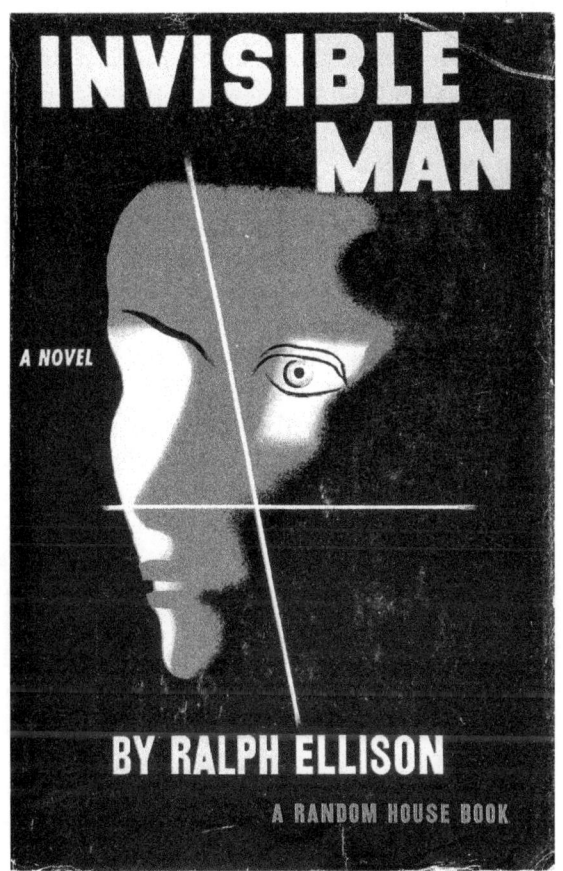

Invisible Man, **Ralph Ellison, published in 1952.**

Hartman and I went through the chow line for dinner together and again seated ourselves at one of the empty plastic tables. By 1969, the long wooden tables and benches I'd seen in prison movies from the forties and fifties had been replaced by colored plastic chairs and sturdy, round, white plastic tables designed to seat four or five inmates. White plastic cups and plastic trays of different colors had also replaced the metal trays and tin cups. Winters followed us, this time bringing another man with him. "I'd like you guys to meet a homey of mine," he said. "This here is Spike. Him and me used to ride bikes together back in Spokane." We nodded at Spike, he nodded at us, then he and Winters engrossed themselves in talk of old times in Spokane, catching up on what had happened to other members of the motorcycle gang they had been part of.

"How's your old lady doing?" Spike asked Winters.

"That's a long story," said Winters, shifting uneasily in his chair. "I'll fill you in some other time."

Clearly, Winters didn't want to talk about his private life in the presence of a couple of hippies he'd just met. He seemed to be slowly warming up to Hartman and me, but his business was still his own business. Far be it from me to pry. I had my own number to do.

The four of us finished our dinner quickly and agreed to head out to the yard to see what was going on. I wanted to get some fresh air and exercise after being cramped up in the marshals' car for two days and in the county jail in Portland for ten days before that. I also wanted to make contact with Surratt, who struck me as an intelligent guy with information about the prison that might be useful to me. Winters and Spike led the way. "This way, guys," said Winters. "I hope you aren't carrying anything you shouldn't be carrying, because the hacks pat you down as you enter and leave the yard."

Over the next several months I found that I could size up the other men by watching their behavior in the yard. Throughout most of the day, we followed orders of one sort or another. In the yard, we were free to choose our own crew.

"Hippies over there," said Winters, pointing to a section of the yard off to our left. I saw a concrete volleyball court with a game going on and small knots of inmates sitting on the sidelines. Several men strummed guitars or played harmonicas.

"See you guys later," said Spike. "Nothing personal, but Winters and me don't hang out much with hippies in the yard."

I watched as Spike and Winters walked slowly around the dirt track that circled the yard, heading toward a large cluster of men. Winters was greeted with handshakes, slaps on the back, and shouts of recognition.

"Low riders," said Hartman. "It's the same in every joint these days. Hippies and low riders are your basic choices if you're a white dude. Winters and Spike will have lunch at our table, but they won't hang out with us in the yard. Low riders think hippies are soft. Check out the weights."

I looked across the yard to where Hartman was pointing and saw twenty or so inmates working out with free-standing weights. Most of them were low riders.

It felt good to be outdoors, walking in the early evening before the sun went down. Hartman and I took several laps around the track, surveying the yard as we went. Just beyond the weightlifting area, we passed two basketball courts. On the first, two different half-court games were going on, Blacks at one end, Whites at the other. On the second, a full-court game was in progress, five players to a side; the players were all dark-skinned, most of them on the shorter side. I assumed they were Mexican Americans or Chicanos.

"I'd sure like to play some hoop," I said.

"I'm not much for sports," said Hartman. "Let's see if we can find that guy Surratt, the guy we met at lunch. You can play basketball tomorrow."

"Fair enough," I said. "I want to ask Surratt how he got his job working as a clerk. I remember what you told me up in Portland about the clerks having time to read on the job. As long as I have to be here for two years, a job that gives me time to do some reading sounds pretty good." *I can prepare for graduate school if I go back and have my room and board paid for by the federal government,* I thought. *Maybe these two years don't have to be a total loss. Maybe they can be preparation for what comes next.*

We took several more laps around the track, talking and looking for Surratt but with no success. The soft, cool breeze felt invigorating as we circled the yard. Neither one of us felt like going back inside yet, so we sat down on the grass in the infield, talking and watching what was going on around us. As the sun began to dip toward the horizon and the air began to cool, we decided to take one last lap around the track to see if we could find Surratt. As we passed the ramps that led into the yard, I heard someone call our names.

"Newhall. Hartman."

There was Surratt, walking into the yard with several other men he seemed to know. "Come on over here," he motioned to us. "Sorry it took me a while to get out here. I had to take care of a couple of things."

We walked over to the grass that bordered the volleyball court and joined the small circle of men clustered around Surratt. Scattered around us on the grass were sixty or so other men. Several were strumming guitars while others talked or listened. One guy played along on a wooden flute. A few sat apart, writing letters, or reading.

"You getting to know Boss Schwartz in A & O?" Surratt asked us after we'd introduced ourselves to the other men. "He rotates with Boss Stockton and Boss Garcia, but Schwartz is the one you need to look out for." He writes up the report on you when you're ready to move out of A and O and into the general population.

"I don't really have a sense of him yet," I said. "He just seems to sit there at his desk up front and fiddle with his papers. Every once in a while, he'll come into the unit and walk up and down the aisles. He doesn't say much."

"Don't let him fool you," said Surratt. "His job is to observe you for thirty days, then write a report on you for your file. He doesn't miss much. He reads all the incoming and outgoing mail of new arrivals."

"Is that even legal?" I said. I was incredulous. "Isn't that a violation of our privacy, tampering with our mail?"

Surratt's three friends, Adams, Cohen, and Denham, all snickered.

"Welcome to the joint," said Adams. "Be careful what you say in your letters because someone reads every word you write, at least while you're in A & O being evaluated. You lose all your rights when you walk in through the front gate. In here, you're just another number. Most of the hacks think we're animals, and that's how they treat us—like animals."

"They need to believe that" said Denham, so quietly that I had to lean forward to hear him. "Otherwise, they'd have to deal with the fact that they're in here with us doing time too. They need to believe that they're better than somebody, and we're that somebody."

Denham's observation was punctuated by a loud rumbling noise off in the distance. When I looked up for signs of rain, I saw nothing but clear blue sky, not a storm cloud in sight.

"Is that thunder?"

"Yeah, that's thunder all right," said Cohen. "Rolling thunder. It's the guns from Vandenberg Air Force Base about ten miles up the coast from here."

Everyone stopped talking to listen to the guns. They really did sound like thunder to me. The foreboding of distant thunder. It was a threatening sound.

"Can you imagine what that would sound like if you were caught in the middle of it?" said Surratt. "Can you imagine having bombs big enough to make a noise that loud dropped on your village, on your family?"

No one answered. We just sat there, listening to the guns thundering in the distance.

"Damn," I said. "It doesn't sound as though the Resistance is winning the hearts and minds of the American people. It doesn't sound as though anyone is planning to end the war soon. In fact, it sounds as though they're just getting warmed up."

"I hear you," said Surratt, looking north in the direction of the guns.

"How many of the guys here are in for the draft?" I asked.

"About thirty," he said. "Thirty out of a population of around twelve hundred. Not a lot."

"You're damn right that's not a lot," Denham chimed in, again so softly that I strained to hear him. "When the riot comes later this summer, we're all going to wish there were more hippies in here."

"Riot?" said Hartman, who'd been quiet up to this point. "What riot?"

"The race riot," said Cohen. "I've been here for four years, going on five. Every two or three years, just like clockwork, going back at least ten years, there's been a race riot during the summer, usually July or August."

"That's just nuts," I said. "I'm not going to participate in any race riot. To come in here for refusing to fight in a war against Asians, then take part in a race riot against Blacks and Latinos? That makes no sense. I won't do it."

"When the shit hits the fan, you won't have a choice," said Cohen. "There's no middle ground in a riot. You're locked in here; you have to pick a side or go down alone. Summer before last, some of us were sitting in the yard, right where we are now, when it broke out. It started down in the machine shop when a brother and a low rider got into a fight about some cigarettes. Low riders had wrenches and screwdrivers. And some of the brothers got hold of baseball bats from the equipment shed. They came after us with bats and sharpened broom handles. They had us pushed up against that fence right over there. I thought we were done for, and we might have been, except the goon squad came out in riot gear and made everyone give up their weapons and lie flat on the ground. It's the only time in my life I've ever been happy to see a cop."

"There's got to be a better way to go," I said. "I didn't come in here to fight brothers in a race war."

"There *is* a better way to go," said Surratt. "A much better way."

"Which way is that?" Denham wanted to know.

Just then a buzzer blared. The yard was closing for the day. Men began drifting back to their units.

"Let's talk some more tomorrow," said Surratt as we filed into the building. The six of us agreed to meet at the same place in the yard after dinner. I was bothered by what Adams had said about the likelihood of a race riot and curious about what Surratt had in mind when he suggested there was "a better way to go."

Back in A&O I could still hear the thunder of the guns. It had been there all along, an endless drone, but I hadn't noticed it echoing within the thick concrete walls of the prison. Now that I knew what I was hearing, I heard it clearly. The hammering of the guns seemed overwhelmingly powerful, like an immutable force of nature; it also made the war seem closer, more real. The guns roared every day except Sundays. They took Sunday off. To this day I think of those guns whenever I hear thunder.

I was deep into *Invisible Man* when the guard up front called my name. I rolled off my bunk and walked up to his desk to see what he wanted.

"Boss Schwartz asked me to talk to you about this letter you wrote to your parents," he said. According to his nametag, he was Mr. Stockton. He held the letter I'd written to my parents that morning; Boss Schwartz had circled various words and phrases with red ink.

"You're going to have to make some changes before we can send this letter out," Boss Stockton said. "What's wrong with it? I'm just trying to let my parents know how I'm doing."

"There's a policy against inmates making critical comments about the institution. You shouldn't say that the food is bad."

"But it *is* bad."

"This ain't the Ritz Carlton, son."

"I know that, but the food should at least be healthy."

"The warden thinks it's healthy enough," said Boss Stockton with a chuckle. "Whether it's healthy or not, you can't criticize it in your letters. It's also against institutional policy for inmates to make comments about other inmates."

"I don't mention anyone else in my letter."

"Yes, you do. See right here, where Boss Schwartz circled this paragraph? You say that 'the inmates are generally segregated by race.' You can't talk about other inmates like that."

"Look at the yard or the mess hall. People *are* segregated by race. I'm talking about the institution, not other individual inmates."

"Didn't you hear me? You can't make critical comments about the institution." He pointed to another paragraph Schwartz had circled. "You say right here that 'this place seems designed to break people down, not to rehabilitate them.' We can't have that sort of comment going out of here. The public is liable to get the wrong impression of what we're trying to do here." He tore up my letter and tossed the pieces into the wastebasket next to his desk. "You'll have to write it over," he said.

"What *can* I say?" I asked him, trying to control my anger.

"Tell them about the weather," said Stockton. "Tell them you're doing fine." At that point, a thought crossed his mind. "You're a college boy, I saw that in your file. Tell them about the educational programs we have here at the institution. Which reminds me, Boss Schwartz says this other letter can't go out either."

The second letter was a brief note I'd written to Professor Lewis Brittenden, my academic advisor while I was an undergraduate. He'd encouraged me to go on to graduate school, and I was thinking seriously about returning to UCLA when I was released. I'd simply asked him to recommend some books that would help me to prepare for a graduate program in literature if and when the time came.

"What's wrong with *that* letter?" I said, through clenched teeth.

"This guy, Professor Brittenden, isn't a family member," Stockton said. "Until his name is approved by the correspondence committee, you can't write to him. Fill out this form and list the people you'd like to communicate with. Mostly, people put family members on their lists. In fact, people mostly don't write letters at all."

"I can't see why," I shot back, a little too quickly.

"Are you going to be a hard case, Newhall?" he said, jutting his head forward and glaring at me. "Are you? If you are, you're going to do some real hard time. Keep your nose clean and a college boy like you won't have any trouble landing a job as a clerk out on the farm. You can do some real easy time as a clerk out on the farm if you stay out of trouble. You just need to get with the program."

"I just want to be rehabilitated," I said.

"Get out of here," Stockton said, with a dismissive wave. "And re-write that letter."

As I went back to my bunk, my mind was boiling. I lay there on my bunk trying to sort out my thoughts. *Fuck this place. Why should I cooperate with them in any way? Why should I help them run their fucking prison? This place isn't helping people to prepare for life on the streets. Why shouldn't I be allowed to write a letter to one of my former teachers asking him for some reading suggestions?*

Later that evening, as I lay on my bunk after lights out reflecting on my first full day in the joint, I decided that it didn't make any sense to refuse to cooperate with the draft on the outside only to cooperate with the same system once it had locked me up. The system had physical control of my body, but it didn't—and never would—have control of my mind. I decided to write a totally bland letter to my parents in the morning, just to let them know that I was doing all right. I'd have a chance to tell them how the system really works at Lompoc—in person.

The next day passed uneventfully until right before the 4:30 count, when Dwight came walking into A and O along with two other men I recognized from County Jail up in Portland. After count was over, Hartman, Winters, Dwight, and I walked to the mess hall. Dwight's initial response to Lompoc was like mine. "This place gives me the willies," he said, as we walked down the corridor to the chow hall. "It doesn't seem to be built with human beings in mind. The scale is wrong. My first impression, when we pulled up, was that all the thick blocks of gray concrete seem designed to crush souls," he said. *Spoken like the son of a minister*, I thought.

I told Dwight about Surratt, and about the conversation we'd had in the yard. I wanted to introduce him to Surratt, so I was frustrated when an announcement over the P.A. system ordered all new arrivals from the previous three days to report to the medical center for a series of inoculations, and then to another room where we took an I.Q. test and a personality test, designed to assess our frame of mind. After that we were taken to another room where the associate warden, a sour little martinet of a man named William Keith, gave us a brief custodial sermon about Lompoc's correctional philosophy. Lompoc, he assured us, was a state-of-the-art institution, and he and the other members of the staff were dedicated to rehabilitating every one of us in the hope that henceforth we'd lead productive lives. After Associate Warden Keith's spiel, we had dinner and then headed out to the yard.

We found Surratt sitting on the grass talking with Denham, Cohen, and Adams—the "hippies" Hartman and I had met the day before.

"What kept you guys?" Surratt asked. "We've been waiting for you to show up."

I told him about the inoculations, the standardized tests, and Associate Warden Keith's pep talk.

"Isn't Boss Keith a trip?" said Surratt. "I think he really believes his own bullshit about rehabilitating people."

"Eric told me you have access to the files of all the new arrivals," said Dwight.

"Knowledge is power," said Surratt. "I don't really like working around the hacks in the Administrative Office, but it's useful to know who's coming into the joint. In particular, I make it a point to connect with all the hippies when they drive up. Some of us who've been here for a while can help some of the first timers to stay out of trouble."

"Speaking of trouble," I said, "I want to talk about the race riot Denham was talking about yesterday when the buzzer went off. You were saying you think there's a better way to go. I've been waiting all day to hear what you have in mind. I didn't refuse to kill Asians ten thousand miles away just so I could come in here and get caught up in a race riot."

"Be cool, be cool, everybody," said Denham, under his breath. "Bacon approaching."

Two guards walked by, circling the track. Once they were out of earshot, Surratt picked up where he'd left off. "A better way to go? Easy to say, hard to do. The hacks want to keep us divided so they can control us. The answer is solidarity. The answer is the same as it's always been for oppressed groups of people—and every convict in here, regardless of his offense, is a member of an oppressed group. Inmates are the waste that society throws out. They see us as trash, and the joint is where society throws its trash. If Black trash wants to destroy White trash or vice versa, the hacks are fine with it."

"So, what can we do?" I said. "What can we do to keep from playing into their hands?"

"We have to raise the consciousness of every inmate in here—or at least try to," said Surratt. "We have to make people see whose interests are served by a race riot and whose interests are not. Only the hacks benefit from racial violence. We have to make everyone see that there are only two classes of people in here—the keepers and the kept. There are more of us than there are of them. The only way they can control us is to divide us against each other. We have to unite with each other. We need to build solidarity. If we don't speak with one voice, we *will be* the trash they think we are."

This is exactly what Surratt said, almost word for word. I'm emphasizing this because some readers may find it hard to believe that these comments could come from a convict in a federal prison. The prison population in the United States in the late sixties was better educated, angrier, more politicized, and less passive than it had been a decade earlier. There was a spirit of change in the air in those days; it was palpable, and it was pervasive. It was present not just among the draft resisters and the dopers, the so-called hippies, but in Black and Latino working-class neighborhoods as well as working class and middle-class White neighborhoods. The desire for change was there, in factories and prisons as well as on the streets and in the universities. People who had dropped out of high school absorbed the thirst for change along with students on college campuses.

All of this was part of the complicated mix at Lompoc while I was there. There was anger in the air, no doubt, and a constant sense of impending violence, but there was also a great deal of hope for something better.

Our conversations in the yard were central to everything that happened at Lompoc later that summer. The yard served the same function at Lompoc that the *agora* did in ancient Athens. My father used to take great pleasure in explaining to us the crucial role played by the *agora*, the marketplace that served as the town square for the citizens of ancient Athens. Open to all male citizens, it was a free space that encouraged conversations and nurtured democratic ideas. At Lompoc, the guards could censor the mail and starve us for information from the outside world, but they couldn't control what we talked about during our free time in the yard.

"How are you going to organize a bunch of convicts?" Hartman wanted to know. "You have a lot of ignorant fools in here. Some of these guys can't even read. Besides, the brothers are angry right now, and have been ever since Martin Luther King was killed. Didn't you see the riots on TV after King was shot? The brothers want some payback. And even if we have a protest instead of a race riot, the hacks will beat the hell out of us just the same. They have all the guns, all the tear gas, and all the gas masks. We won't stand a chance, even if it's all of us together."

"I'm not talking about a riot," said Surratt. "I'm talking about a movement for change. Riots are always used to justify harsher conditions. I'm talking about a sit-down strike where we just refuse to help the hacks run the prison until things get better. I think that's possible. It's happened before. Why should we run their prison for them? Why not let them mop the floors and cook the food? Why not let them file their own damn folders?"

§

Over the next few weeks, our little group got together after dinner just about every day. One evening, Surratt told us the story of how he wound up in the joint. He'd gone to the University of Oklahoma for two years and studied political science, he said. His real love was political theory, but he also believed that the purpose of theory is to create change in the world. During the summer after his sophomore year, he'd become deeply involved with a student organization called Students for a Democratic Society (SDS), in Norman, Oklahoma. He became so disillusioned with the war in Vietnam and by the poverty he saw all around him in Oklahoma that he dropped out of school and became a full-time community organizer.

After he dropped out of school, where his full scholarship had covered the cost of his room, board, and tuition, he'd had trouble making ends meet. To get by, he started selling marijuana to friends who were still in school, but one day he got careless and sold some to an undercover narc. His sentence was a "zip-six," meaning: he could be released at any time, from day one up to the last day of year six. It was an "indeterminate sentence" that gave prison officials, the parole board, and the judge a great deal of discretion. If you wanted to get out of prison sooner rather than later, you got with the program, kept your nose clean, didn't cause trouble. Yet here was Surratt talking about organizing the prison population for a sit-down strike.

"I'm with you all the way," I said, when he first brought up the idea of a strike. I told him about my argument with Boss Schwartz over my letter. "Why should I do anything to help them run their prison? I've even thought about going on a hunger strike." Listening to Surratt had gotten me worked up, and I blurted out some things I hadn't really intended to say.

Surratt looked at me for a while. "I'm not talking about an individual protest," he said. "Moral individualism is all well and good, but that's not what I'm talking about. If one or two guys refuse to work, they'll get thrown in the Hole and nothing will be accomplished. I'm talking about collective action to shut this place down. I'm talking about trying to change the living conditions of everyone in here."

"I've been feeling the same way as Eric about this place since I got here six months ago," said Adams. "I don't want to cooperate in any way with their bullshit, but they have the power. Are you saying that we should continue to cooperate?"

"Only until we can persuade everyone, or almost everyone, to join us," said Surratt. "We choose the time when we're ready to go on strike."

"You guys are nuts," said Hartman, swatting at a bee that was buzzing around his ear. "Either that, or you're dreaming. People aren't going to lose all their good time and run the risk of getting the shit beaten out of them just to make some sort of political statement. It ain't gonna happen. All you're going to do is get yourself some hard time." He gave me an intense look. "Eric, you need to calm the fuck down and think about what you're saying. You need to get with the program for a while, get yourself a clerk's job out on the farm, do your time, and get out of here."

"What's the next step?" asked Adams, undeterred. "If we want to change this place, what's the next step?"

Surratt looked around at all of us. "Who's in and who's out?" he asked. Adams, Cohen, Denham, Dwight, and I were all in.

"Count me out," muttered Hartman, looking extremely uncomfortable.

I didn't begrudge Dale his "nay" vote. He had a point: the guards *did* have all the guns and tear gas and the Blacks *were* angry about racism in the U.S. in general and the assassination of Martin Luther King in particular. To be honest, I wasn't as certain as I sounded. Still, even though Hartman was probably right from a practical perspective, my heart was with Surratt.

Surratt stared at Hartman long enough to make him squirm. "You know you need to keep all of this to yourself," said Surratt.

"Are you calling me a snitch?" Hartman snapped. "I'm just saying that I don't think a strike will work. Most of the Blacks and Mexicans in here barely even speak to Whites. How are you going to get them to agree to go along with your plan, a plan that's going to cost them any chance they have of being paroled?"

"We're going to organize," said Surratt. "That's how we're going to make it happen. We're going to organize."

"What's the next step?" Adams was eager to know. "How do we get started?"

"First thing is, we all need to stay out of the Hole," said Surratt. "You can't organize anything in isolation. That means we accept whatever work assignment we're given. Then, the six of us need to reach out to the other groups in here. The Blacks, the Mexicans, the low riders, and the Indians."

"How will that work?" said Cohen. "Eighteen months ago, the

brothers had me up against that fence over there, ready to bash my skull in with baseball bats. How am I gonna talk to them?"

"Maybe we need to expand our core group," said Dwight. "What if we agree to meet on Saturday—four days from now—and each of us brings one more person who agrees with us?"

"Good idea," said Surratt. "That would make twelve. Twelve is just the right size for a steering committee. Six is too small and anything more than twelve gets to be too big."

Surratt knew exactly what he was doing from the outset. That's why he kept such a close tab on new arrivals. He had a plan from the beginning, and Dwight and I, along with Adams, Cohen, Denham, and the others, were part of that plan.

When I got back to A & O after our conversation in the yard, I was excited and energized. Surratt's comments suggested that my time at Lompoc could be more than just dead time. We could work for change from inside the prison; we didn't have to wait until we got out. I thought about whom I might ask to join what we all began to refer to as the "strike committee." Winters didn't strike me as particularly political, but he was angry about being back at Lompoc after only a short time out on the streets. He seemed like a possibility, at least. Maybe Dwight could approach Winters and draw him in. Then, Winters would be our link to the bikers and low riders since he already knew a lot of them from his previous time at Lompoc.

It was clear to me that as a first-time offender and recently arrived fish I was not in a good position to organize a strike against conditions at the prison. I didn't know enough people, and people didn't know me. I had no credibility and no standing with the other men. Truth be told, as a draft resister in a violent, hyper-masculine environment, I had *negative* credibility. Still, Surratt was right: to stop another race riot and to organize a strike against conditions in the prison, we needed to reach out to other groups, and we couldn't do that if we were stuck in the Hole for refusing to work.

During the next several days I made a point of starting conversations with other men in A & O, hoping to recruit one more member for our group before we met on Saturday. On Thursday a couple of guys were looking for a third to play a game of hearts, so I joined them. They were a Laurel-and-Hardy pair, one tall and thin and the other short, red-haired, and round as a bowling ball. They seemed friendly enough, but as soon as I began to steer the conversation to problems I saw in the prison, both became uneasy.

"I'm just going to do my own time," said the tall, thin one. "I didn't come down here to reform no prison. I want to do my number and go back to Seattle."

"Me, too," I said. "I just want to do my number and go back to Portland. But I don't like to be messed with, and they're messing with all of us. Boss Schwartz wouldn't let me send a letter to my parents a few days ago unless I changed the wording to suit him."

"That's some bullshit, all right," said the round, red-haired guy. "But you can't do anything about it. Prison's prison. It's not going to change—at least, not any time soon."

The game of hearts ended when I went over one hundred and fifty points, and the three of us went back to our bunks. My career as a political organizer was off to an inauspicious start.

I'd nearly finished *Invisible Man*, so I decided to read the last couple of chapters before it was time for lunch. I remember savoring the novel the first time I read it and trying to make it last. *Invisible Man* is a profound reflection on the destructive power of the color line that runs through American history and American lives. I say this even though today I don't agree with all of Ellison's conclusions. I understand the unnamed protagonist's very Emersonian desire to be free from plots, schemes, and manipulators. I also understand his anger about being invisible to the White society around him. I understand why he comes to distrust unions and the shadowy political organization, the Brotherhood. What I question when I teach the novel today is the novel's conclusion. The narrator winds up isolated, powerless, and underground—literally: fleeing an angry mob, he drops into a pitch-black hole, into a large underground room.

Ellison sees his protagonist's escape in positive terms, arguing that underground, the Invisible Man is finally free from the controlling groups intent on taking away his autonomy. Over time, however, I've come to believe that the only thing certain for Ellison's narrator is that, in his underground hideout, he can have no impact on the society above. To be fair, the narrator does *talk* about returning to the surface to take action, but it's also true that he's never able to do so successfully. When he tries to emerge from his hole, he can't avoid the machinations of the power brokers. Ellison's narrator needs a supportive, non-manipulative, political organization like the civil rights movement that supports his social goals, but in 1952 when *Invisible Man* was published, the Supreme Court decision in Plessey v. Ferguson was still the law of the land, and the Montgomery Bus Boycott had not yet taken place. Ellison could see no viable social or political option for his narrator.

I continued my recruiting efforts but got nowhere. A few men simply walked away as soon as I began to talk about the need to change conditions at Lompoc; others listened politely, but argued that, as inmates, we didn't have enough power to make real change.

After lunch on Saturday, Dwight and I went directly to the hippie section of the yard. We found Surratt in his usual spot on the grass by the volleyball courts. I noticed several new faces in the group. Cohen had brought in two new men who worked with him in the machine shop. Adams had recruited a man he worked with in the garment factory. There were nine of us now. After the new members were introduced, we talked over our successes—and failures—in trying to bring new recruits into our group.

"Everyone told me they just wanted to do their time and go home," I said. "They don't want to lose their good time, and they don't want to do hard time in the Hole. I tried to talk with a couple of the brothers, but they clearly don't trust me. Why would they? White people have never done them much good."

"You have to figure out what people want, then persuade them that our group can help them to get it," said Surratt. "Most people are willing to run calculated risks if they think it's in their self-interest to do so."

Surratt suggested that we should all continue to look for recruits, and we should try to reach out to non-hippies. We needed to connect with Blacks, Latinos, and low riders if we wanted to expand our influence.

"It will be easier to make new contacts after they move you out of A & O and into the general population," Surratt said to Dwight and me. We must have been looking a little downcast, because I sensed that he was trying to encourage us. "No one really trusts anyone when he first arrives unless he knew them on the streets before they got here. When you have the whole population to draw on, it's easier." He laughed. "We have plenty of time."

"On a different note," I said. "Does anyone have a good book that I can borrow?"

"I don't," said Surratt, "but I know where you can get one. There's a dude named Barber who's over in M-unit. Busted for LSD up in Berkeley. Dude has an M.A. in literature. You and he'd get along real well."

"Be careful if you try to find him in M-unit," said Denham softly. I wondered if he always spoke this quietly or if prison had somehow changed him. "You're not supposed to be inside any unit other than your own," Denham said. "The hacks don't always write you up if they catch you, but sometimes they do. Get in and get out quickly. Tell Barber that Denham sent you, and he'll have something for you."

The following Monday after breakfast Boss Schwartz called Hartman, Dwight, and me up to the front desk. "You guys have been here long enough to settle in. Time to put you to work. Morrill and Newhall, you guys are assigned to latrine duty. Scrub out those toilets and mop down the floor in the shower room. Hartman, sweep your half of A & O every day after breakfast and dinner. These assignments will hold you while you're in

A & O. Then you'll get a regular work assignment when you're moved out into the mainline population."

A week earlier I think I would have at least considered refusing to clean the toilets, but the conversations in the yard with Surratt and the others had changed my thinking. The idea of building a movement inside the prison aimed at changing the living conditions for the entire population appealed to me. *It's what Gandhi would have done*, I thought. *It's what Martin Luther King would have done. Start a movement. Build a movement. There's strength in numbers. Resist.*

"Sure thing, Boss," I said. "Just give us some brushes and some Ajax and Dwight and I will have those toilets so clean you can eat your lunch off them."

Schwartz gave me a long look, wondering, I think, if I had just insulted him in some way.

This job assignment lasted for the next few weeks, the rest of our thirty days in A & O. Boss Schwartz watched Dwight and me carefully, looking for any sign of insubordination. He made it clear that he had no use whatsoever for draft resisters—or "draft dodgers," as he referred to us. "You guys would be speaking German right now if everyone had your attitude during World War II," he told us one morning. "If everyone refused to fight, you guys would be working for the Nazis."

"If *everyone* refused to fight," Dwight told him, "There would have been no World War II."

Dwight and I spent our remaining time in A & O trying to find three more recruits to join "the movement," as we had all begun to refer to it. I had no luck whatsoever, but Dwight managed to make some progress with Winters, who was from Spokane, Washington, where Dwight had been going to school until he received his draft notice.

Winters was angry at "the system," as he called it, for revoking his parole and separating him from his wife over the issue of marijuana. "I'd never violate someone over a few ounces of a plant," he grumbled. "I'm in my own house doing no one any harm, and these motherfuckers violate me for possession of a *plant*." Despite his anger, however, he couldn't be persuaded to close ranks with a group of "hippies."

"I like you guys better than I did when I first saw you up in county jail in Portland," he said, "but in general I don't have a lot of use for hippies. In here, I hang out with my own kind—the bikers. When the riot comes this summer, I know they'll have my back. No disrespect, but when the shit hits the fan, I don't know for sure what you guys'll do. It'll be interesting to find out. Besides, I don't want to lose all my good time. I just want to get home and kick back with my old lady."

Prison policy mandates that 30 percent of your sentence will be subtracted if you obey prison rules and stay out of trouble. It's a sort of discount designed to produce "good behavior." On a five-year sentence, for example, eighteen of your sixty months could be subtracted for "good time." The longer your sentence, the more good time you would stand to lose for violating prison rules. Winters did not want to lose his good time by getting involved in our "movement."

Our remaining days in A & O dwindled down. I was scheduled to be moved out into the general population on May 28, one month to the day after I'd arrived at Lompoc. Dwight would join me in the mainline population two days later. The prison officials, from the warden down to the lowliest guard in a cellblock, were remarkably efficient when it came to processing prisoners. They didn't miss a beat. Their system of admitting, numbering, counting, housing, feeding, and releasing prisoners functioned like a well-oiled machine.

What gets lost in the smooth flow of this process is the damage it does to the human beings who pass through it. Most inmates leave prison more racist, more misogynistic, and more violent than when they entered, having learned no skill that will help them to find employment. Support from friends and family can help them to stay afloat for a while, back on the streets, but eventually most ex-convicts are sucked back into one illegal activity or another, unable to escape what Michelle Alexander refers to as "their permanent pariah status."*

The move out of the Fish Tank and into the general population is a life-changing transition for every inmate. In A & O, behavior is scrutinized closely by the guards, and although the guards' constant surveillance of the mail, for example, can be annoying, the close observation also provides a degree of security. Out in the general population, there is much less supervision, and more can go wrong.

During my last days in A & O, I went in search of Barber in N-unit. As it turned out, he ran a sort of lending library out of his cell for incarcerated men who liked serious literature. How he managed to do this remains unclear to me to this day, but he supplied me with good books from the day I tracked him down in N-Unit, third cell on the bottom tier, until the morning I left Lompoc.

I went looking for Barber after dinner. I was nervous because I knew I was breaking prison regulations by entering a living unit other than my own, but also because I didn't know anyone in N-unit. Nevertheless, I walked briskly through the door as though I belonged there and approached the cell Denham had directed me to. Several Black men were

---

*Michelle Alexander, *The New Jim Crow: Mass Incarceration in the Age of Color Blindness* (New York: The New Press, 2010), 95.

playing dominoes at a plastic table, slapping each piece down hard and taunting their opponents as they made their moves. They stared quizzically at me as I walked past, then went back to their game.

I approached the third cell and saw a White man about my size sitting on his bunk writing.

"Barber?" I said, through the bars.

"Who's asking?" he said in a tone that was neither friendly nor unfriendly.

"I'm Eric Newhall. I hear you trade or loan out books. Denham told me to tell you that he sent me."

"Denham's good people," he said, brightening. "What do you have for me?"

"*Invisible Man* by Ralph Ellison. What can you give me for it?"

"Ralph Waldo Ellison. Who turned you on to him?"

"I heard about *Invisible Man* in college," I said, "but I didn't read it until now. I found it when I was in County Jail up in Portland before they sent me here. I think it's a really good book."

"It's a fine novel," said Barber. "I read it on my own, too. When I was at Berkeley, they didn't assign anything by Black writers, which was getting to be an issue about the time I graduated. Where did you go to school?"

I told him that I'd attended Occidental College in Los Angeles and that I'd been an English major. When he heard this, the expression on his face changed and he began to sort through the piles of books on the floor underneath his bunk.

"Let me see what I have here that you might like," he said. He cracked his knuckles several times as he pawed through his collection. "Have you ever read *A Death in the Family* by James Agee? And what about this? *A Connecticut Yankee in King Arthur's Court*? It's by Mark Twain."

"I've read *Huck Finn* and *Tom Sawyer*," I said, "but not *A Connecticut Yankee*. I've heard of *A Death in the Family* but haven't read it. I'll trade you *Invisible Man* for those two."

"Deal," said Barber, handing me the two novels through the bars. "You'd better get out of here now before Boss Morgan catches you." Some of the hacks will cut you a break if they catch you in a unit other than your own, but Morgan isn't one of them.

Back in A & O, I started *A Death in the Family*. Between scrubbing toilets and spending time in the yard talking politics with Surratt and the rest of our circle, I finished it in two days. Two days later, Barber saw me sitting out in the yard and walked over. He nodded to Cohen and Denham, and then turned to me.

"You read those books yet?"

"One of them. I finished *A Death in the Family*."

"Well?"

"Well, what?"

"Well, what did you think of it?"

"I thought it was pretty good."

"'Pretty good,'" he said, framing my judgment in air quotes. "You think *A Death in the Family* is *pretty good*. Holy fucking shit. Where did you say you went to school?" Barber's tone was a mixture of incredulity, amused contempt, and genuine outrage.

One of the guards on yard duty heard the edge in Barber's voice and started walking rapidly in our direction. Cohen saw him coming. "No problem here, Boss," he said with a laugh. "Just a little literary dispute out here in the yard at Lompoc Federal Penitentiary."

A Death in the Family, James Agee, published in 1957.

All of us cracked up, and the guard looked at us as though we had lost our minds. In my four years as an undergraduate English major, I'd never had my taste in literature called into question with such vehemence or conviction.

"Maybe it's that I'm not a Catholic," I protested, in a game attempt to placate Barber who clearly wasn't going to go away until I gave him some sort of explanation.

"What about the tension in that opening section?" he said, still peeved. "How can you not respond to that?"

"What can I say," I said. "I like it, but there are books I like better. I'll get back to you when I'm done with Twain."

Barber walked off muttering grimly about "fucking semi-literate philistines."

Chapter 3. Fish Tank

"There's someone we ought to recruit into our movement," said Surratt. "Barber's one of those guys who doesn't do things half-way. When he believes in something, he goes all the way with it."

"I can tell," I said. "I'll see if I can bring him around—that is, if he's still speaking to me."

Near the end of May, the West Coast had shifted to daylight savings time and the weather had turned warmer. The guards regularly let us stay out in the yard until 8:00 p.m., sometimes even 8:30. One evening, Dwight and I walked four or five laps around the track, then stopped by the basketball courts to see what was happening. On one court, a full-court game was in progress. The men in this game were Indians, Adams told me, not Chicanos as I'd assumed when I first arrived at Lompoc. The other court was divided, as usual, between a Black game at one end and a White game at the other. The Blacks were to our right, yelling and smack talking after every basket. Fifteen or twenty Black men were shouting at the players from the sidelines. Dunks were frequent and wildly applauded as were behind-the-back passes. Defenders who got burned were ridiculed. Three or four of the guys in the game at that end of the court had obviously been well-coached in the fundamentals at some point before coming to prison.

Dwight and I sat down next to the White end of the concrete court. I've played a good amount of basketball in my life, and I have to say, this game was pretty sorry: six White guys who couldn't run, jump, or shoot. After they finished a game, two of the six players headed back toward the main building and the remaining four looked over at Dwight and me.

"Hey," one of them called. "Do you guys want to play some three on three?"

"Sure," Dwight and I responded in unison. We introduced ourselves to the other four players and took a few shots to warm up. Then we divided up into two teams of three. Dwight and I and the third member of our team, who called himself Low Rider, won the first game easily by a score of eleven baskets to two. Low Rider was short, about five feet, eight inches tall, with curly brown hair and blue eyes that constantly darted from person to person, never making eye contact with anyone.

"You guys are hippies, aren't you?" said Low Rider as we got a drink of water between games.

"Why do you say that?" asked Dwight.

"Because I've seen you sitting over there with the other hippies," he said. "You own a bike?" he asked.

Dwight and I both responded that we didn't, and our opponents all shook their heads.

"Thought so," said Low Rider. "You guys play pretty good basketball, but I bet you can't ride no Harley Davidson."

"That's probably true for me," I said. "I see guys riding them out on the streets, but I like the control I have in a car with a steering wheel. Harleys look pretty heavy and hard to control."

"Let's play one more game, then I got to go," said Low Rider. "I can't afford to be seen playing too much hoop with no hippies. Sometime though, you ought to get you a bike out on the streets." Two of our opponents nodded in agreement. They introduced themselves as Dog and Dusty. No last names. Just Dog and Dusty. Both men had intricate tattoos that covered their necks and arms. "You really haven't lived until you've taken a Harley out onto the freeway," said Dog with a smile. Dusty agreed. "There's just nothing like taking a bike out on the open road. It feels like flying."

"A friend of mine owns a Harley," said Dwight. "I just might ask him if I can take it for a test run when I get out of here."

We played another game and again won easily. Dwight was a tall, rugged guy who played down low near the basket—in the paint, as sportscasters refer to it—and I was a sniper from the outside. Dusty was as tall as Dwight and, if anything, heavier and a bit more muscular, but Dwight was far quicker, and better coordinated. Between the two of us, we were too good at basketball for the bikers and low riders at Lompoc Federal Prison that summer. The four bikers headed back inside after the second game.

I was just getting warmed up, and I wanted to play a few more games. My shot was dropping, and I was, as they say, "starting to feel it." Dwight and I played some one on one at our end of the court; I found that he was too strong for me to stop inside, close to the basket. He was very agile for someone his size, and he had good moves around the basket. If he were playing today, he would play what has come to be called the "power forward" position. He'd back me down low in the paint, and then simply shoot over me or, in some cases, through me. I, on the other hand, was a shooting guard. I was not what they call "a shot creator," but in those days, if you left me open at nineteen or twenty feet, I'd generally make you pay some sort of price.

Out of the corner of my eye I could see some of the Black players at the other end of the court checking us out. I was hoping they'd need two more players so we could play in a real game, but no one said anything to us. We sat next to the court and watched their game for a while, then headed back to A & O for the night.

Chapter 4

Mainline

Three days later I was moved out of A & O and into M-Unit. Hartman was moved into N-Unit as was Dwight, two days later. I was disappointed, because I'd hoped that the three of us could stick together, not only for security, but also because talking with both of them made the time pass more easily.

My cell in M-Unit was up on the third tier. M-Unit resembled what most people think of when they think of prison: tiers of individual cells stacked one on top of another. I've moved several times in my life; this move was my quickest and easiest. I simply put all the contents of my locker—clothing, toiletries, the journal I'd begun keeping since I arrived, some letters from family members, a couple of books, a few photographs—over my shoulder or into my pillowcase and carried them down the corridor to M-unit. Once inside my cell in M-Unit, it took me about five minutes to arrange things the way I wanted them, and my move was complete.

I looked around at my new dwelling. The cell measured five by seven by nine feet. It contained a metal cot with a mattress, two sheets, a pillow, a blanket, a small sink, a metal locker with two shelves, a set of earphones tuned to the same four stations available in A & O, and an open toilet in full view of any passerby. The walls on three sides were built of cinderblock. The fourth wall consisted of steel bars, half of which slid open and slammed shut every forty-five minutes or so to allow inmates to leave or return to their cells. A guard stationed at the front of each unit controlled the doors electronically.

Odd as it may seem, I felt more at ease in M-Unit than I had in A & O. Although I didn't know anyone in this new unit, I felt less vulnerable inside my cell than I had in the open design of A & O. I learned over time that other inmates felt the same way. Prisoners are assigned to cell blocks in rotation as they come into the prison. They're not grouped according to their personality, demographic background, or, as you might think, the severity of the offense that brought them to prison. First offenders are housed with repeat offenders, conscientious objectors with muggers, drug addicts with drug dealers. I rarely slept soundly in A & O because I was always worried about the violent nature of some of the other inmates in the fish tank. As it turned out, my time in A & O was peaceful, but the threat of violence was always there, and there were violent incidents every day somewhere in the prison.

Lompoc's lone psychiatrist met occasionally with ten of the draft resisters who expressed interest in meeting with him. He was a conscientious objector assigned to work at the prison for two years in lieu of serving in the military. He told us at one of our meetings about a number of violent incidents that had taken place during his two years at Lompoc. The one that shocked me most at the time involved an inmate who was gang raped in the laundry room for meditating out in the yard earlier in the day. Apparently, the act of public meditation offended the sensibilities of four or five low riders. Too many asocial individuals were packed into the same small space. From this perspective, an individual cell actually provided a feeling of security.

That first morning in M-Unit I just stayed in my cell. This was my first day out in "the population," and I decided I'd take it slowly. The cell doors opened and shut at regular intervals, but I just stayed on my bunk reading. Other inmates walked back and forth on the walkway outside the cell doors, some returning to their cells and others on their way to work assignments, appointments with their caseworkers, the yard, or who knows where. After the noon count, I left my cell along with the rest of M-Unit for lunch. As I went through the chow line, I saw Dwight and Hartman sitting at a table with one of the bikers we'd played basketball with. I got my food and joined them.

"Eric," said Dwight as I sat down. "This is Dog. You remember him from playing hoop last week?" We nodded and shook hands.

"What kind of work assignment did you guys get?" Dog asked as we ate our lunch of hamburgers, coleslaw, and under-cooked French fries. "We have a couple of openings in the machine shop if either of you are interested."

"Thanks," said Hartman, "but I'm already assigned to the kitchen. That's what I put in for when I got here. I'll be cooking for you guys in a couple of days."

"What about you, Dwight?" I asked. "Have they told you what you'll be doing yet?"

"I start working out on the farm day after tomorrow," said Dwight. "When I filled out those forms when I first got here, I told them I'd prefer some sort of outdoor work. I was thinking of working in the flower gardens, like those guys I saw when we drove up the first day, but I guess the farm won't be so bad."

"I didn't express any preference on those forms," I said, "so they have me cleaning the chow hall."

"Why didn't you do what I told you and put in for a job as a clerk?" said Hartman, frowning at me. "You could do some easy time working as a clerk out on the farm."

"At the time, I just didn't feel like stating any preference at all. So, I didn't."

"You're not going to like working for Boss Redburn," said Dog. "He's in charge of the mop detail after lunch. You'll want to get off that detail as soon as you can get a transfer. He's one of the baddest bosses in here. He'll fuck with your time just for the hell of it. Trust me on this. The dude's a motherfucker." With that, Dog stood up to leave. "Guess I'll head back to my house," he said.

"If you guys ever hear me call my cell my 'house,' please smack me," I said quietly to Dwight and Dale after Dog was out of earshot. "I can't believe anyone can call a cell his 'house.' I think maybe Dog's been locked up too long." Dwight and Dale left at that point, and I walked up to the front of the mess hall where I saw five other inmates gathered around a guard whose nametag identified him as "Mr. Redburn."

"Let's get started," Boss Redburn said to us as the last few inmates filtered slowly out of the mess hall. "If you guys concentrate on what you're doing, we can knock this off in half an hour. If you screw around, it can take all day. It's up to you."

Boss Redburn pointed to the center of the mess hall where I saw some buckets, large sponges, and several mops—not the type of mop with a sponge on it that my mother had always used at home to mop the linoleum floor in our kitchen, but a string mop, the kind you see sailors swabbing the deck with in movies. "You four, sponge off the tables," said Redburn. "You other guys grab those mops and get to work on the floor."

I picked up a bucket of soapy water and a mop and followed the other three inmates who'd been assigned to the mop detail. I dipped my mop in the soapy water and squeezed most of the water out by using a wringer attached to the bucket. Then, I started mopping. My three co-workers were faster than I was, and I had to hurry to keep up with them.

"What the hell do you think you're doing?" Redburn shouted at me from across the room. He stormed over. "You're missing spots," he snapped. "Here, here, and over there." *You need to relax you little pissant,* I thought to myself. But when I looked down at the floor I had just mopped, I saw that what he said was true. There were, in fact, some spots I'd missed. I went back over them with my mop until I was even with the rest of the crew. When we reached the far end of the mess hall, we reversed direction back toward the other end of the room. The four of us had just reached the end of the room when Redburn came rushing over again.

"You call that clean?" he snarled at us. "You call that clean? I call that some bullshit. Do it again until you get it right."

The four of us pulled our buckets back over to the third of the floor we had just mopped and started to retrace our path. The floor seemed clean to me, but I did as I was told.

Redburn left us to mop this section of the floor again while he berated the four members of the cleanup crew he'd ordered to sponge off the tables. *There's something off about this guy that reminds me of someone I know*, I thought, as I listened to him rant. *No, not someone I know; someone I saw in a movie one time. On a ship.* The Caine Mutiny, *that's the one! The sailors used mops just like these. Swabbing the decks.* Then it came to me: Boss Redburn reminded me of Captain Queeg! *He's just like Captain Queeg, the unhinged ship's captain in* The Caine Mutiny, I thought. Dog was right. I regretted not following Hartman's advice about requesting a job as a clerk out on the farm.

Each time we mopped a section of the floor, Redburn found some problem with what we'd done. I noticed that he was wearing a pair of white gloves, the sort that I associate with a military dress uniform. He'd walk over to a table that had just been wiped by one of the guys with a sponge. "You call this table clean?" he'd say, running his index finger over the top of the table. "Look at this dirt. Just look at this." And the sponge detail would begin to clean the tables all over again.

For the next three weeks this scene was repeated three times each day, after breakfast, lunch, and dinner. Redburn rarely changed. He always made us mop the floor or sponge the tables at least twice, sometimes three times, regardless of how well we cleaned them. None of us had the faintest bit of respect for the man. I'm a non-violent person, but I'm willing to admit that after listening to Redburn's ranting for a few weeks, I had a strong impulse to throttle him. So did the rest of the crew, I'm sure, but we kept our thoughts to ourselves. If a guard "writes up" an inmate for disrespectful or insubordinate behavior, the report goes into the inmate's file and decreases the likelihood of early release or parole.

Dale, Dwight, and I continued to meet in the yard after dinner with Surratt and the other hippies, discussing "the movement" and our efforts to build support for a strike. Our conversations always began with planning for the strike, but that's not all we talked about. Sometimes we would just socialize and talk about other joints people had done time in or occasionally how someone had gotten busted. There were about twelve hundred inmates incarcerated at Lompoc while I was there, and other than the draft resisters, I can remember only five or six of them admitting they'd committed the crime for which they'd been convicted. Most inmates who talked about their "beef" claimed to have been framed or "given up" by their crime partner or unfairly punished by a harsh judge who had it in for them. I did not encounter many penitents in the penitentiary.

One evening around the middle of June we were talking in the yard after dinner, and I sensed a tension in Surratt that I hadn't felt before. He seemed to be on edge, snapping uncharacteristically when anyone asked him a question. Finally, Dwight asked him what was bothering him.

"Well, it's like this," said Surratt. "The last several days all the hacks in the main administrative office have been talking about the race riot this summer. To hear them talk about it, you'd think it's a formal event, pre-scheduled on the institutional calendar. Their conversations assume that it's going to happen and it's only a question of when. Some of them seem to be looking forward to it."

"When do they think it's going to happen?" said Hartman. "I'd like some advance notice."

"After the weather warms up," said Surratt. "Most of them are guessing sometime in July or August, early September at the latest. If we're going to do something to head off a riot, we need to get moving."

"I've tried to reach out to a few people in N-Unit," said Dwight, "but they just look at me like I'm nuts or something. They're afraid of losing their good time or being sent to the Hole or both. I've tried talking to Dog and his buddy Low Rider, to see if I could get some of the bikers to come along, but they just want to do their time and move on."

"You know what we need?" said Surratt.

"What's that?" asked one of the new members of our group, a stocky, redheaded guy named Breintnall.

"We need a list of demands," said Surratt. "People won't go out on strike unless they think it's worth the risk. We need to give people a list of concrete reasons to strike. We need to show them how their lives will get better if they join the strike. People won't strike for vague generalities or abstract ideas. They want something concrete that they can hold on to."

"Makes sense to me," said Cohen. "Let's put together a list of concrete demands right now."

The nine of us sat there in a circle in the yard at Lompoc, composing a list of demands until the buzzer indicated that the yard was closing for the day. I don't remember the exact date, but I know that it was around the middle of June; Dwight and I had been moved out of A & O a couple of weeks earlier, at the end of May. We asked each other a question that I've been asking myself, my family, my colleagues, and my students ever since: what is there in this world that you want or need so much that you would be willing to risk something significant to get it?

In some ways, the list of demands we came up with seems trivial. From another perspective, however, the fact that we were even talking about a strike seems remarkable. The guards and prison officials had all the Billy clubs, all the guns, all the tear gas and gas masks—in short, all the coercive power. As we sat there in the yard creating our list, we heard the ever-present guns at the Air Force base up the coast rumbling in the background. If the warden should happen to need reinforcements, the military police at the Air Force base were only a phone call away. From a tactical perspective, you might say that our position was untenable.

Nevertheless, with the guns rumbling in the background as a kind of mocking accompaniment, we came up with a list of demands around the middle of June. True to form, Hartman's first thought was about food. Although he remained skeptical about the notion of a strike, we continued to include him in our conversations. We trusted him not to snitch on us, and we also hoped he might eventually come around and join us. "We need a better grade of meat than we're getting," said Hartman. "I'm in the kitchen every day, and I can tell you that somebody's cutting corners on the meat they order. I'm not sure what's in the mystery meat they serve, but I am sure that it's not all ground beef."

"While we're on the subject of food," said Cohen, "I think we should demand more fresh fruit and vegetables and less of this canned shit they give us. Here we are in motherfucking California, and we can barely get any fresh fruit on the menu."

"Enough about food," I said. "People on the streets aren't going to support changes that cost them more money. What about some changes that will help us but won't cost them a cent?"

"Like what?" said Cohen.

"Like letting us have books sent in from the outside," I said. "I'd like to read some books in here that will help me when I get out, but they won't let my parents or any of my friends send books to me. My father mentioned in his last letter that a shipment of books he had mailed to me had been returned to him with a form letter telling him that such shipments were 'against institutional policy.'"

"No shit," said Surratt. "What did he try to send in?"

"Three novels by William Faulkner and three by Herman Melville," I said. "I'd like to learn more about both of those writers, and Barber has nothing by either of them."

"You ought to talk to your case worker," said Denham. "Sometimes they can help to work something out."

"Another thing," I said. "Why shouldn't we be able to correspond with anyone we want to correspond with? I'm trying to stay in touch with my advisor from school, and they won't let me put him on my correspondence list because he's not a family member."

"They don't want you corresponding with any radical college professor," said Dwight.

"This guy's not a radical," I said. "In fact, I suspect he may be a Republican. I just want to get some reading suggestions from him in case I decide to go back to school when I get out."

"People strike over bread-and-butter issues," grumbled Cohen. "Do you really think the bikers will strike for more books and more people to write letters to?"

The group in general wasn't thrilled with either of my suggestions, but they agreed to put them on the list. "We need a list that has a little something for everyone," said Surratt. "If Barber and Newhall want more books in here, that's good enough for me. Books, ideas, and writing always play a role in creating social change."

"What about the fucking medical care in here?" said Cohen? "One or two doctors for twelve hundred inmates and only one shrink. The warden and the guards don't really care if we live or die. They do just enough to cover their butts against a lawsuit and bad publicity, and that's all."

"Right on," said Adams. "And dental care. We ought to be able to have our teeth cleaned and examined at least once every other year. Going to prison shouldn't mean that you have to lose your teeth."

"Their whole philosophy has to change," Dwight chimed in. "There's a guy named Dawkins in N-Unit with Dale and me who can't read. He's twenty-four years old, and he can't read. That's the real reason Dawkins is in here in the first place. He went to an elementary school that didn't teach him how to read, and he went to a high school that let him graduate anyway. He can't fill out a job application because he can't read the instructions. He should be spending every day learning how to read, but they have him pushing a broom all day instead."

"Vocational training in here is a joke," said Surratt, who up to this point had simply been jotting down notes. "They talk about learning a trade in prison so that people can get a job on the streets when they get out, but it's just rhetoric. I was talking to a dude named Dusty the other day about the auto mechanics program. He knows cars because he's worked as a mechanic on the streets. He says that the equipment in the auto shop is so out of date that even if you learn how to use it, you're still nowhere, because no shops on the outside use equipment that old."

"We'll demand vocational training programs with up-to-date technology and equipment," Surratt said. "They make the public think their tax dollars are being put to good use, but the vocational programs in here are a sham."

That was as far as we'd gotten with our list when the buzzer rang. Surratt told us to keep thinking of additional demands. "This isn't a bad list," he said. "It's a good start, but we need to have a little something for everyone. Right now, this looks like just the sort of list that a group of hippies would come up with. Fresh fruits and vegetables and books. We need to find a way to reach those guys over there." He pointed over to the basketball courts and the weightlifters. "We need to bring in the low riders, the brothers, and the Mexicans," he said. "Building a movement is about building solidarity. We need a list of demands that attracts everyone, regardless of background."

Surratt was always talking about the need for solidarity. In the beginning, his talk sounded vague and abstract to me—just words. Over time, that would change.

When I went back to M-Unit after the yard closed that evening, I found a group of about twenty men gathered in front of the television, watching a professional basketball game. By June the NBA playoffs were into the semi-finals. In those days the Boston Celtics and Bill Russell were riding high in the East and the Los Angeles Lakers were the favorite in the West. I stopped to watch for a while before going up to my cell on the third tier. All the plastic chairs were occupied already, so I leaned against the wall and watched. The twenty inmates were about half Black and half White. Most were from southern California, judging from the cheers that went up whenever Philadelphia scored. Most Laker fans were tired of losing to the Celtics and hoped that Philadelphia would put the Celtics out in the semifinals so the Lakers wouldn't have to face them in the finals.

One of the Black inmates seemed to have it in for the Celtics. I recognized him as the best player I'd seen playing in the game on the Black end of the court a few days earlier. His friends called him Crow, I assumed because he was Black and could practically fly. In those days, Philadelphia had two very good guards. Every time they scored, made a good pass, or stole the ball from the Celtics, the Crow would shout his approval. "Bill Russell is old," said Crow. "He's old and worn out and so is K.C. Jerry West and Elgin are going to eat these motherfuckers up if Philly don't do it first." He was talking to another Black inmate I recognized as one of the four guys on sponge detail in the mess hall. The cell doors clanged open reminding all of us that we needed to get back into our cells promptly or be shut out of them for the next forty-five minutes. I decided to watch the rest of the game and sat down on one of the chairs that opened when several men returned to their cells. Sports in general and basketball in particular were among the most "normal" experiences I had during my time in prison. This time of year, I always watched the NBA playoffs; it made no difference whether I was locked up or on the streets. The same is true of playing hoop. Pickup basketball games in the joint weren't that much different from pickup games on the street. A little rougher maybe, but essentially the same game.

After dinner the next day I felt like playing some hoop. When Dwight and I went out into the yard, we saw Surratt and the other guys sitting in their customary spot by the volleyball court, talking about our list of demands, no doubt. Dwight wanted to join them, but I persuaded him to head over to the basketball courts. "They'll be there tomorrow and the next day," I told him. "Politics is all Surratt thinks about. The guy is totally committed. I get it. And I respect him, but I need a break. I really want to play some ball today." Last night, I'd joined a crowd of guys watching the NBA playoffs on the M-Unit TV. The game was between Boston and Philadelphia, the two strongest teams in the Eastern Conference that year. Watching the playoffs had gotten me all fired up.

We walked over to the courts, where the usual three games were already in progress. Low Rider, Dusty, and two other White guys were playing two on two at one end and eight brothers were playing four on four at the opposite end. On the adjoining court, the Indians, with one or two Latinos mixed in, were running full court.

We sat down next to the White game and waited our turn. When Low Rider and his partner reached eleven, the four of them paused and looked over at us.

"You guys want to play?" said Low Rider.

"Yeah," I said. "Give us one guy and we'll take you on."

"No way," said Low Rider. "We got to split you two up. I remember the last time we played. Let's make even sides."

So Low Rider, Dusty, and I took on Dwight, and the other two bikers. We played a couple of games to eleven baskets and worked up a good sweat. Down at the other end of the court, one of the Black guys who'd been watching the playoffs in M-Unit was doing his thing, dunking the ball at every opportunity. I recognized him as the best player I'd seen playing in the game on the Black end of the court. His friends called him Crow because he was Black and could jump higher than anyone else on the court. I also noticed that another Black inmate I'd seen around M-Unit, Bubba, was a very solid player. He could pass, dribble, and shoot. He wasn't as flashy as Crow, but he was fundamentally sound and very strong. The brothers were playing games to eleven baskets, one point per basket, with the winning team holding the court and the losers sitting until it was their turn to challenge again. Crow, the guy named Bubba from sponge detail, and two other guys were on a run that day. Nobody could sit them down.

Two games of half court with the bikers left me warmed up and wanting more, but Low Rider, Dusty, and the other bikers had had enough.

They headed off to the section of the yard where the bikers hung out. Dwight and I shot for a while longer, then sat down on the grass next to the court to watch the brothers.

Crow could really play the game. He was about six feet three inches, very agile, and looked as though he didn't have an ounce of fat on his body. At times he was unnecessarily flashy, but someone had schooled him well; every aspect of his game was solid. He had a good outside shot that set up his drives to the basket. If you sagged off him to protect the middle, he'd pull up and hit a jump shot; if you got up in his face, he'd just blow past you.

Crow, Bubba, and two other guys won several games in a row, at which point several of the Black players called it quits. Drifting off to their units, they left Crow, Bubba, and two other players on the court.

"Let's go two on two," I heard Bubba say.

"No," said Crow. "I don't want to play no two on two. Three on three's a better game." Crow glanced over at Dwight and me for a second, then turned away and called to a couple of brothers walking past on the other side of the court. "Big Bob," he called. "You and Jomo want to play some hoop?"

They didn't. Crow looked at Dwight and me again. He said something under his breath to Bubba and the other Black guys, who laughed and nodded in agreement. Crow strolled slowly over to where we were sitting.

"You boys want to play some hoop?" he asked us.

This was a *very* interesting moment. Crow hadn't called us "boys" by accident. He was playing to his friends and issuing a challenge to us. He was curious to see how we would react. He was testing us. We could take his bait—or we could ignore his taunting "boy" and just play some ball. We wanted to play some ball.

"We thought you'd never ask," Dwight said.

"Let's run," I said.

"Where are you guys from?" Crow asked. "Portland," I said. "Ashland," said Dwight.

"Where are you from?" I asked Crow.

"We're all from L.A.," he said, "except for Tim here. He's from Napa Valley. Owns a winery up there, don't you Tim?"

Crow and his friends all enjoyed a laugh, apparently at Tim's expense. I learned later that Tim worked out on the prison farm, where he surreptitiously made what prisoners called "pruno," a horrible-tasting alcoholic beverage that he sold to other inmates for packs of cigarettes.

"Let's get this here game going," said Crow. "Bubba, me, and this white dude here against Tim, EJ, and the big white dude."

Crow was as good a ball player as I've ever played with—tall, wiry,

Chapter 4. Mainline

and lightning quick. Bubba was six three and muscular, so he guarded Dwight. I covered EJ, and Crow took Tim, or Tiny Tim as his friends called him affectionately.

That basketball game on an ugly concrete court in the yard at Lompoc was the start of something that would drive me for the rest of my life. It was the day six of us broke the color line at Lompoc and began to resist the prison culture of racism and violence from the inside. Crow, Bubba, and I won the first game 11–8. I was pumped up to be playing with players who knew how to play the game but also because I was intensely aware that the six of us were crossing a line.

Other inmates from around the yard gradually began to drift over to the court. They sensed that something was going on too. They'd never seen Blacks and Whites playing with and against each other in the same game—at least not at Lompoc. Some of the spectators were probably wondering if this was where the riot was going to start. Would there be a fight in a game of basketball that eventually spread throughout the yard, turning into a riot? The guards must have been thinking the same thing because they moved in from their usual positions on the outer edges of the yard. They didn't say anything; they just moved closer to our game and watched.

After the first game, Tiny Tim called a time out. He was an excitable sort of guy who wore his feelings on his sleeve, and he didn't like to lose. He *really* didn't like to lose. I could hear him tearing into EJ. "You're shooting the ball too much, motherfucker," he said. "If you were lightin' it up, that would be one thing, but you're not hitting shit. Give the ball to the big man. He's too strong for Bubba." EJ was not at all happy, because, as I later learned, he really did love to shoot, but he could also see that Tim knew what he was talking about. Crow, Bubba, and I had a clear edge if the game boiled down to finesse and shooting. Dwight, EJ, and Tim had a much better chance if they passed the ball inside to Dwight.

That's what they did in the second game. Dwight was simply too strong for Bubba to handle down low, close to the basket. Tim and EJ were both good ball handlers; they slowed the game down so they could work the ball inside to Dwight. Then Dwight would either shoot a hook shot over Bubba or power the ball through him. Crow wanted to win just as badly as Tim, and he began to talk to Bubba. "C'mon, man," he'd say. "You got to stop that white boy. He's punkin' you." This was the first time I'd heard that term. In prison slang, "punkin'" means "turning you into a punk"—"dominating you."

Used between strangers or enemies, it's a serious insult, and generally leads to fights. Used among friends, it's half-insult, half shit-talking banter, but still an insult that requires some sort of response. Bubba started pushing on Dwight, fouling him—hard—when he took his shot. Dwight didn't call the fouls, as he would have in a game on the streets. But he did start playing harder. Tim and EJ kept working the ball inside to Dwight, and at one point, much to the delight of the inmates gathered around the court, Dwight dunked the ball three times in succession with Bubba hanging all over him.

Crow began to yell at Bubba every time Dwight scored. "Damn Bubba. Get up on that big motherfucker."

Bubba finally got tired of Crow's criticism: "You guard him then, motherfucker, if you think you can stop him."

"All right, then, I will," said Crow. Bubba switched to guarding Tim, and Crow matched up with Dwight.

The score was ten to seven, with Dwight's team in the lead. Crow was riding Dwight hard, but Dwight was just too strong. Crow could jump higher than Dwight, but he didn't have Dwight's bulk or strength. Tim bounced the ball inside to Dwight, who took the pass, turned, and dunked the ball right through Crow's outstretched arms. Crow and Dwight came down next to each other, and Dwight landed like a sack of cement on top of Crow's left foot.

"Oh, God damn!" Crow yelled in obvious pain. "That hurts like a motherfucker. You've got some goddamned big feet!" Still cursing, Crow limped to the side of the court and collapsed onto the grass. He took off his left shoe and began to massage his foot. Only then did I notice that he was wearing black Converse All-Stars, the most popular basketball shoe in those days before leather athletic shoes took over the market. Dwight was wearing the only shoes he had—the big, clunky, leather, work boots he'd been given when he arrived at Lompoc. They were fine for his job out on the farm, but they were near lethal on the basketball court.

"You got some big feet," Crow lamented, gingerly massaging his left ankle.

"Yeah, man," added Tim. "You look like Bigfoot out there. That's what we gon' call you from now on: Bigfoot." Everyone laughed. From that day until the day he was released, Dwight was Bigfoot. Over time, "Bigfoot" was shortened to simply "Foots."

Having determined that no bones in his foot were broken, Crow was up and eager to play again. "You guys ready for one more?" he asked.

"Sure," said Foots. "Let's play the tie breaker."

Just then, one of the guards, Boss Jackson by name, declared the game over and the yard closed. "Let's get this yard cleared," he shouted to the other guards.

"What you talkin' about, Boss?" said Crow. "I didn't hear no buzzer."

"You're not in charge here, boy," said Boss Jackson. "I decide when free time is over. You guys get your butts back inside the institution. This yard is shutting down right now."

Fifty or sixty other inmates, a mixture of Blacks, Whites, and a few Latinos, were eager to see who would win the tiebreaker. Some of the spectators began to boo, hiss, and hurl insults at Boss Jackson and, into the bargain, his entire family.

Jackson yanked the walkie-talkie from his belt and called for support. Then he turned and faced the crowd of angry inmates. "Are we going to have an incident here, or are you guys going to go back inside? Free time is over for today."

Consciously or not, Boss Jackson and the other guards understood on some level that their interests lay in keeping the White and Black basketball games separated. An integrated game would strengthen ties between inmates, thus weakening the control the guards had over all of us.

"I guess we'll have to finish this tomorrow," said Crow. "Same time, same place?" he asked Foots and me.

"We'll be here," I said.

"And one more thing," said Crow. "You got to get you some basketball shoes, Bigfoot. Don't come out here tomorrow wearing them killer boots. You're damn sure going to cripple somebody and I don't want it to be me."

Back inside M-Unit, I saw Crow and Bubba watching the Laker game that was being televised that day. I took a seat on the White side of the room. "Get on, Zeke," I heard Crow shout across the room. "Get on, you bad motherfucker!" He was referring to Jerry West, perhaps the best White player of his era and one of the best guards ever to play the game. West was called "Zeke from Cabin Creek" by the commentators, a reference to his hometown of Cabin Creek, West Virginia.

Most of the inmates at Lompoc rooted for the Lakers that summer. In those days, sports were a significant part of my life and my identity, and my time in prison was no exception. At their best, sports function as a progressive force, as common ground that helps to bring people from different backgrounds together. Team sports can cross both class barriers and the color line. When a racially mixed group of men who don't know each other get together in a social situation, it's generally possible to break through an awkward silence by asking something like, "How about them Dodgers?" or "Damn, did you see Zeke light it up last night on the tube?" Obviously, the world of athletics is still tainted at all levels by racism, sexism, and homophobia. At times, however, a more progressive side of athletic competition comes to the fore and helps to break down barriers of race and class that normally divide us from each other. That's the role that basketball played during the summer of '69 at Lompoc Federal Penitentiary.

The next morning, after I was done with my floor mopping assignment, Boss Redburn handed me a note telling me to report to my caseworker's office at 11 a.m. Boss O'Brien opened his office door when I knocked. He was a tall, thin man who looked rangy enough to have played some basketball himself in his day. He motioned me to a chair. "Newhall," he said. "I've been meaning to talk with you for a while, but my caseload didn't allow me to contact you until now. We need to talk about your father."

"What about my father?" I was surprised, because I wasn't aware that my father had had any contact with O'Brien or, for that matter, any prison official.

"Your father sent a shipment of books addressed to you. In fact, he's sent it twice, and we've returned it to him twice."

"Why did you return it?" *Here we go again,* I thought. "What harm can some books do? I asked my father in a letter to send me some books that might help me to get a job after I get out of here. I asked him to send me some novels by Herman Melville and William Faulkner. Those authors are two of the best American writers ever."

"That's not the issue, Newhall," said O'Brien with a bored expression on his face.

"What *is* the issue then?"

"It's against prison policy to have packages of any kind sent in from the outside. If we allowed packages to be sent in, this place would be full of drugs in no time flat. We just can't allow that."

"What if you were to inspect the packages of books? My father is a teacher; he's not a drug smuggler."

"We have to treat everyone the same," O'Brien explained in a patronizing tone. "If we let you receive a package, we'd have to do the same for everyone. We don't have the manpower to inspect that many packages."

He switched gears. "But this letter here is what I wanted to talk with you about."

He handed me a letter addressed to him and signed in my father's left-handed, semi-legible scrawl. The first two paragraphs spoke in general terms about the value of great literature and explained my tentative goal of becoming a college professor. The final paragraph cut to the heart of the matter. "Could you please send me a statement of your educational policy?" it asked. *Good move, Pop,* I thought to myself. "What did you tell him?" I asked. "What *is* your educational policy, anyway?"

I laugh every time I think of this exchange. I've used this move of my father's a number of times during my forty-some years in academic life. Whenever I suspect that I'm dealing with a bureaucrat who doesn't have any sound basis for why he's doing what he's doing, I just ask him or her for an explanation of their policy. I've learned, through multiple humorous experiences, that people are usually at a loss when pressed to explain the reasoning behind stifling bureaucratic policies. It's generally easier for them to give you what you want than it is for them to make sense of petty, arbitrary rules.

"So how are you going to respond?" I asked O'Brien again.

"We've decided to let his books in as long as he doesn't send any more shipments."

"Is that your *policy*, then?"

"Our policy is that you can have hardback literature sent in from the outside directly from the publishers, but you can't have any paperback books sent in."

"I beg your pardon?" I couldn't believe my ears.

"I said that you can have good literature sent in as long as it comes directly from the publishers, but you can't have any paperbacks," O'Brien repeated.

It took me a few moments to figure out exactly what he was saying, and when I understood, I came dangerously close to laughing out loud. "Let me be sure I'm understanding you," I said. "If someone wants to send a collection of hardback novels by Melville or Faulkner, he can do that. But he can't send paperback versions of the same novels."

"That's right," said O'Brien. "Prison policy won't allow paperbacks to be sent in under any circumstances."

To O'Brien, "hardback book" meant "textbook" and "educational material," both of which were acceptable to the Department of Corrections, whereas "paperback" meant violent pulp fiction like detective stories or westerns, or maybe soft-core pornography. "I'm glad we had a chance to talk this over," I said. "The next time I write to my father, I'll ask him to send only hardbacks, directly from the publishers."

"That should take care of it," said O'Brien. "Usually, we can work these things out if people are reasonable." "One other thing," he said casually, as I got up to leave. "I'd be a little careful about getting too close to any of the Black boys in here if I were you."

"What do you mean?"

"We've got established ways of doing things here at Lompoc, Newhall," he said. "I heard yesterday in the Officer's Lounge that you and your partner were mixing it up with the Black boys on the basketball court. Nothing good can come of that. I'd advise you to be careful about trusting any of the inmates you didn't already know before you got here. Some of these more experienced cons will try to take advantage of first-time offenders like you and your partner."

"Thanks for the advice," I told him. "These guys seem like decent guys who just want to play some hoop. But I'll keep my eyes open." *Interesting,*

I thought. *One game of basketball in the yard, and my caseworker already knows about it. And he's advising me to steer clear of Black inmates. The possibility that we might get along with each other threatens him.* I made a mental note to bring this up with Surratt and our group after dinner.

As I was heading back to M-unit, Hartman walked up to me from the direction of the mess hall. "I got something for you," he said. He looked around quickly to see that we weren't being observed, then he handed me a sandwich-sized package wrapped in wax paper.

"Keep this in your pocket until you get back to your cell," he said. "And don't let anyone else see it. There's more where these came from. Oh, yeah," he said. "One other thing. One of the guys I work with in the kitchen just told me that a clerk position out on the farm is going to come open around the middle of July. There's a dude named Stevenson who's getting out in four or five weeks. You'll have a good shot at getting that job if you let them know you're interested. I'll keep you posted." With that he turned and walked back toward the door to the mess hall.

Back in my cell I opened the wax paper and discovered three large chocolate chip cookies. They were still warm. I began to see why Hartman put in for a job in the kitchen. It gave him easy access to food. For reasons I didn't fully understand, food was extremely important to him. He stored different sorts of snacks—cheese and crackers, peanut butter and crackers, Ding Dongs, candy bars—in his locker to eat between meals throughout the day and out in the yard after dinner. My best guess was that his constant snacking had to do with his desire to do easy time. Hartman was a hedonist, and tasty food, particularly sweets, made the time pass by more easily. I can't prove it, of course, but I also began to suspect that not all of Hartman's hunger was physical. Something else was driving his behavior. I think he was searching for something to make sense of his life—and not finding it.

I ate the cookies slowly, savoring every bite. It briefly crossed my mind that the cook, Hartman, or someone else, might have spiked the cookies with marijuana or something else (the joint makes everyone a little paranoid), but I ate them anyway. I spent the rest of the morning in my cell reading and writing a letter home, telling my father about my conversation with Boss O'Brien. I heard back from him a couple of days later that he had placed a book order and that he had paid a few dollars extra so that the publisher would ship his order directly to Lompoc.

The buzzer for lunch went off just as I was finishing my letter. I left my cell when the door opened, dropped my letter into the box for "outgoing mail," and headed down toward the mess hall. Crow and Bubba were going to lunch along with the rest of M-Unit.

"You and your partner still up for some hoop later today?" Crow asked.

Chapter 4. Mainline 89

"We'll be there," I said. "Same teams as yesterday?"

"Same teams. You tell Bigfoot I got something for him."

"What's that?"

"Just tell him that Crow has something for him." Crow and Bubba went off to sit in the Black section of the Chow Hall. I found Foots and Hartman over with the hippies.

"Crow says to tell you that he has something for you," I told Dwight.

"Something for me?" asked Dwight. "What does he have for me?"

"He wouldn't say," I said. "I guess we'll have to wait until after dinner to find out."

After dinner that day when I finally got out to the yard, I looked over at the basketball courts. The Indians were already running up and down, playing their special brand of fast break basketball or "rez ball" as they called it, but there was no sign of Bubba, Crow, EJ, or Tim. I saw Foots over by the volleyball court, talking with Surratt and the other members of our group.

"What's going on?" I asked Foots. "I thought we were going to play some hoop today."

"We are," Dwight said, "but Crow's going to be late."

"Listen to those guns," said Surratt, shaking his head slowly. "All day, every day, except Sunday. There are thousands of guys over there at the Air Force base, training and going off to Vietnam. Everyday hundreds of young guys being shipped off to fight and maybe die in a war that we have no business being in."

"It's a tragedy," I said. "Someday, people will see that we're on the wrong side of history in this war."

"I'm not so sure of that," said Cohen. "I'm not so sure people will think differently about Vietnam twenty years from now. In fact, I think there's just as good a chance that you and Dwight and everyone else in here for the draft are going to feel a lot of heat for being disloyal in time of war. You've read about the witch-hunts during the McCarthy era. Nam has been so ugly that the witch-hunts after this war are going to make McCarthy look like fucking Tinkerbell. Ten years from now I'll be working for some business making a good salary; everyone will have forgotten about my little drug bust up in the Bay Area. Ten years from now you and Dwight are still going to be feeling the heat. This country won't forgive draft dodgers, particularly if we don't win the war."

"Draft *resisters*," I said. "We didn't dodge shit."

Before anyone had a chance to respond, Tim came running over. "Let's play some hoop! Crow's done with his business and he's ready to run." Over on the court, Crow, EJ, and Bubba were starting to warm up.

"See you guys later," said Dwight. "We got to play some hoop."

"Keep your wits about you," said Surratt. "The guards have their eyes on your game, and they don't like it. You saw what Boss Jackson did yesterday. He shut the yard early just to break up your game."

When we got over to the court, Crow handed Dwight a large brown paper bag.

"What's this?" Dwight asked.

"Open it up and see," said Crow.

Inside the bag, Dwight found an extra-large pair of black Converse All-Star basketball shoes. They weren't new, but they looked as though they'd only been worn a few times.

"Where did you get these?" asked Dwight.

"I got a friend in the supply room who gets things for me every once in a while. I told him that you were going to kill me with those boots of yours if somebody didn't get you some basketball shoes to wear. Consider these to be on loan until you can get your own from the Commissary."

Dwight sat down on the grass and put the shoes on. They were size fourteen and they were still a little tight, but he laced them up and we started to play. I was feeling good that day and happy to be playing basketball with some guys who knew how to play. The rim looked huge; it felt as though everything I put up was going to go in. I was in the zone that day: I hit my first four shots, and Bubba and Crow did what I'd always been taught to do—get the ball to the man with the hot hand.

"Get on, New," shouted Crow, when my fourth shot went in. "Get on, you bad motherfucker."

Once again, a crowd of inmates began to gather around the court, Blacks on one side, Whites on the other. The crowd started to whoop and holler with every basket.

"That White boy's lighting you up," shouted one of the Black bystanders to EJ who was guarding me again. This irritated EJ, who shot a hard look at the guy who had made the comment. The next time I got the ball, EJ fouled me hard on my left forearm as I was going up for a shot.

"That's a foul," said Crow when I didn't say anything. "That's a goddamned intentional foul."

"He didn't call nothing," objected EJ. "The man with the ball didn't call nothing."

"I don't care if he called a foul or not," said Crow. "I'm calling a fucking foul."

EJ threw the ball to Crow, a little harder than necessary, and the game continued.

"Damn," said Crow, after Dwight scored with one of his inside moves. "You're wearing rubber shoes, but it still hurts when you land on me. You got some righteous feet."

Everyone laughed because it was true. Foots was like the proverbial bull in a china shop. He meant no harm, but if he landed on you, you'd be in a world of pain the next day.

The teams were evenly balanced, and the score went to ten all. Bubba set a pick on EJ, and I drove off it, pulled up, and hit a jump shot from the top of the key.

"Lights out," said Crow. "Eleven to ten. Game over." The Black fans howled at EJ for being lit up by a white boy. The White fans, a mix of hippies and some low riders who had wandered over from the weightlifting area, stayed quiet, but nodded their heads vigorously.

"This is bullshit," said Tim. "The game's not over. Everyone knows you have to win by two baskets. Ain't no game over when it's 11 to 10."

"Bullshit my ass," said Crow. "Everyone knows that the first team to eleven wins. And we have eleven. What do you say, New?" That's what I was called most of the time in prison—New.

"Well, on the streets, different gyms have different rules," I said. "What are the house rules here at Lompoc?"

"Ain't no fucking house rules here," said Tim. "It's about whoever's in charge. And I say you have to win by two."

Tempers were starting to heat up on both sides; someone needed to cool the situation down. "From now on, let's say that to win you have to win by two points," I said. "The score's 11-10 in this game, and it's our ball since we scored the last basket."

Crow didn't look happy, but he went along with my suggestion. We ran the same play as before. Bubba set a pick for me at the top of the key. I rubbed EJ off on the pick and looked for my jump shot, but Foots moved up on me quickly to help EJ out. This is the oldest play in basketball—the pick and roll. When Foots left Bubba and picked me up, Bubba rolled to the basket. I fed him a quick bounce pass for a lay in. Game over. Or so I thought, but Tim wasn't done yet.

"What you yellin' about," he asked Crow. "Everybody knows a series ain't over till one team wins three out of five. Two out of three ain't no series. A series is three out of five games. Even ignorant motherfuckers know that."

"Fuck it then," said Crow. "We'll beat your ass three out of five."

So, we started a fourth game, and I could feel the tension mounting. By this time, the noise around our court had attracted most of the inmates in the yard along with the guards, who wanted to keep their eyes on what was going on.

In the fourth game, Dwight's strength gradually began to wear Bubba, Crow, and me down. Bigfoot was one of the strongest men at Lompoc that summer. In a full court game of five on five we could have double teamed him and made him give up the ball. When we tried to do this in a three-on-three game he simply did what he had been coached to do: he passed the ball to the open man—Tim or EJ—for lay ins or short jump shots. We had no good answer for his power, and we lost the fourth game 11–6.

Crow, it turns out, was a little bit of a ham. "All right now," he said to us but also to the inmates watching from both sides of the court. "Counting yesterday's games, we each won two. We got us a one game series now." He spoke into his fist pretending that he was a TV announcer commenting on the game into a microphone. Crow was hamming it up for the crowd that continued to grow as word spread about our game, and more inmates came into the yard to watch. "It's even up after four games, folks. Will the power of the big man be too much for Crow, New, and Bubba or will the Crow fly one more time?"

The spectators applauded his imitation of a television announcer and shouted comments at all of us out there on the court. "Get on, Crow," shouted someone from the Black side of the crowd. "Show Tim how the game is played."

"Don't tell me no White boys can't play no ball," said one of the White spectators. I looked over to see where the comment had come from and found that it had come from a low rider who had a large eye tattooed right in the middle of his forehead.

"Ain't that right," he said again. "Don't tell me that no White boys can't play no basketball. Keep shooting that ball, Slim," he said to me. "Keep dunking the ball, big man," he said to Foots.

"You tell 'em, Cyclops," shouted one of his friends. "You get on, you bad motherfucker." Cyclops had a shaved head, a muscular build, and yellow teeth that looked as though they were rarely, if ever, brushed.

We started the fifth game with both teams intent on implementing their strategy. EJ and Tim dribbled around the perimeter until they could work the ball inside to Bigfoot, who would overpower Bubba or Crow, who took turns guarding him. We would run our pick and roll; Crow and I would shoot high percentage jump shots or try to hit Bubba for lay-ins as he rolled to the basket.

The score went to six all, at which point two guards stepped out onto the court and ended the game, just as they had the day before. The spectators on both sides of the court hooted and hollered their objections.

"I didn't hear no fucking buzzer go off," shouted Cyclops from where he was seated on the grass. "What kind of bullshit is this?"

One of the guards walked over to where Cyclops was sitting. "You just can't stay out of the Hole, can you Morrison? I said free time's over. Get back inside."

"The Hole don't mean shit to me," said Cyclops.

He and the guard glared at each other, just long enough for each man to show everyone present that the other didn't intimidate him. Then Cyclops got up and walked slowly back inside, and so did the rest of the inmates on and around the basketball court. I heard a lot of grumbling as I walked along. The grumbling was widespread and angrier than it had been the day before. It wasn't just the few inmates the guards considered "troublemakers." Everybody resented the arbitrary decision by the guards to close the yard early when we were enjoying ourselves and breaking no rules.

"What harm would it do the hacks to let those guys finish their game," said a low rider I'd never seen before.

"No harm at all," said Crow. "With these bulls, it's all about control. They don't want us to have nothin' we can feel good about. They want to let us know who's in charge. And they want to keep us down. It's just like it is on the streets. They want to keep us in our place."

"Ain't that the truth?" said Bubba, shaking his head in disgust. "Ain't that just the motherfucking truth?"

"New," Crow said to me. "You never seen nothing like this before, have you? I bet you've never been hassled like this by the police on the streets before. Am I right?"

"Yeah, you're right. In fact, I don't have much contact at all with the police on the streets."

"Now you and your partner are getting a taste of what Bubba and me live with every day," said Crow. "It don't feel too good, does it?"

Hearing the mounting anger in the voices around me as I walked back toward M-Unit, it dawned on me that this moment was an opportunity to recruit more inmates to our strike committee or what I had come to see as Surratt's group.

"We ought to do something about this," I said to Crow, Bubba, and two bikers who were walking next to us toward M-Unit. "Like what?" asked one of the bikers.

"Like we should stop cooperating with these motherfuckers. We should all refuse to work until this sort of bullshit stops. They shouldn't be able to close the yard right in the middle of a game that everyone is enjoying. It's not even eight o'clock yet. It's still light out here. There should be a set time for the yard to close, and all the guards should stick to it."

"You refuse to work, they'll throw you in the Hole and throw away the key," said one of the bikers. "They'll just let you rot in there. The chow's worse in the Hole than what they serve in the mess hall."

"You fuck with the man, and the man will fuck with you," said Crow, giving me a long look.

"The man's already fucking with me," I said. *The man's already fucking with all of us*, I thought. As I turned away and started up the stairs to my cell on the third tier, someone grabbed my arm from behind. When I turned around, I saw that it was Crow.

"Say, my man," he said. "Just a word to the wise. You seem like a good guy. In here, you got to be a little careful who you talk to."

"What do you mean?" I asked him.

"I mean like suggesting to those bikers that we all stop working. Some guys in here are solid but others will snitch you off for a pack of cigarettes. You understand what I'm talkin' about? Bubba and I are solid, but I don't know those two bikers."

"Thanks for the advice," I said. "I'll be more careful, but I'm really tired of how they jerk us around. We need to do something about it."

Bubba and Crow looked at each other and laughed.

"How long you been here?" Bubba wanted to know.

"About seven weeks," I said.

"How long you got to do?" asked Crow.

"A little less than two years now," I said. "How about you?"

"I have a zip-six," said Crow. "I've done three here in this motherfucker and I got three more to go. Less if I keep my good time. I could do two years standing on my head," he said. "You were short the day you drove up. You ought to do your number and get the fuck out of here."

Crow and Bubba walked over to join the perpetual game of dominoes that went on in M-Unit the whole time I was there, and I went up to my cell on the third tier to write in my journal.

Since moving out of A & O and into M-unit, I had noticed that my letters weren't checked as carefully as they had been when I first arrived. Surratt and Adams had suggested to me while I was still in A &O that this was the case, and they seemed to be right. "They watch every move you make when you first drive up," Surratt had said. "After you move out of A and O and into the mainline population, they don't have time to watch you as carefully. They focus on the new arrivals. What I do is slip a sensitive sentence in here and there in the middle of a bland paragraph about something like the weather or what I saw on television. You might try doing that if you want to say something you think the hacks might not like."

In the letter I wrote home that night, I slipped in two sentences that would undoubtedly have been censored in A&O by Boss Schwartz or Boss Stockton. "There is widespread discontent among the inmates about how we are treated." Two paragraphs later in the middle of a discussion of the shipment of books that I'd finally received, I wrote, "You should know that all of the mail—incoming and outgoing—is censored by the guards." I waited for several days to see if my comments would be caught and censored by someone reading the mail, but they were not. My letter reached my parents intact, apparently: in her next letter, my mother said, "We'll be coming down to Lompoc to visit you near the end of July. We can talk about 'sensitive issues' in person then." *This is her coded way,* I thought, *of letting me know that she'd caught my reference to censorship of the mail.*

The next day out in the yard there was no one on the basketball court. Apparently, Crow, EJ, Tim, and Bubba were otherwise occupied, so Foots and I sat down with Surratt and his crew. Hartman was there too, although he continued to tell us openly that he was skeptical about any sort of strike or work stoppage. Foots and I told Surratt and the others about the grumbling we'd heard the day before when the guards arbitrarily stopped our basketball game and shut down the yard early.

"We ought to be able to do something with that sort of discontent," said Surratt. "We ought to be able to channel it."

"What do you think we should do?" I asked him.

"Look over there," said Surratt, pointing to the part of the yard we referred to as "Muscle Beach." "What do you see over there?"

"I see a bunch of bikers and low riders pumping iron," I said.

"That's right," said Surratt. "And do you also see that there's no brothers lifting weights with them right now?"

"Sure," I said. "The brothers wait until the bikers are done lifting, and then they do their own lifting. It's like two different shifts. It's been like that the whole time I've been here."

"That's right," said Surratt. "And that's a problem for us. As long as we're split into different shifts and different factions, the guards can treat all of us however they want to. If they keep us divided, we have no chance of changing anything. We need to persuade every inmate in here that there's only two groups here at Lompoc—them and us, the keepers and the kept."

"Our movement needs a slogan," said Cohen. "Like 'Give me liberty or give me death.'"

"I don't think that will sell too well in here," said Foots. "Especially the 'death' part." A chuckle rippled around the circle.

"What about something simple like, 'Them and us, the keepers and the kept'?" said Foots.

"That's better," said Surratt, "but we need to keep it short and simple." What about, "Them and us?"

"That works for me," said Adams. "I think everyone in here will understand what that means. 'Them and us.'"

We all agreed to begin spreading the slogan whenever we had the chance. "Them and us." And we all agreed to support, within reason, all other inmates, regardless of color.

Surratt understood exactly what he was doing—and what the guards were doing. He saw that we really were going to have another race riot if we couldn't create a sense of solidarity among the inmates. He also saw that the guards understood that they could control the inmate population much more easily if we continued to distrust each other. They knew their jobs would be harder, more dangerous, if the inmates were united.

My first opportunity to act upon our resolution presented itself unexpectedly a week or so later. It was near the end of June, and the weather was growing warmer. I had just finished a particularly unpleasant session with Boss Redburn on the floor mopping detail after lunch and was on my way back to my cell in M-Unit when a Latino inmate approached me just as I was starting up the stairs to my cell on the third tier.

"Hey man," he said. "Hold up a minute." He looked around a bit nervously, as though he didn't want to be overheard. "I talked to Crow and Bubba about you, and they say that you're a solid dude. You got a minute?"

"Sure," I said. "In fact, I have a couple of years. I've got plenty of time. What's on your mind?"

"I'm Chuy," he said, extending his hand. I noticed that on his right forearm he had an elaborate tattoo of an eagle holding a snake in its talons. He had black hair, dark eyes, and struck me right away as a thoughtful person.

"I'm Eric," I said, as we shook hands.

He again looked over his shoulder to be sure that no one was listening to us. "What do you think about the food in here?" he asked.

His question took me by surprise. I didn't know this guy, and that made me wary. I had no idea where he was heading with his question, but since Crow and Bubba seemed to have steered him in my direction, I decided to see why he wanted to talk with me. "The food's not good," I said, "but to tell you the truth, it's not the main issue I have with this place."

"I hear what you're saying," said Chuy. "There are a lot of things I'd change about this place too, but the food here is one of them. We have to start somewhere. Some of the Chicano brothers have a plan for improving our diet, but we need some help to put it into action."

Again, I was puzzled. I was only about four weeks or so out of the Fish Tank and still feeling very much out of place.

"Have you ever stolen anything before?" he asked me.

I thought about some baseball cards I had once swiped from a boyhood friend who had a much larger collection than I did, but this seemed too trivial an example to bring up with real thieves housed on every tier.

"Nothing to speak of," I said.

He smiled and said, "That's what I thought. That's why you're perfect

Chapter 4. Mainline

for what we have in mind. None of the guards would ever be looking for you to steal anything."

"What's the plan you have in mind?"

"It's all about protein," he said. "When you walk around the track, do you notice all the guys pumping iron?"

"Sure," I said. "It's hard to miss them. Seems like there's three separate shifts: Low Riders, Blacks, and then Mexicans, usually in that order."

"Chicanos," he said. "Not Mexicans. We're Chicanos. We're American citizens of Mexican descent."

"My mistake," I said. "I hear you. I try to call people what they want to be called."

"Don't worry about it," he said. "You're not the only one who still calls us Mexicans. Anyway, you're right about the weightlifters. Separate shifts, but they all have a common need."

"What's that?" I asked.

"Protein," he said. "All athletes, particularly weightlifters, need protein. In here we don't get enough protein. That means that anyone who wants to pump some serious iron is going to get broken down rather than built up."

"I see what you're saying," I said. "How are you going to steal meat out of the meat locker? And even if you manage to get it out, how will you cook it? You can get real sick from eating meat that isn't cooked enough."

"That's the beauty of it. We're not after meat," said Chuy.

"What are you after then?" I asked him.

"Eggs," said Chuy.

"Eggs?" I repeated in surprise.

"That's right," he said. "Eggs are one of the best sources of protein there is. We want to steal some government eggs from the kitchen, and we need your help."

"How do you think I can help?"

He looked me directly in the eye. "You promise me that you'll keep this to yourself, one way or the other?"

"Of course," I said. "There's only two groups in here—them and us, the keepers and the kept. We have to stick together."

Chuy looked at me. "I like that," he said. "I like that a lot. 'Them and us, the keepers and the kept.' I like that a lot. Listen up: we want to steal eggs out of the kitchen. We know we can get them from the kitchen out into the mess hall, but we need someone to carry them through the door of the mess hall and back to M-unit. That's where you come in."

"I get it," I said. "I don't look like a thief to the hacks, so they won't search me."

"Bingo," he said. "That's it. What do you think? We know you're on mop detail after every meal. The mess hall will be emptied out. Only one hack in charge of the cleanup detail, and he can easily be distracted. You come up to the front counter to wring out your mop and one of the brothers hands you ten hard boiled eggs taped to a piece of cardboard. You put them under your shirt in back and tuck your shirt in loosely. No one will notice a thing. You finish mop detail and take the eggs back to M-Unit and give them to me when I come by your cell."

I thought about his request for maybe ten or fifteen seconds. I knew I had to give Chuy an answer right then, one way or the other. Multiple thoughts flashed quickly through my mind. A few days before, I had followed Hartman's suggestion and sent a note to my caseworker, Boss O'Brien, indicating an interest in the clerk's position on the farm when it opened up. It sounded like an easy job, and it would give me plenty of time to read during the day. If I were caught stealing eggs, I could kiss that job good-bye and probably be stuck on the mop crew for at least another couple of months. I was also getting eager to move out of M-Unit, and I had heard that E-unit was quieter and housed fewer of the "hard cases." I thought all of this over in less time than it took to write it down here and made a snap decision. This wasn't about right and wrong—stealing private property or anything along those lines. This was about solidarity. Surratt was right. Two groups. The keepers and the kept.

"I'm in," I told Chuy. "When does Operation Protein start?"

"Hey," he said. "I like that too. 'Operation Protein.' It sounds kind of official."

"It sounds kind of like resistance," I said. "When do we start?"

"We're ready to go after breakfast tomorrow if you are," he said.

"I'll be there on mop detail," I told him. "Who's going to give me the eggs?"

"His name's Art," said Chuy. "He's over in N-Unit right now. I'll tell Art that it's on for tomorrow." We shook hands again and headed back to our respective cells.

That evening after dinner, Foots and I headed over to the basketball court to see who was there. We had worked out a sort of informal schedule for ourselves that allowed us to play as much hoop as we wanted and also talk with Surratt and his crew about politics. When we got over to the court, I saw Crow and Bubba sitting on the grass waiting for the next game.

"Hey, fellas," said Crow. "We need two. Do you want to run with us? We're up next."

"Sure," Foots and I answered in unison. "Let's do it."

"By the way," Crow said, looking at me. "Did a dude named Chuy ever get in touch with you?"

"Yeah, he found me after lunch today."

Crow looked at me intently. "Is everything cool?" he asked.

"Chuy and I are cool," I told him.

"Cool," said Crow. "That's cool. I told him I thought you and Foots were solid."

Just then the game ahead of us ended and it was our turn to play. Word had spread around the yard, and eventually around the prison, since our previous games: two White guys were playing in what had previously been an all–Black basketball game. More and more inmates gathered around the basketball court. In addition, more players wanted to play in the game; every day, some new ball player showed up. On this occasion, one of the new players was a brother named Big Frank. He had heard on the grapevine about this White dude named Bigfoot, and he wanted to check out his game.

If it seems strange that a pick-up basketball game could generate this much interest, bear in mind that not much else was going on at Lompoc. Dostoevsky called the prison where he was incarcerated "the house of the dead" for a reason. On the basketball court, we all felt a little bit more alive. The basketball court was a relatively free space. On the court we made the rules; throughout the rest of the institution, we had next to no autonomy and generally did what we were told to do.

Big Frank was one of the only ball players at Lompoc that summer who was strong enough to match up with Foots. I'm guessing he weighed about 260 or even 270 pounds, which means he outweighed Foots by about thirty-five or forty pounds. They were roughly the same height—about 6'5". Big Frank clearly had a weight advantage on Foots, but Frank must have been in his mid-thirties in those days and Foots was just twenty years old. Frank had massive arms that were as thick as many people's legs. It was rumored that he had played a couple of seasons with the Los Angeles Rams, but the joint is rampant with rumors of that sort that can't be confirmed one way or the other. What *was* clear, however, was that Big Frank was enough of an athlete to cause Foots some real problems on the basketball court.

Frank was playing with Tiny Tim and two other guys I had never seen before named Curly and Blue. Tim was a good ball handler and extremely quick, but not much of a shooter. Curly and Blue were both good athletes, though they were better athletes than they were basketball players. When it was our turn to play, Crow set our defensive matchups, because he knew all the players. He put me on Tiny Tim and Foots on Big Frank. If Tim had been a better shooter, I would have had to move away from the basket to guard him, and then he would have used his quickness to drive past me. Since he was a below average shooter, I simply played him the way my coaches had always told me to play quicker guards. I sagged off him a couple of steps and tried to keep him from driving past me.

Frank started fast and scored the first four baskets for his team. Foots was leaning on him and bumping him the way post men always do, but all to no avail. Frank was just a little too strong and he was still remarkably agile for a man his size and age. It makes me laugh, even now, to think of Frank and Foots, the grizzled veteran, and the fresh young rookie, going all out against each other. The two big men were the show that day and everyone on the sidelines knew it. Once again, a crowd gathered around the court and people began to whoop and shout with each basket that was scored. Once again, Boss Jackson and several of the other guards positioned themselves in the yard so that they could observe what was happening on the basketball court and take any action they deemed to be necessary.

After Frank scored his fourth basket and Blue followed with a short jump shot and a lay-in on a nice pass from Tim, Crow called a quick time out to regroup. We were behind six to nothing and going down fast.

"We got to give Foots some help with Frank," Crow said. "Let's double team Frank every time he gets the ball and make somebody else beat us. Ain't a one of these guys can shoot from the outside. Let's pack the middle and make Frank give up the ball."

"My thought exactly," said Foots. "And one other thing. Let's make Frank work on defense. I'll move away from the basket so that he has to move more to guard me. He's starting to huff and puff a little bit. I think he's beginning to get tired."

We all nodded our agreement with this plan and resumed play. Foots moved out to the free throw line when our team had the ball. He was not a long-range shooter, but from fifteen feet on in he was effective, and he could pass the ball well. Bubba, Crow, and I would set picks for each other to get open and Foots would feed us the ball if he didn't have an open shot himself. Every basket from that point on was hard fought. Occasionally there was a hard foul followed by a brief argument and much whooping and hollering from the spectators, but for the most part it was just good basketball, the sort you'll find on weekends in gyms all over America where players of all ages gather just because they love playing the game.

Our strategy gradually began to take its toll on Big Frank. He found himself double and sometimes triple-teamed and forced to give up the ball. And when he passed the ball off to open teammates, their shots would clang off the rim. Crow began to taunt Tiny Tim and Blue after each miss.

"Brick," he'd shout out. "Another brick. You can't win if you can't put the ball in the hoop."

Frank never said a word in response the entire game, but Crow's trash talking gradually enraged Tiny Tim who began to foul me on almost every shot. I was never one to call a lot of fouls in pick-up basketball games, but Crow wasn't about to let Tim win by consistently fouling whoever on our team happened to be shooting the ball. The fans also began to get on Tim for his tactics. This seemed to enrage him even further, but it also put a stop to his most blatant fouls. We gradually overcame our slow start, turned the momentum of the game around, and evened the score at nine all. At that point Curly finally hit a ten-foot jump shot, but Dwight answered immediately for our team with a soft hook that arched just over Big Frank's outstretched arm. When Dwight's hook went in, I thought we were going to win the game, but it was not to be. With the score tied at ten all, Tim hit the only long jump shot he made the entire day. We failed to score on our next possession, and Big Frank ended the game with a resounding dunk that drew a roar from the crowd. It seemed to me that he drove his shoulder into Foots on the play, but Foots wasn't about to call a charging foul in a pick-up game any more than I was. That we were part of this game was far more important than who won it.

Getting to know Crow and Big Frank played a major role in what happened later. In any group there are some natural leaders—guys who hold no official position, but who lead through example and are followed because they have the respect of those around them. Everyone who knew Big Frank and Crow respected them, and no one at Lompoc messed with either of them. It's interesting how this worked for Foots and me in the joint. When Big Frank and Crow put the word out to the brothers that Foots and I were "okay White boys," it made our lives easier, but it also made life easier for our entire group, the so-called "hippies." As time went on, I began to see more and more conversations out in the yard that included both Blacks and Whites and occasionally Latinos. I don't want to exaggerate this in any way. I'm not trying to suggest that, suddenly, everything was sweetness and harmony at Lompoc that summer. But something was happening.

The next morning, I woke up early. I felt tense as I thought about Chuy and our covert operation with the eggs—Operation Protein. At breakfast I sat with Foots and Hartman. Big Frank and Tim were seated at an adjoining table; we bantered back and forth about the previous day's games. A few tables over, Chuy was sitting with a guy I guessed was Art, the kitchen worker who was going to pass me the eggs. Chuy and I made eye contact; when Chuy nodded meaningfully at Art, I knew my guess was right. I nodded back and we were confirmed.

After breakfast I grabbed a mop as usual and swabbed the mess hall floor under the close supervision of Boss Redburn. Out of the corner of my eye I saw Art up at the front of the chow hall busily making a show of wiping down the stainless-steel counter of the serving line. This was standard procedure, so Boss Redburn paid no particular attention to him. Up and back we went, our mops in unison, moving gradually from the left to the right side of the mess hall. A tired-looking inmate emerged from the kitchen and approached Boss Redburn, drawing his attention away from the mop detail.

"Boss," I heard him say. "I need to go to sick bay."

"What's wrong now?" Redburn asked. The guards were generally skeptical of unusual requests. Inmates did, in fact, frequently claim to be sick in order to avoid their work detail.

"I think I have a fever," said the prisoner. "I have chills, and I feel hot. Real hot. I need someone to check my temperature."

Boss Redburn turned his back to the mop crew, giving the inmate his full attention. Seizing the moment, Art, handed me a piece of brown cardboard that had ten hardboiled eggs attached to it with scotch tape. I quickly tucked the eggs under my shirt, against my back. I left my shirt loose so that the eggs would be less visible. Unless someone frisked me, I thought it unlikely that I would be found out. Nevertheless, I was nervous. I'm not a thief by nature. My palms were sweating.

Redburn, with a look of disgust on his face, finally waved the inmate off to the infirmary to see a medic and turned his attention back to the mop crew. "Not bad," he said to us. "You guys may actually be getting a little better at this. That's it for breakfast. Be back here right after lunch."

He opened the door to the mess hall and motioned us all through to the main corridor. I moved quickly past him and returned to my cell, where I hid the eggs under my pillow. Half an hour later, Chuy came by to pick them up, and Operation Protein was officially underway.

At times the prison grapevine can be a remarkably efficient mode of communication. As I was going through the lunch line that same day, Hartman emerged from the kitchen carrying a large metal container of rice up to the line. This struck me as odd because Hartman's job description was "cook." Other inmates who had no experience on the streets as short order cooks generally worked as runners, removing empty serving containers, and replacing them with full ones. Hartman waited until I got to the rice and potatoes section of the serving line with my mop. Then he stepped up with his container of rice.

"Fresh rice," he said to the server. "Get that empty container out of there so I can replace it."

As the server removed the empty stainless-steel container, Hartman turned quickly to me.

"What the hell are you doing?" he asked quietly.

"What do you mean, 'what the hell am I doing'?" I replied. He looked around him and spoke even more softly.

"You know damn well what I mean," he said. "Eggs."

"Either you're part of the solution or you're part of the problem," I said. "Let's talk out in the yard after dinner," he said.

"See you then," I said. "And remember, two groups. There are only two groups in here. Them and us." He just looked at me, once again, as though I'd taken leave of my senses, picked up the empty rice container, and vanished back through the door to the kitchen.

I got out to the yard late after dinner, because Boss Redburn was in a particularly bad mood, markedly different from his demeanor that morning. He made us mop down the floor three extra times. I didn't know a thing about the man's life away from his job at the prison, but I'm guessing it wasn't much. He seemed to compensate for whatever was going wrong in his life on the streets by requiring us to spend unnecessary time mopping the floor. I've rarely encountered such a venomous and thoroughly spiteful person. Almost never a positive word for any of the inmates in his crew. You didn't have to have a degree in psychology to figure out that this was about power. Other members of the mop crew joked about Redburn behind his back.

"Small man's complex," said a White guy who sometimes hung out with the hippies in the yard. "What's that called?" he asked, looking at me.

"I think it's called a Napoleon complex," I said. "The little emperor." Being a college graduate hadn't caused me any problems in the joint so far, but I still didn't feel comfortable being singled out in this way. I just wanted to fit in and be seen as "one of the guys."

"He ain't gettin' none at home," suggested Fred Thompson, a muscular Black inmate from San Diego.

"Shit," said another brother. "That sorry ass motherfucker ain't married. Ain't no woman, no matter how sorry, can put up with his bullshit. He ain't getting none, period. Probably never did unless he paid for it."

If my time at Lompoc taught me anything, it's that solidarity among oppressed groups comes from two things: external threat and internal ideology. That summer, guards like Boss Redburn, along with the upper-level prison officials, were the external threat. They did everything they could to keep us pitted against each other. The longer I observed the workings of the prison as a system, the clearer it became to me that despite all the rhetoric about rehabilitation, prison was helping few, if any, inmates "get their lives back on track."

Prisons do lasting damage to most people who spend time in them. When inmates are released, they're generally *less* prepared to survive on the streets than they were when they were sentenced. Prisons reassure frightened citizens by making them feel that something is being done to protect them. In actuality, prisons punish all of us in the long run because the men who spend time there typically become more hostile and anti-social while they are incarcerated, and then are released to live in an unwelcoming environment with a razor-thin social safety net. To one degree or another, prison damages nearly every prisoner's sense of self, grinds down his dream of a better life. I've always felt lucky that my stay wasn't longer than it was.

When Redburn finally let us go, I went out to the yard and found Hartman waiting for me over with the hippies. He reminded me of a big mother hen clucking at Foots, Surratt, me, and the other inmates who were gradually connecting, at least occasionally, with our group.

"You guys don't know what you're fucking with," he said, singling me out for special disapproval. "If I already know you're helping to steal eggs, how long do you think it will be before the hacks find out? There are snitches all over this place. Guys will sell you out in a minute if they think they can get something out of it for themselves. My buddy out at the farm says that his boss has your file on his desk. He's put in to have you replace one of his clerks who has a release date in the middle of July. You could be doing easy time from July until you get out of here. Why would you want to fuck that up?"

"Look, Dale," I said. "I appreciate your concern, I really do. And I still want that clerk's job out on the farm. But there's something about helping those guys get the eggs they want that just feels right to me. It feels right to me in my gut, and I've got to go with that. It's a calculated risk."

"What feels right about it?"

"It's symbolic. I like the idea of stealing the prison's eggs to make 'the people' stronger—building up our strength with their resources. I also like the idea of stealing eggs right underneath Redburn's nose. He's such a pompous little asshole. The other thing is, my loyalty is to the inmates, not to the guards. It really *is* 'us and them.' We're the only ones in here who care about 'us.'"

"It's going to cost you one of the best jobs in the joint. Why would you want to do hard time when you can do easy time?" I said, "I don't want to do hard time. I still want that clerk's job out on the farm. But I don't want it at any price. Chuy asked me for support. I think I should try to help him. I'm also thinking that if we help him with the eggs, he may join our group and eventually bring some of the Chicano brothers into the strike."

"The Mexicans are just using you because you're naïve. Why don't they get one of their own guys to be the mule?"

"I thought about that. Chuy's right when he says that the hacks watch them more carefully than they do some of us. They're harder on Black and Latino prisoners than they are on whites."

"That'll change real quick if you get caught."

"You're right," I said, "but sometimes you just have to go with your gut."

"It's your funeral," he said. "Don't say I didn't warn you." He turned to move away, then stopped and walked slowly back toward me, a serious expression on his face.

"Can we talk over there for a minute?" he said, pointing to a bare patch of dirt where no one was sitting because the grass was more comfortable. "There's something I want you to know about. Something serious. Something that's going down back in the kitchen."

We walked far enough away from the others so that no one could overhear us.

"What's up?" I asked him.

"Do you remember that dude named Billy Brown, the fish Winters yelled at in A and O?"

"Sure. I remember him. You said he'd better wise up or he was going to get himself into trouble."

"Exactly," said Hartman. "Billy Brown was assigned to work in the kitchen, and he hasn't wised up. He doesn't know when he's being set up."

"Meaning what, exactly?"

"Big Mama Cutler, the big hack who's stationed in the kitchen during lunch, has a little sex club going on back there." There seem to be seven or eight guys involved. He usually doesn't have to force or pressure anybody to participate, because he picks guys who are already willing. They give him what he wants, and he gives them special favors—time off work or things they want from the commissary. For the most part everybody's happy, but right now there's a problem.

"Where does Billy Brown fit into this?" I said.

"That's the problem. Mama Cutler is hitting on Billy, apparently, and Billy isn't interested in having sex with guys," said Dale. "Boss Cutler is moving up the pressure on Billy to join his little club, and Billy doesn't know what to do. He's freaking out. He's terrified that he's going to be assaulted, and he can't sleep."

"Why doesn't Billy report Cutler to the warden or to his caseworker?" I asked.

"Cutler's smart. After Billy turned him down, Cutler's been using inmates to pressure Billy. A couple of guys who work in the kitchen threaten him every day. He's really stressed out."

"What can we do to help him out?"

"Not much," Hartman replied. "It's Billy's word against Cutler's, and some of the inmates who work in the kitchen will back Cutler up. When I told Cutler that he should back off and leave Billy alone, Cutler got pissed; the next day, the same two guys who threatened Billy threatened me. They told me to back off and keep my mouth shut."

"Did Boss Cutler ever approach you about having sex?" I asked him.

"Not really," Dale said. "I don't think I'm his type. He did ask me to be his lookout one day, but I told him I didn't want any part of what he was doing. The whole thing is messed up. Yesterday Cutler asked me to bring Billy to the back of the kitchen during lunch to talk with him. I know what he wants to do, and he's trying to make me a part of it."

"It sounds to me as though both of you should request a transfer to another job," I said. "I had a conversation with an old convict in county jail up in Portland about how to get along in the joint. One thing he said stuck with me. He said, 'When you get down to Lompoc, don't go into no room that don't have no back door out of it.' The kitchen doesn't have a back door. I think you and Billy should both get out of there."

"I've thought about that," said Dale. "But I really don't want to change jobs because I'm learning how to cook new things. I want to get a job as a short-order cook when I'm released."

"Let me think about this overnight and get back to you tomorrow," I said. "There's got to be a way to make Mama Cutler back off, but you're right: if it's your word against his, you lose."

"If you can think of anything, let me know," he said. "Billy Brown is at the end of his rope. The pressure is getting to him."

Hartman walked off to take a few ambling laps around the track. He was already overweight when Foots and I first met him in Rocky Butte, but he seemed to have put on at least ten pounds since going to work in the kitchen at Lompoc. Hartman was a pleasure seeker, an epicure. I used to think of him as the "Emperor of Ice-Cream," the central figure in one of Wallace Stevens' poems. Stevens saw *pleasure* as the dominant power (the emperor) in the humanistic world that emerged for many writers after the devastation of World War I undermined belief in more traditional values.

I walked back over to where Surratt was sitting with Cohen, Denham, and Adams. Breintnall was strumming on a guitar I'd never seen before. As usual, the group was focused on organizing.

"Eric," said Surratt, "I've seen you and Dwight over there playing ball with the brothers a lot recently. Do you ever hear any talk about a race riot?"

"Not a word," I said. "Although I'm sure they wouldn't talk about anything like that around Dwight and me. Some of the brothers think Foots and I are all right, but that's just on the basketball court. I understand why they won't talk about a race riot with two White guys they just met."

"You need to start talking some politics with the brothers you know the best. You need to take it beyond basketball. The guards in the front office are talking with each other about 'the riot' all the time these days. They make it sound like it's a done deal. We have to move faster if we're going to head this thing off."

"I'll talk to Foots about how to raise the subject with the brothers," I said. "This isn't the sort of topic we can just bring up out of the blue. We have to ease into it. All the brothers respect Crow and Big Frank. If we can persuade Crow and Big Frank that a race riot will only help the guards keep us down, maybe we'll have a chance."

"Speaking of next moves," Surratt said, "I hear on the wire that you're up for a job as clerk out on the farm."

I laughed. "Is there anything going on in here that you don't already know about?" Obviously, he used his position as clerk in the administrative office to gather information from the files; he also kept his ears open, eavesdropping on the guards' conversations.

"You're right," I said. "I like the sound of the job out there. It will get me away from Redburn and leave me four or five hours every day to read. Good preparation for life after the joint, whatever I wind up doing."

Surratt looked at me for a while. "You can only ride the fence for so long in this world," he said. "At some point everyone is forced to choose. When push comes to shove, you'll have to choose between joining the strike and doing easy time out on the farm. Don't let them buy you off with an easy job and a key to your cell in the Honor Unit. The only thing in the middle of the road is yellow lines and dead armadillos."

About a week after that conversation with Surratt, I received a note from my caseworker. When we met, Boss O'Brien told me that he'd approved my request to be moved into E-Unit when there was an opening. About a month earlier, at Surratt's suggestion, ten of us had agreed to apply for transfers to E-unit on the grounds that it would make it easier and safer for us to have conversations about the strike; E-unit was a barracks, like A and O, rather than tiers and single cells. In the yard we were a little too visible, sitting together with the other "hippies." In E-Unit we would be living where we were "supposed to be" and would be less likely to attract attention. Since I had never heard anything back officially about my request to be moved to E-Unit, I had nearly forgotten about it.

"Well, Newhall," Boss O'Brien said as I sat down in the chair next to his desk, "I hear you've been keeping your nose clean in M-Unit. No shots in your file so far. I called you in to tell you that your request to move into E-Unit when there's an opening has been approved."

"Glad to hear it," I said. "I thought you wanted to talk to me about the clerk's job that's going to open up out on the farm."

"Let's not get ahead of ourselves," he said to me. "Your time will go easier if you just let things happen as they happen. One step at a time. Just get with the program."

There was a lot I could have said about "the program" at this point. I thought briefly about asking O'Brien to help Billy Brown out of the situation with Boss Cutler that Hartman had told me about, but decided it was a waste of time. O'Brien, like most of the inmates at Lompoc, was interested in doing easy time. He wanted to pick up his paycheck and go home. He was not about to disrupt the system or confront a co-worker over something as inconsequential—to him, at least—as Billy Brown's well-being.

"When do you think I might move into E-Unit?" I asked him.

"Stay out of trouble and you'll have a new home by the middle of July," he said. "Stay clean and your next move after that will be to C-Unit and then to B, the Honor Unit, where you get to have your own key."

"It sounds like a plan, Boss," I said as I got up to leave.

That evening out in the yard Surratt told us that seven of our group had been informed that a move to E-Unit was coming up some time in July. "Most inmates have no interest in E-Unit," said Surratt. "It's too much like A & O for them. There's not enough privacy, and if they have a beef with someone, there's no safe place to retreat to. The only reason I suggested that we put in for transfers is that it makes it easier for us to talk with each other without being obvious about it."

"Good point," said Cohen. "In E-Unit we'll be less isolated. My daddy was a union man from way back. He always told me, 'Together we stand, divided we fall.' Seems like a good thing to be somewhere we can talk in groups without being as visible to the hacks as we are out here in the yard."

Before I left M-Unit, Foots and I both talked to Crow, Bubba, Big Frank, and a few more of the brothers we'd been playing ball with about making the move to E-Unit and refusing to work. Neither one of us could drum up much enthusiasm for the idea of a strike.

"I ain't going to play no fuckin' games with the man," Crow told me. "This whole system is bullshit."

Foots told me that Frank just looked at him and shook his head. "You crazy White boys are going to get yourselves into a heap of trouble. Don't say I didn't warn you. You don't know what you're fuckin' with. I'm just going to do some easy time and walk on away from this motherfucker after I flatten out my sentence."

I got the same response from Chuy and Art when I suggested that they put in for a move into E-Unit. They were willing to run the risk of stealing eggs from the kitchen—at least thirty a day, maybe more for all I knew—but not willing to run the risk of refusing to work. They were fine using "hippies" as mules to smuggle eggs, but they didn't want to join us in a movement to create broader change. Clearly, they had no confidence that some White boys from Oregon and their "hippie" friends could have any impact on Lompoc whatsoever. Which made sense, though I was too naïve at the time to know it; their life experience prior to arriving at Lompoc had given them no reason to trust White people and plenty of reasons not to.

§

I moved from M-Unit into E-Unit on August 3, 1969, one month to the day after my 24rd birthday. It was also the day of the most memorable basketball game I've ever played in. I felt good when I got up that Saturday morning. I had received a letter from my parents the day before, telling me that they would be coming to visit me near the middle of August on their way to Santa Ana to visit my mother's mother. "I'll be here," I wrote them.

After breakfast, Foots and I went out to the yard as we always did on weekends. We headed straight for the basketball court. Surratt was holding forth with his group over by the volleyball courts, and he beckoned us over, but I pointed to the court. Playing hoop helped me do my time, and that's what I wanted to do that morning. Playing basketball on that ugly concrete court was about as close as I could come to feeling free at Lompoc. Surratt would just have to wait for an hour or so. We both had plenty of time.

When we got to the court, we found Crow, Bubba, Curly, and Big Frank sitting on the grass next to the court. Crow was twirling the ball on his index finger, seeing how long he could keep it spinning. The court where we usually played was empty. The bikers were apparently doing something else that morning. Over on the adjoining court the Native Americans were already running.

"What's happening?" I asked Crow and Bubba. "Why's everyone sitting around? Let's play some hoop."

"Actually, I wouldn't mind a break today," Foots broke in. "Big Frank's been pounding on me all week. My whole body is one big bruise. I feel more like watching than playing."

Big Frank laughed when Foots said that. "*You're* sore?" he said, shaking his head. "You're too young to be whining like that, Bigfoot. When I was your age, I could take a whuppin' and be back at it the next day. But right now, you done tired me out. I ain't playin' no ball today."

Crow, Bubba, Curly, and I wanted to play, so we got up and started to warm up, waiting to see if someone else might show up. Crow looked around the yard, but he couldn't spot any of the other players who sometimes joined our game.

"Ain't this a motherfuckin' bitch," said Crow. "Here it is the weekend, and I can't find eight guys to play a basketball game."

At that point an argument broke out on the court behind us where the Native Americans were playing—nothing major, just a typical disagreement over a foul call. "Say," said Crow, looking over at the adjoining court. "Let's see if those little dudes want to play us. Ain't nobody else out here this morning."

"What you talkin' about?" said Bubba. "Those dudes can't play with us. They can't rebound with us. We got too much height for them. All they do is run up and down."

"Come on," said Crow. "They're the only game out here today."

Crow walked over, and I saw him exchange a soul shake with a tall Native American named David Running Wolf. They talked for a while; then David and four of his teammates began to walk over to our court.

"We got a game," said Crow. "Except there's one condition. David says his guys won't play unless we go five on five, full court. They want to run. What do you guys say?"

"I'm in," I said. Bubba and Curly said they were up for it, but the two big men held back. Finally, under pressure from the rest of us, Frank and Foots agreed to play if they could rotate with each other every five minutes or so.

What happened over the next thirty minutes caught my teammates and me completely by surprise. When the game started, I was certain that we would simply overpower the Native Americans. It never even crossed my mind that they might give us a close game, let alone beat us. We were much taller, jumped higher, and outweighed our opponents by at least twenty pounds at every position. On paper, we looked like the stronger team.

On the court, however, the Native Americans turned out to be far too quick for us, and they knew how to use their quickness to their advantage. The combination of an effective full court press and some exceptional passing and shooting by David Running Wolf and a forward called "Phenomenal Snuffy" demolished us in about half an hour. Fifty years later, I still have occasional nightmares about having the ball stolen from me in this fast-paced game of what has come to be called "rez ball." Snuffy was lightning quick, moved constantly without the ball, and was a deadly shooter from the baseline on either side of the basket.

Crow, Curly, and I were the guards on our team, with Foots at center and Bubba playing inside at a forward. No sooner did Bubba pass the ball inbounds to me than two of the Native Americans were all over me slapping and clawing at the ball. I had faced some pretty good full-court presses when I was younger, but I'd never faced anything quite like what

I ran into that day in the yard at Lompoc. As I turned to dribble the ball up court someone swooped in from my blind side, stole the ball from me, took it in for a lay in. We were down two-zip, and we hadn't even taken a shot yet.

I picked up the ball and passed it to Crow, the best ball handler on our team. He managed to get the ball over the half-court line, but as soon as he did, he was double-teamed. Two Native American players waved their arms and harassed Crow into picking up his dribble. He tried to give me the ball with a bounce pass, but the Native Americans were anticipating this move. As I reached for the ball, Snuffy streaked in for another steal and scored at the other end. We were down three-zip and going nowhere fast.

"Time out," shouted Crow. "Time god damned out." Our team huddled at the half-court line to talk things over while the Native Americans quietly drank from the plastic coke bottles they'd filled with water. "Haven't you guys ever seen a full-court press before?" shouted Crow. "We got to handle the damn ball and get it inside to Foots. They don't have anyone who can stop Foots or Big Frank inside. Take care of the ball and get it inside to one of the big men. These guys have no answer for Foots or Frank."

He sounded like my high school coach. I knew that was what we should be doing, but I was having a hard time doing it because these guys were so quick and, for a pick-up team, so well-coordinated. There seemed to be Native Americans swooping in from every direction, regardless of which way I tried to go. It felt to me as though they had seven or eight players on the court, but when I stopped and counted, there were only five.

The Native Americans never stopped running; whether we scored or missed a shot, they just kept running. They were relentless. After about ten minutes Foots began to tire. I could hear him beginning to breathe heavily with each lumbering trip up and down the court. He was used to playing half court games at this point, and the pace was too fast for him. Finally, he raised his hand and signaled Big Frank that it was time to come in for him. In fact, the fast pace of the game was taking its toll on our entire team.

A crowd had gathered around the court. Shouts of encouragement rang out for both teams; bets were placed on the outcome. Most of the bets were for cartons of cigarettes, the standard currency in most prisons, but some of the Latinos and Native Americans were betting eggs. Ten eggs against one carton of cigarettes. The Native Americans were smart. They moved David away from the basket so that Frank would have to run to guard him. Doing that also opened the middle of the court for quick cuts and passes that led to lay-ins. I could hear Big Frank breathing heavily after only three trips up and down the court. Sweat was pouring out of every pore in his body. Big Frank had heart. He was giving it everything he had, but the pace of the game was just too fast for him; like Foots, he was used to playing half court games where he didn't have to run too much. David would cut through the middle looking for the ball and then continue running on the perimeter while someone else cut through looking for a pass. Frank just couldn't keep up. Finally, David got the ball at the free throw line and faked a jump shot. When Frank went up to block the shot, David drove past him for a lay-in. Nine–five.

I was so shell-shocked at this point from having the ball stolen that I had almost given up looking for my shot.

"Shoot over that little dude," said Crow. "Use your height, New. You can't score if you don't shoot!"

Crow set a pick for me at the top of the key, and I took a jump shot that bounced on the rim a couple of times and then dropped in. Nine-six.

At this point Foots relieved Big Frank and scored two quick baskets. The rest had helped him to get his second wind. Nine to eight. We began to feel that we had a chance, that our size was wearing the Native Americans down, but David and Snuffy were not to be denied. Snuffy called for the ball and nailed a long jump shot from the left-hand corner, making it ten-eight.

"Get out on him, Bubba!" Crow shouted. "Guard that motherfucker. At least get a hand in his face."

"Fuck you, Crow," responded Bubba. "You guard him if you think you can. Dude was twenty-two feet away from the basket."

"All right," said Crow. "Switch men with me. I'll guard him."

Crow gave it everything he had, and he did manage to block one of Snuffy's shots, much to the delight of the crowd. But the next time down court Snuffy knew that Crow wanted to block his shot again. He gave Crow a head fake, watched Crow fly past him, and then drove the ball to the basket. Foots left David to pick up Snuffy, but Snuffy fed a nice bounce pass to David who rolled to the basket and dunked the ball to win the game.

A loud shout went up from the crowd in response to David's dunk. Even the Black spectators who were rooting for Crow and Big Frank's team applauded David's play.

I walked over to Running Wolf, who was standing on the side of the court drinking water from his empty Coke bottle. He was strong without being bulky and obviously in very good condition. The game had been fast paced, but he wasn't breathing hard and had barely broken a sweat.

"Nice game," I said. "You guys are too quick for us."

"Thanks," he replied.

"Where are you from?" I asked him.

"New Mexico," he said. "How about you?"

"Oregon," I said. "Portland, Oregon."

"You guys want to go again?" he asked.

"Let me ask the other guys," I said. No one on my team wanted to play another game.

"Hell no," said Crow when I asked him. "That ain't basketball. That ain't no basketball. I didn't come out here on a Saturday morning for no god damned track meet."

"That's right," said Bubba. "These guys don't play basketball. They just run up and down till we get so tired we can't shoot or guard them. Crow's right. It's a damned track meet."

"It ain't a track meet," chimed in Curly. "It's a fucking marathon. That's what it is."

I couldn't help but laugh and that seemed to exasperate Crow even further. In his entire time at Lompoc, I'm sure he hadn't been on the losing side of a basketball game more than three or four times.

"What you laughin' about, White boy?" he said. "You got your ass whipped same as we did. What you laughin' about?"

"I know, I know," I said. "But we got beat, fair and square. Those guys may not be big, but they know how to play. That full court press is straight out of John Wooden's playbook."

"Bull," said Crow. "That's not basketball. That's a damn track meet."

I saw David listening to all of this, and I could swear that I saw the hint of a smile flicker across his face. It was there for just a second, and then it was gone.

"I guess we're done for today," I said to David. "Nice game."

David shrugged his shoulders and without a word he and his teammates walked back to their regular court and started to run again. A feeling of sadness swept over me as I watched them running up and down that grey concrete court. Here were descendants of the original inhabitants of the continent, locked up in a prison, running up and down a concrete basketball court with little to look forward to when they got out. *The guards don't see any of us as human beings. We're all expendable to them*, I thought, looking around me at the men in the yard. *We've all been written off by the culture. Every single one of us here at Lompoc is expendable. We're just part of the can that's being kicked down the road by the politicians and the voters who elect them.*

Whenever I hear people in Los Angeles complaining these days about the "exorbitant profits" Native Americans are making from their casinos and how they "aren't paying their fair share," I think of David, Snuffy, and the others running up and down on that concrete court at Lompoc. Whatever reservation they're on today, I hope it has running water that's safe to drink.

§

After dinner that day I was transferred down the corridor to E-Unit, and within the next seven days so were Foots, Surratt, and most of Surratt's hippie crew. My frame of mind during the time I was in E-Unit was different from what it had been in A&O and M-unit. I had much more peace of mind in E-Unit because I knew the people around me. In A&O I was new, a fish, and primarily concerned with survival in a world that was alien to me. The same was true during my time in M-unit, where I had to demonstrate that I could survive out in the general population. Foots and I were put in separate units, so for the first time I didn't know anyone in my immediate area. In M-Unit I had felt isolated, powerless, and alone.

One of my colleagues at Occidental College is a political theorist whose primary scholarly interest is the French thinker Alexis de Tocqueville, and his masterpiece, *Democracy in America*. Combining travel writing with social analysis, Tocqueville discusses, among other things, the relationship between isolation and tyranny. He believes that when citizens isolate themselves in their homes, engage in little or no discussion of social issues, and in general withdraw from civic engagement, tyrants find it much easier to control the populace. I hadn't read Tocqueville when I was twenty-four, but I've read and talked about his theory of democracy with my colleague frequently over the last four decades. Contemporary thinkers apply Tocqueville's theories to modern mass culture, noting the degree to which Americans have retreated into their private homes and electronic media, withdrawing from social engagement with the important issues of the day, frequently failing even to vote. Egalitarian democracies become vulnerable when citizens are isolated, divided into hostile factions, and disengaged.

My experience in prison was consistent with much of Tocqueville's thinking about civic engagement. As long as my fellow inmates and I remained divided into racial groups and isolated in our separate cells, we posed no threat to the prison administration and its abusive policies and practices.

In E-Unit, however, there were no cells. We were free to move about within the unit as we wished. We were free to gather and talk about whatever we wanted: the arbitrary behavior of the guards, the food in the Chow Hall, race riots, the need to resist. We were free to organize. In short, the communal living arrangement in E-Unit gave us more power than we had in the other units where we were isolated in our individual cells. Within the prison, E-Unit was a small pocket of free space, much like the yard, but indoors and less public. Democracy flourishes in free spaces where individuals can come together to discuss common issues and problems. Solidarity grows in free spaces; it withers in isolation.

As I got to know Surratt better, I learned that he was steeped in the writings of Karl Marx but was also widely read in political theory from the Greeks to the present. Before the rest of us, Surratt saw the advantage of moving into E-unit where we could talk freely. That's why he suggested that we all transfer to E-unit in the first place.

"We need to get people who support the idea of a strike into this unit," he said. "E-Unit will be our base. We don't need everyone to go out on strike with us, but we need a clear majority if we want to have any impact." He turned to me. "Have you talked to Chuy about moving into E-Unit?"

"No, but I will," I said. "I'll talk with Art too. Both of those guys are fed up with how we're being treated. They can see through the bullshit the hacks spout about programs and rehabilitation. They just don't think a strike can be successful. They don't think we can win."

§

Much to my surprise, Crow and Bubba came walking through the door of E-Unit about a week after our game with the Native Americans, carrying their belongings with them.

"Did you bake us a cake?" Crow asked.

"If I'd known you were coming, I would have," I said. "Or better yet, I'd have asked Hartman to bake you one. You wouldn't believe what that guy manages to bake back there in the kitchen." And it was true. Hartman had decided not to request a move into E-Unit with the rest of us. He remained in N-Unit, but he stayed in touch with our group out in the yard. Every other day or so he would pull cookies or some other sort of dessert out from under his shirt and pass it around as we sat there in the yard talking. Hartman felt comfortable with our group, and he enjoyed hanging out with us, but he also continued to believe that we were on the verge of getting into serious trouble with the warden.

Crow and Bubba took two adjoining bunks halfway down my row. As time went on, I found myself talking with them about as much as I talked with Surratt and his group. After dinner Dwight and I would go out to the yard to play basketball. After an hour or so of basketball, we would go talk politics with Surratt and the hippies, and Crow and Bubba would go lift weights or hang out with the brothers. When the yard closed for the evening, everyone came back to E-Unit.

We all had a lot of time on our hands, and we did what people the world over do to make time pass: we talked. Dwight and I talked for hours with Crow and Bubba during the time we were in E-Unit together. We talked about major life questions and smaller, less consequential things. At some point in our end of the day conversations, we touched upon just about anything you can think of.

Take the evening Crow and Bubba were talking about various brands of shoes they liked. At one point Crow turned to me. "New, what kind of shoes do you wear on the streets?" He asked.

"I like black Converse All Stars," I said. "That's what Bill Russell and Sam Jones wear. I sort of like that Celtics look."

"We're talking about when you're styling with your lady," said Bubba. "When you go out to clubs and shit. What kind of shoes do you wear then?"

"I don't go to clubs," I said. "I like to listen to music, but I can't dance at all."

"Damn, New," said Bubba. "I'm starting to get concerned about you. You starting to sound like some sort of a slug or something. Don't he, Crow?"

"Don't be calling my man New no slug," said Crow. "New's young and he ain't had much of a chance to develop his game yet. But I don't think he's no slug. Slugs can't shoot a basketball the way this White boy can shoot it. What kind of shoes do you wear out on the streets, New?"

"I wear Towncraft work boots on the streets," I told him. "They're comfortable, and they last a long time."

"Where do you get them Towncraft work boots?" Crow asked skeptically.

"I get them at J.C. Penney's."

Crow and Bubba looked at each other for a moment and then exploded with laughter. Crow was laughing so hard that tears were streaming down his face. Bubba rolled off his bunk, into the aisle between the rows of bunks, and lay there, helpless with laughter. "Damn, New," gasped Crow. "I'm startin' to get concerned about you. You starting to sound like some sort of slug or something. You need to get yourself a better brand of shoes. You should get yourself a pair of lizard skins. No, no; hold up. I'm not sure you're ready for no lizard skins yet. You should get yourself a pair of Florsheims. They're a good White boy brand of shoes."

"That's right," Bubba agreed. "When you get out, New, get yourself a pair of Florsheim Wingtips. You want to be lookin' sharp when you go out with your lady."

Playing basketball with each other had opened some space for this sort of friendly smack talk. Friendly smack talking is a sign of trust.

When I got out of prison, the first pair of dress shoes I bought was a pair of black Florsheim Wingtips. I wore them to the Modern Language Association Convention when I was fresh out of graduate school and looking for a job. Crow would laugh if he knew I wore those conservative White boy shoes, the most expensive shoes I'd owned up to that time, for the next twenty-five years. I didn't wear them often, but on the rare occasions when I wore a coat and tie, those shoes went with them. Over the years, I put new heels on them four or five times. I finally threw them out when Angela told me that I needed some shoes that didn't look "so clunky."

Over the years I've thought a lot about my conversations with Crow, Bubba, Chuy, and the other guys I got to know at Lompoc. What struck me was how different their view of the world was from mine. Because we were locked up together and had time on our hands, we spent hours and hours talking. We talked about clothes, cars, and sports—the usual straight-guy male-bonding stuff—but we also talked about death, money, women, marriage, the war in Vietnam, living (and doing time) in America, our parents, school, and just about anything else you can imagine. Our conversations went on for hours.

I had never had long, serious, personal conversations with young Black and Latino men my own age before. As time went on, it became clear to me that we really did live in different worlds. Our experiences were different, and because of that our assumptions about life were different. Coming to understand at least something about these differences at a relatively early age—I turned twenty-four while I was at Lompoc—has served me well in the classroom for the last forty-four years. Understanding something about the color line, before I started teaching, taught me that my own perspective is just one of many possible perspectives, an insight that helped be more effective in the classroom. Too many professors seem to confuse their own perspectives with objective reality, and this tendency makes it difficult for us to communicate with students who don't share our backgrounds, values, and assumptions about the world.

Take work, for example. When I was young, growing up in Portland, Oregon, I was always told that if I worked hard and "kept my nose to the grindstone," I could achieve most if not all my goals. I had been taught that if I wanted a good job, I should get good grades so that I could go on to a good college. I had been taught that Benjamin Franklin was a good role model for any young man aspiring to be successful in the United States. I had been taught that anyone in the United States could achieve the American Dream if he or she were willing to work hard enough. Start at an entry-level position, demonstrate merit, and rise in the world, went the Horatio Alger gospel.

As I got to know Crow and Bubba better, I began to think that I might be able to help them out once we were all released. Prison was a world they knew far better than I did, and they had given me a lot of advice and support that helped me to stay out of trouble in the joint. The simple fact that they played basketball with Foots and me and were willing to be seen talking with us helped us out in all sorts of ways. Most of the Black inmates at Lompoc came to view us as "okay white dudes," and some of the low riding White inmates probably hesitated to mess with us because we had some Black friends in addition to our White friends.

One evening in E-Unit after the yard shut down, Crow, Bubba, and I started talking about how many people returned to the joint multiple times. Both Crow and Bubba knew older men in their neighborhoods who had spent fifteen, twenty years or more of their lives in various prisons or jails.

"Seems like almost everyone I know who ever goes to the joint comes back again and most of the time they come back more than once," said Crow.

"I hear you," said Bubba. "Dudes spend so much time in here that they get institutionalized. They get so they feel more comfortable in the joint than they do on the streets. What about you, New?" he said. "Do you think you'll be back again?"

"No way," Crow interjected. "Ain't no way in hell New's coming back to the joint. He wouldn't be here in the first place if it weren't for the war."

"I don't want to come back again unless I have to," I said. "Much as I like playing hoop and talking with you guys, I'd much rather do it out on the streets where I don't have some hack yapping at me every time I turn around. Do you guys think you'll come back?"

"Sure," they said, in unison. "We'll probably be back," said Crow. "That's the way the game goes."

"What do you mean?"

"Well, let me run it down for you, New," said Crow. "When Bubba and I are on the streets, we do what we need to do to get over. You understand what I'm talkin' about? We do our thing, get our money, buy a car and clothes, get a nice pad, hang out in clubs with our women, and live the life for as long as we can. Then, when we get busted again, we come in here and do easy time. We play some ball, smoke some weed, and sharpen our game by talking to the older cons so that the next time we get out there, we stay out longer. When you in the joint, you got to do what you can to sharpen your game. When you get out, you run as long as you can."

"So, you're telling me that you both assume you'll be back?"

Both of them agreed: "that's the way the game goes." Crow was philosophical. "Sooner or later, everyone gets busted. It's part of life. Don't make no difference how sharp you are, sooner or later the man gets you. Those are the rules." Bubba nodded his head in vigorous agreement. Those were the rules.

"Can I ask you something?" I said.

"Sure, New," said Crow. "We don't have no appointments this afternoon." He turned to Bubba. "Do you have any appointments this afternoon?"

"No, man, I ain't got no appointments," Bubba said. "All I got is time. Ask me anything you want, New."

"Come on, now," I said. "I'm serious. You only get busted because you're doing something that's against the law. Have you ever considered getting some sort of job that isn't illegal?"

"Sure," said Crow. "I tried that once or twice. Right after I graduated from high school, I got a job as janitor in an office building, but it didn't pay shit. Minimum wage. No car. I was taking the bus to work and home again. Run down pad, and no clothes to speak of. I tried that for about three months, and I'd had enough. It was like I was walking uphill on a treadmill."

"But the job was legal. You didn't wind up in the joint, did you?"

"That's right," said Crow, "but I didn't have no life, either. Not the kind of life I wanted to have."

"So, what you're telling me," I said, "is that you'd rather live high on the streets for a while, get busted and come back to the joint than stay out of here but work for less money."

"That's it," said Crow. "That's it exactly. When I'm on the streets, I'm livin' large. When I'm in the joint, I'm sharpening my game, learning from guys who know more than I do. Those are the rules. What you shakin' your head about?"

"That's a pretty sorry future to look forward to," I told them. *If you can't imagine a future for yourself, you may not have one*, I thought. "There's got to be a better way to go than that. I hate to think about the two of you coming back here over and over again. What if I could help you find a legal job that would earn you a decent income? I know some people who might be able to help you find a good legitimate job."

Again, they shook their heads.

"Ain't no one gonna give a Black man with a felony on his record and only a high school diploma a job that pays no money," said Crow. "And I damn sure ain't gonna work my ass off for no bullshit slave wages. Listen here: Why would anyone in his right mind slave away for minimum wage when he can make $2,000 for one or two hours' worth of work? Tell me that, New."

"Because you can start with minimum wage and move up the ladder," I said. "Because you have no freedom when you're in prison."

"I don't have that much more freedom when I'm on the streets," said Crow.

"I hear you, brother," said Bubba. "On the streets, you still playing by the man's rules. You still trying to get ahead walking uphill on a treadmill.

Don't shake your head, New. The man makes the rules, and we play by them. We choose how we gon' play the game. Ain't no use cryin' about it. If you were Black, you'd do the same thing Crow and me are doing. But you white. You have choices. I understand why you think the way you do."

When I wasn't talking with Crow, Bubba, or Foots, I was talking with Surratt and his crew. After Surratt moved into E-Unit he hardly ever stopped talking about the strike he envisioned.

"Are you and Foots talking to the brothers about the strike when you're out there playing ball?" he asked me one day. "Or are you guys just out there playing ball?"

"Damn, John," I said. "I told you before that we talk to them all the time about the conditions in here. They understand better than we do that this system is fucked up, but they don't seem eager to join in a strike, either. They just don't think we can change anything."

"What kind of organizer are you, anyway?" he said. "Are you committed to what we've been talking about since the day you drove up? If we're going to pull this off, we all need to be committed. How much do you really want to make this happen?" His eyes were blazing. "The only reason I get up in the morning is to organize for change," he said. "Why do you get up in the morning, Eric? It can't be just to play basketball."

It was a fair question, and I knew it. Surratt could see it: I was conflicted. One part of me still believed in Ben Franklin and the American Dream. I still wanted to do easy time in the joint and achieve success in traditional terms when I was back on the streets. Another part of me was angry about being put in a cage and wanted to push back on the people who put me there. Most people I know who've spent more than a few weeks in the joint have realized quickly that the prison system is a billion-dollar failure that punishes society at least as much as it punishes the felons it puts in cages.

"I'm starting to think I'm an incompetent organizer," I said. "Most of the guys I've approached don't think we can make any difference; others just look at me as though I've lost touch with reality."

"It's hard," said Surratt, "but it's not impossible. A lot of people are educable if you approach them right. We just have to find them and talk to them in terms they understand."

"Don't you ever get tired of talking to people and coming up empty handed?" I said.

"Tired? *Tired?* I can't afford to get tired. They're trying to crush our spirits in here. They take reasonably good care of our bodies, despite what we say about the food. I'll give them that much. The real problem is that they don't care about our lives. They don't respect us as men—as human beings. They don't give a damn about what happens to us while we're here or after we get out. All their talk about rehabilitation is just empty rhetoric, designed to hide what they're really doing. Doesn't it piss you off? We're just a job to them. They talk about rehabilitation, but they practice custody and control. That's the reason I get out of bed in the morning—to resist what they're trying to do."

Surratt gave me a lot to think about while I was at Lompoc and in the years since then. I've read about people who were truly committed to social change and justice—people like Martin Luther King, Cesar Chavez, Mahatma Gandhi, Nelson Mandela—but they were larger-than-life heroes, iconic figures. When it comes to people I've known personally, Surratt is right up there, close to the top, in terms of his willingness to run risks to create change. Every day, before I walk into a classroom, I think about the question he asked me there in E-Unit: "Why do you get up in the morning, Eric?" More than fifty years later, I can still hear Surratt's voice, challenging me with that probing, fundamental question.

A few days later, my caseworker called me in to tell me that my request had been approved: I was going to be transferred off Boss Redburn's mop brigade and out to the farm to work as a clerk.

"A lot of guys in here would give their right arm to have this assignment," Boss O'Brien told me. "Don't screw it up. You sit at a desk in a nice office and type up some memos and forms. When you're done with your work you can read whatever you want to until it's time to break for lunch or dinner. In here, it won't get much better than that. You can do some easy time, flatten out your sentence, and get on with your life."

"I appreciate your support, Boss," I told him. "I think I can handle the job without too much trouble."

The following morning, I climbed into the back of a black pickup truck with seven other inmates and rode out to the prison farm. I was assigned to Boss Bradford, who oversaw the fruits and vegetables division. The prison farm grew some of the produce that was served in the mess hall. In addition, some of the produce grown on the farm was sold to markets outside the prison. It was never entirely clear to me what happened to the profit from these sales, but there was no doubt that the profit was based on the labor of prisoners who were paid around thirty cents an hour for their efforts. With the passage of time, this practice has led to the booming, for-profit, private prison industry around the United States today. It's slavery, by another name.

Boss Bradford gave me a thirty-minute orientation, then left to supervise the inmates out in the orchards and vegetable fields—the guys who were doing the picking and cultivating of the crops. I typed up a few forms and filled out a few invoices and in less than an hour had emptied the "to do" basket on my desk.

I could see why Hartman had encouraged me to apply for this position. The workload was very light, affording ample time for reading. That evening, I wrote a letter home asking my parents to send another shipment of hardback books. I asked them to send some major pieces of American fiction, books that would help me if I did decide to go on to graduate school—*Moby Dick* by Herman Melville, *The Scarlet Letter* by Nathaniel Hawthorne, Twain's *Huckleberry Finn*, Henry James's *Portrait of a Lady*, and Faulkner's *Light in August*. I also asked them to include a copy of Ellison's *Invisible Man*. I'd traded the copy I'd found in county jail to Tom Barber, and he'd lost track of it. I wanted another copy to give to Crow and Bubba. I wanted to hear what they thought of it.

That evening back in E-Unit Foots, Crow, Bubba, and I were sitting around talking. I mentioned that I'd had asked my parents to send me some books and asked if any of them had read *Invisible Man*. Foots and Crow had read it before; Bubba had not.

"I don't like fiction that much," said Foots, "but I had to take a general education requirement in literature up at school and our English teacher assigned *Invisible Man*. It really grabbed me. In fact, it was my favorite book in that class."

"What about you, Crow?" I said. "How did you like *Invisible Man* when you read it?"

"No disrespect, but I don't really like that dude Ellison," he said. "You know I think both of you are solid, even though you're both White as a couple of polar bears. I know you like his style and his big words, but I don't like all that. It's like he's writing for White dudes in schools and such. I couldn't get into it."

"His main character is a rebel," I said. "Eventually, he figures out that he's got to do his own thing rather than letting everyone else tell him what to do. That's what I like about him. By the end of the novel, he's free."

"Free, my ass," said Crow. "By the end of the novel he's all by himself, living in an underground hole where he don't get no pussy or weed or any other god damned thing. He's underground and away from all the action. What kind of motherfuckin' bullshit is that? That ain't my idea of freedom. There ain't no freedom down below ground in a hole."

I couldn't help laughing. He had a point. "But he's metaphorically free," I said. "Symbolically, he's free to go on with his life."

"Metaphorically free don't mean shit to me," said Crow. Bubba was nodding in agreement. "I'm talking about real freedom," Crow said. "Hungry motherfuckers aren't free. People living in holes aren't free." His face grew serious. "You know a book you ought to read?"

"What's that?"

Chapter 4. Mainline

"*Native Son*. That brother understands how me and Bubba think about things."

"Say it loud, my man," said Bubba, slapping hands with Crow. "That brother knows how to write. What's his name again?"

"Richard Wright," said Crow.

"That's it," said Bubba. "That's a righteous book he wrote."

"Have you read that one, New?" Crow asked me.

"No, I haven't," I said. "No one ever assigned *Native Son* in any of my classes."

"You bet they didn't," said Crow.

He switched gears, shifting to a conversational thread that had a lasting impact on my view of Occidental College and the education I had received there.

"Any brothers or sisters teach at that school you attended?"

"No," I said. "There were no Blacks on the faculty where I went to school. No Latinos either."

"And you say you went to school in Los Angeles," said Crow. "And they couldn't find no Black or Latino professors? That's a goddamned shame."

"Right on, brother," said Bubba. "It's a damned shame."

"New," said Crow, "when you get out of this motherfucker and become a teacher, I want you to promise me that you'll teach some books by Black folks. And I ain't talking about no damned white-ass niggers, neither. Teach some books by Black folks who tell it like it is."

"I'll try to do that," I told him.

"Don't fucking *try*," he said. "*Promise* Bubba and me."

"All right," I said. "I promise you."

"And one more thing," said Crow.

"What's that?"

"Promise me you'll hire some Black folks to teach at whatever school you're at. Black folks understand some things that White folks really need to know."

"I promise," I said.

"That's good enough for me," said Crow. "I believe you're a man who keeps his word."

§

After I was transferred out to the farm, my days fell into a comfortable and regular rhythm. A buzzer would wake us up at 6:30 a.m. After breakfast, we went to work until we returned to the cellblocks for the morning "count." Then lunch, followed by more work until 4 p.m. Another count before dinner, followed by dinner followed by a "free period" until 9:30 p.m. when everyone returned to his cell, or in our case, our unit. Lights out at 10:30.

Just about every day after dinner Bubba, Crow, Foots, and I would play basketball for an hour or so in the yard and then come back to E-Unit to read, write letters, or talk. Sometimes Surratt and his crew would join in on our conversations. I think Crow and Bubba enjoyed these conversations as much as Foots and I did. They told us that they had never known any White people before, and they sure had never known any Whites who had gone to college. I enjoyed hearing Crow and Bubba talk about their lives on the streets, even though I suspected that neither one of them ever owned an Armani suit.

A few days after I was transferred to the farm, I was sitting on my bunk reading when Crow walked over.

"What you readin,' New?" he asked.

"A novel by William Faulkner," I told him. "He's one of the best writers I've ever read. I'm starting to think that if I do go back to school, I may try to write something about him."

"Never heard of the dude," said Crow. "You know a book I'd like to read?"

"What's that?"

"You know about Malcolm X?"

"Sure," I said. "Everyone knows about Malcolm X."

"What do you think of him?"

"I have a lot of respect for the man," I said. "He gave his life for a cause he believed in. It's hard not to respect that kind of commitment."

"Don't lie to me," said Crow. "Malcolm scared White folks. He called you all kinds of White devils and pale things, and so forth. Don't tell me you liked him."

"I didn't say I liked everything he said," I said. "I said I respect him, and I do. And anyway, by the end of his life, he didn't view all White people as 'White devils.'"

"How do you know that?"

"Because I read his autobiography. If you read it all the way to the end, you see that Malcolm grew a lot during his lifetime. In fact, for me, that's one of the main points of the book."

"What's that?"

"The idea that people can change and grow when they think deeply about their experiences."

"Ain't this a bitch?" Crow announced to the room in general. "Ain't this a motherfuckin' bitch?"

"Say what, Crow?" asked Bubba from down the aisle. "What's happening over there?"

Chapter 4. Mainline

"This White boy's lecturing me about brother Malcolm, and the warden won't let me have a copy of the book so I can read it myself. Motherfuckin' White devil!"

"I hope you're talking about the warden and not me," I said. "I don't believe in the devil, white or otherwise."

"I'm talking about both of you all," said Crow. "I asked the Librarian to order *The Autobiography of Malcolm X* for the library, and he turned me down. He told me that the warden had told him that the book would just stir up trouble."

"That's bullshit," I said. "The warden's more likely to stir up trouble by denying you access to the book. When did you put in the request?"

The Autobiography of Malcolm X, Malcolm X in collaboration with the journalist Alex Haley, published in 1965.

"Over a month ago," said Crow. "I saw Malcolm speak on the TV news before they killed him. That dude had it together. Brother Malcolm would chew your Ralph Ellison up and spit him out."

I said, "My parents got permission to have some books sent to me as long as they come directly from the publisher. I'll ask my caseworker if I can have a copy of Malcolm's *Autobiography* sent in."

"They won't let you have it," said Crow. "But I appreciate your trying."

At that point Surratt joined the conversation. "It's the same story all over again," he said. "It's ironic. Malcolm X used to point out to people that the history books we used in high school were just a lot of crap. They left out poor people and focused on the rich and powerful. They also left out anyone who wasn't White. Malcolm used to say that history in this country had been 'Whitewashed.' It's ironic that his *Autobiography* is being banned in places like this."

"I don't know if it's ironic or not," said Crow. "But I do know it's a bitch. Why should New get to read whatever he wants to read, and I can't get what I want? That's not right."

"Of course it's not right," said Surratt. "That's why we have to do something about it. We have to organize and change things in here. This is a prison, not a plantation."

"There you go again," said Bubba. "All you ever do is to talk about 'we got to organize.'" "You just going to make things worse. All Crow wants is one fuckin' book. He don't want no part of no strike. Right, Crow?"

"That's right, my man. I just want to get hold of that one book, and I'll be happy for a month."

"Let me ask you a question," said Surratt. "What will you guys do when the riot comes down?"

"What riot?" said Crow and Bubba, simultaneously. "We don't know nothin' about no riot."

"Bull," said Surratt. "You're hearing the same things I am. All the guards are talking about it. In fact, they have a pool about the start date. Some say end of August. Some say the first two weeks in September. All the guards think it's getting close."

"I won't take part in any race riot," I said.

"Me either," said Foots. "I don't have anything against Black people or anybody else in here."

Bubba and Crow exchanged a quick glance.

"We don't have anything against any of you guys," said Crow. "But when the shit comes down in the yard, if it does, I'll stick with my own kind. I was in the last riot two years ago before you guys got here, and it was ugly."

"That's why I'm saying we need to organize," said Surratt. "Once it starts, it gets out of control. Anyone can get hurt. That's why we need to organize. We have to change things in here so we don't have a riot."

"I agree with you about the riot," said Crow. "Anyone can get hurt. I'm not going to start anything with anyone, but if someone comes after me first, he'll wish he hadn't."

"Me too," echoed Bubba. "I was talking to Big Frank the other day. He don't want no race riot, but if someone comes after him, he's going to hurt the dude. Big Frank don't play."

"We need to talk to Big Frank," said Surratt. "Next time you guys play hoop with him out in the yard, see if you can get him on board with a strike."

"No way that's happening," said Crow. "Big Frank just wants to do his time and get out of here, like the rest of us."

"Just talk with him," said Surratt. "Every day I hear the guards talking about the riot more and more. They want it to happen. If we beat each other up, they don't have to. Can't you see the game they're playing?"

"I'll talk to Big Frank tomorrow," said Foots. "He and I work together out on the farm. I'm getting to know him a little better."

"See what you can do, Foots." With that, Surratt walked off to talk with the rest of his crew.

§

The next day after breakfast I was called in to see Boss O'Brien. He wanted to talk with me about my new work assignment, see how things were going out on the farm. Things were going well, I told him, a lot better than working on the cleanup crew.

"How long have you been here now, Newhall?"

"A little over three months. Why do you ask?"

"I'm just wondering if you've had any second thoughts about your decision not to go into the military?"

"Not a one. In fact, the longer I'm here, the better I feel about resisting."

"Why's that?"

I paused and thought about whether I wanted to have this conversation with Boss O'Brien. He wasn't going to budge any more than I was. But I went ahead anyway. In fact, from this point on during my time at Lompoc, I moved into a new mode of conversing with the guards. I never swore at them or spoke disrespectfully the way some inmates did. Instead, I tried to engage with them, asking them questions when it felt right. If you want to make change, you can't talk only with people who already agree with you.

I said, "Every day I get up and read in the paper about more and more people being killed in Vietnam. And every day it seems clearer to me that we aren't going to win this war."

"Well, you're wrong there, Newhall," he said, with a frustrated look on his face. "Just flat out wrong. Uncle Sam's never lost a war. Never. Not one. You've been reading too many books. You've lost touch with reality."

"*Someone* has lost touch," I said, "but I'm not sure it's me."

Boss O'Brien wasn't really a bad man. I came to see him as a decent man working in a destructive system. We'd have our occasional arguments about foreign policy or social issues, but on a personal level he reminded me of some of the moderate Republicans I'd grown up with in Portland.

One on one, they were decent people, good neighbors, but they supported policies and trusted institutions that over time had produced some terrible results, probably because those results were out of sight—in Vietnam, or in the Black and Latino neighborhoods Crow and Bubba and Chuy came from, or the reservations David Running Wolf and Snuffy lived on—and therefore out of mind.

"Do you think that anyone gets rehabilitated in this place?" I asked him.

"What are you saying?" he said, looking at me suspiciously. I'm pretty sure that in all his time at Lompoc no inmate had ever asked him this question before.

"I'm just asking if you think that anyone gets rehabilitated here at Lompoc?"

He looked at me seriously for a while before he responded. "Sure," he said. "I think a lot of people get rehabilitated in here. We've got educational programs and vocational training programs for anyone who's motivated enough to sign up. The problem is that most of the guys who wind up here are screw offs who don't want to make anything of themselves. They don't really want to stay out of jail."

"I think you're wrong about that," I said. "I'm living with these guys right now in the general population. They don't want to be in here anymore than I do, but most of them don't have the skills to get a job on the streets that will pay them a decent, living wage. That's the real problem. And the vocational training programs in here are a joke. You can fool the public because most people out there don't really care anyway. But the fact of the matter is that if you train a man on equipment that's ten or fifteen years out of date, you're setting him up for failure."

"Look, Newhall," O'Brien replied. "You and I both know that all the draft dodgers in here are not like the typical inmate. You're in here because you made a bad choice, and I can tell that you're not going to change your mind about Vietnam any more than I am. I tried to get you a job as a clerk out on the farm so that you can do some easy time and leave when you've served your sentence. I hope you don't ever have to come back here."

"I'm not talking about me," I told him. "I'm talking about the guys in here who never graduated from high school and who don't have any job skills that they can use on the streets. This place isn't helping those guys, and, in fact, it's damaging them."

"How's it damaging them?" O'Brien asked. "We take pretty damn good care of people in here. A lot of these guys didn't have three square meals a day and a roof over their heads out on the streets."

"I'm not talking about physical care, Boss," I said. "For a prison, it's not bad. I'm talking about something else."

"What's that?"

"I'm talking about what this place does to people's frame of mind, to their spirit. This place destroys people's souls. It breaks most people down; it doesn't build them up. Most of these guys are in here because they were born into a rough neighborhood and at some point, they made a bad decision. How is it going to rehabilitate them to keep them in this place where they aren't allowed to make even the smallest choice on their own?"

"You're a dreamer, Newhall. Warden Keimer does the best he can with the budget they give him. If he had the money to hire a shrink for every convict in here, I'm sure he'd do it. This isn't Boy Scout camp." He looked quickly at the appointment book on his desk. "Anything else on your mind today?"

"Actually, there is," I said. "I'm wondering if I can add one more book to the list of books my father is having the publisher send in?"

"What's that?"

"*The Autobiography of Malcolm X*."

"What do you want with that book? That's no book for a White man. Don't you know that he hated Whites, yourself included?"

"It's still an important book. I'd like to read it."

"I'm afraid I'll have to deny that request. I'm trying to be reasonable, but that book will just stir up trouble in here. We've got enough racial tension as it is. Stick with books by those other authors you requested. Who were they again?"

"William Faulkner, Nathaniel Hawthorne, Herman Melville, Mark Twain, and Henry James." *All White guys, Boss*, I thought. *They should be fine.*

"Stick with William Faulkner, Herman Melville, and Nathaniel Hawthorne, Mark Twain and Henry James."

§

Right after count that day, before we went to dinner, I saw Surratt circulating around E-Unit, talking to people. Eventually he made his way over to Foots and me. His eyes had that intense burning look I'd come to recognize. Close up, he looked even more agitated than usual.

"Give me an update," he said. "Have you guys had any luck persuading anyone in your basketball game to join us? We're already a week into August. That's when the last riot happened: August of 1966. I checked the records today in the main office."

"I'm still not getting any takers," I told him. "It's not for lack of trying either. I talk to guys on the basketball court all the time, but Crow and Bubba just want to do their number and go home. I talk with Chuy and some of the Chicanos he passes the eggs to every day, but they just don't think we can change this place."

"That's about what I'm hearing, too," said Foots. "Big Frank and I talk about stuff as we go up and down the rows of potatoes we're digging, out on the farm. He agrees with what we're saying, but he doesn't think we can change anything. He tells me that the man has all the guns and all the tear gas. He doesn't want to play against a stacked deck."

Surratt shook his head slowly. "Everyone in here knows that the system is set up to warehouse people, not to help them stay out of the joint once they're released. The hacks and the warden talk a good line about rehabilitation, but they laugh every time one of us gets busted and comes back to the joint. Think about it: If we don't come back, they don't have jobs. They're rewarded for failure and punished for success. The inducements are all wrong."

"Well," I asked Surratt. "What do you suggest? I'm drawing blanks when I try to persuade other people to join us." "We just need to keep doing what we're doing," said Surratt. "There's no magical formula for creating change. The conditions have to be right, and right now they aren't right. We're too divided and disorganized. We have to be patient. We have to be long distance runners, not sprinters."

That was the first time I'd ever heard the term "long distance runner" applied to social change. I've been using it myself ever since, passing it on to my students and my kids. Social change is not about short bursts of fired-up activism. It's about long-term commitment. If you're serious about change, profound and lasting change, you've got be a long-distance runner.

As we moved into the second week of August, the atmosphere all over the joint felt increasingly tense. The weather turned from warm to hot, and everyone, guards and inmates alike, was on edge. Over in the weightlifting area, one of the bikers crept up behind a Black inmate and hit him in the head with a fifteen-pound bar bell. I didn't actually see this assault, but word about it spread quickly around the prison. The injured inmate did not die, but his skull was fractured. He was taken to the prison infirmary and later treated at a hospital in Santa Barbara. I never saw him or heard anything about him again.

We could all feel the growing tension. There were more arguments than usual on the basketball court and a few shoving matches that nearly turned into fights. No punches were thrown, but the tone of the game changed. Foots and Big Frank played the role of peacemakers, cooling things down when they threatened to boil over, but we all sensed that something was in the air. The guards were on edge, too. If their instructions were not followed instantly and to the letter, they barked out their orders. They began to frisk us more frequently and more thoroughly, and they frisked the Black and Latino inmates far more frequently and thoroughly than they did the Whites.

For the first half of August, I went all out, trying to persuade people to support a strike. I gave it everything I had but got nowhere. Surratt brought in a few more dopers, but even he couldn't persuade any of the Blacks, Latinos, or low riders to support a strike, and he knew that a strike supported only by the "hippies" would not be effective. We'd hit a brick wall. For the first time, even Surratt looked battle-weary and a little downcast.

A few days later, Boss O'Brien, my caseworker, called me in to his office. "Your father sent you another bunch of books," he said. "As long as they're hardbacks sent directly from the publishing company, we'll accept them, but tell him that we have a library here and there's really no need for him to send all these books."

Boss O'Brien handed me a cardboard box that had already been opened. "The guys in the mail room open all packages," he said. "It's prison policy. We inspect for contraband. Weapons, drugs, and so on."

"Is that all?" I said, getting ready to leave.

"There is one more thing," he said. "Just what is it you're so unhappy about? You're working on the farm. You have time to read these books that your parents send you, books we've agreed to allow you to have sent in, even though we don't have the manpower to inspect a lot of packages. Why are you so angry?"

Boss O'Brien seemed to be truly puzzled. I decided to give him a serious answer. "What gives you the impression that I'm angry?" I asked him.

"Word gets to me on the grapevine that you and some of your friends are not happy with the way the warden is running this place."

"I'll give you a straight answer to your question, Boss," I said. "I've been here for more than three months now, and it didn't take me that long to see how this system works. Or rather, to see how it doesn't work."

"I'll give *you* a straight answer," said O'Brien. "I've been here for twenty-two years, and it seems to me that the system works fine. The prison is doing its job. It's protecting people who obey the law from people who don't."

"On the surface it might seem that way," I said, "but from the inside it's clear that that's not really what's happening. You lock people up, but when they get out, they're angrier, and in many cases more violent, than when they went in. In a nutshell, that's what's wrong with this system: we're treating the symptoms of the problem rather than the problem itself. We have too many prisons and not enough teachers, schools, and decent jobs that pay a living wage."

"You're a dreamer, Newhall," he told me. "You're not living in the real world."

"I'm one of the few practical people in this place," I told him.

Boss O'Brien just laughed and waved out me of his office. "Enjoy your books," he said, "and stay out of trouble."

I went back to E-Unit. My plan for the rest of the day was to start reading one of the novels my father had sent me, have lunch, and then go out to the farm for the afternoon shift. I laid the six books out on my bed. All six were novels by William Faulkner: *The Sound and the Fury*; *As I Lay Dying*; *Light in August*; *Absalom, Absalom!*; *Go Down, Moses*; and *Intruder in the Dust*. *That's odd*, I thought. *He already sent me a copy of* Light in August. *He must have forgotten.*

I picked up *Light in August*, turned to the first page, and started to read. I've always loved the opening chapter of this novel. Lena Grove, young, unmarried, and pregnant, walking barefoot along a dirt road in Mississippi, in touch with the earth and nature, as her name suggests. Belly swollen with child, Lena embodies freedom and the life force itself—everything that concrete prisons threaten.

But as I read the first few sentences of the book I was holding, I was puzzled. The opening paragraph was not about Lena Grove at all. Instead, I read: "When my mother was pregnant with me, she told me later, a party of hooded Ku Klux Klan riders galloped up to our home in Omaha, Nebraska, one night." I was puzzled. My eyes dropped down to the second paragraph. It began, "My father, the Reverend Earl Little, was a Baptist minister, a dedicated organizer for Marcus Aurelius Garvey's U.N.I.A. (Universal Negro Improvement Association)." I was shocked: the book in my hands was *The Autobiography of Malcolm X*. Then, the other shoe dropped. My father had guessed that the guards would not check his shipment of books carefully enough to be sure that the books he sent corresponded to their jackets. *Good old Pop*, I thought. *Always resisting any sort of censorship. Always supporting John Stuart Mill, freedom of speech, the free exchange of ideas.* I laughed silently to myself. *Don't judge a book by its cover.*

After I got out, he told me the whole story. During the spring semester of 1965, he'd had a student in his "Introduction to Philosophy" who was in danger of failing.

"Professor Newhall," the student said, "I'm flunking your class, and if I flunk your class, they'll kick me out of school. And if they kick me out of school, I'm pretty sure I'll be drafted. I'm I-A (draft category), and they're drafting the older guys first before they go after they younger guys who are I-A."

"The young man was very pale, and his eyes were blood shot," my father recalled. "He looked as though he had been losing a lot of sleep and not eating properly. I told him that I couldn't give him a grade he hadn't earned. I told him that I knew other students who were in predicaments similar to his and that I believed in equitable treatment."

"What did he say to that?" I'd asked.

"He told me that I was signing his death certificate if I gave him an F for the class."

"That's pretty heavy pressure," I said. "What happened to the guy?"

"I told him that I'd work with him for one hour each week to help him understand the readings and some of the concepts he was having difficulty with. He took me up on my offer and eventually earned a legitimate C+ in the class."

"What's the connection?" I asked my father. "I mean, what's the connection between this guy and that copy of Malcolm X's *Autobiography*?"

"After the young man graduated, he came by my office to thank me for the extra help. He told me that if there were ever anything he could do to reciprocate, he'd be happy to do so. A year or so later I received a letter from him. He was working in the Bay Area for the West Coast Division of Random House. He sent his business card along with the letter."

That student, or someone he knew at Random House, had helped my dad slip the *Autobiography* past the guards at Lompoc by sending it directly from the publisher's warehouse with a book jacket from *Light in August*. It's like Crow used to say: "What goes around, comes around."

It made me feel good to pass that book along to Crow, and to watch him reading it in E-Unit every spare minute he had. When he was done reading it, he passed it along to Bubba, who read it with the same intense interest. When Bubba finished it, he passed it along to Big Frank, at which point I lost touch with it. Most likely, it circulated among the Black prisoners who liked to read. For all I know, it may still be making its way through Lompoc's cellblocks. Not a year goes by that I don't include *The Autobiography of Malcolm X* in my seminar on "The Social Movements of the 1960s." And every time I teach it, I think of the look in Crow's eyes when he was reading it.

Aside from that small success on the literary front, however, I was forced to accept the fact that I was an abysmal failure as a political organizer. As an undergraduate, I had read about labor struggles in novels like Steinbeck's *In Dubious Battle* and *The Grapes of Wrath*; I had studied the Depression era history of the labor movement; I had gone with some friends to see *The Battle of Algiers*, a film about the Algerian struggle for independence from France. My senior year, I had gone to hear Saul Alinsky, a noted community organizer, speak about tactics people could use to fight against their own oppression.

Like many people in the anti-war movement, I admired rebels, rebellion, and political organizers like Alinsky. I respected his commitment to his calling and privately wondered if I might develop the skills required to do what he was doing. Two months of abject failure as a political organizer at Lompoc forced me to give up any illusions I may have had about moving the masses with my inspiring oratory. Despite persistent attempts to persuade other prisoners to join our movement, I had failed to recruit anyone. Zip. Zero. Nada.

Nonetheless, I was doing "easy time," for what it was worth. I did have, as far as I could tell, one of the best jobs in the joint. As a clerk out on the farm, I was free from the threat of violence that was an ever-present reality for inmates assigned to the laundry room, the machine shop, or the furniture factory, where most of the daily fights at Lompoc took place. As long as I finished the specific tasks Boss Bradford gave me each day (typing invoices, filing paperwork), he didn't care what I did with the rest of my time. My assigned work took two hours a day at most, usually less. During my first ten days on the farm, I read three of the Faulkner novels my father had sent to me.

As the second half of August loomed, I continued to float along easily and relatively comfortably by Lompoc standards. Each day was like the one that preceded it, and more or less like the one that followed. Boss Bradford seemed satisfied, and so was I. I could keep my position as a clerk on the farm for the next year and a half, if I wanted to, read some good books, stay in shape playing basketball, finish off my sentence, and move on with my life. Easy time. Aside from being in prison, it seemed like a pretty good plan.

Or maybe not. On August 25, I was in the Chow Hall eating lunch with Foots, Cohen, and Adams when Surratt sat down at our table. Something was up. His eyes were afire.

"Fellas," he said, "I heard a couple of hacks talking in the administrative office right before lunch about trouble down in the furniture factory this morning."

"What sort of trouble?" asked Cohen.

"The guys who work down there want their earnings for the last two weeks to be entered on the books by Friday, tomorrow, so they can go to Commissary over the weekend. The hacks in the furniture factory don't want to do that. They want to wait until next week to put the money on the books."

"That doesn't sound like such a big deal to me," said Foots. "I hear they only pay twenty-nine cents an hour in the furniture factory. It's like modern-day slavery. What difference does it make if their money goes on the books this week or next Monday?"

"It makes a lot of difference to some of them," said Surratt. "The guys want to use the money to buy zu-zus and wham-whams from the Commissary over the weekend. They don't want to wait until next week."

"What are 'zu-zus and wham-whams?'" I asked. I'd never heard the term before.

"That's joint slang for cigarettes and candy bars," said Cohen. "You don't smoke, do you?"

"No," I said.

"If you need a cigarette," said Cohen, "you don't want it next week. You want it right now. That's why some of these guys are getting so worked up. They're tired of these cheap, bullshit, Bull Durham, roll-your-own cigarettes. They want Camels, Lucky Strikes, and Marlboros."

"Some of the guards were saying there was a lot of talk in the furniture factory about inmates refusing to work unless the money went onto the books this week," said Surratt. He underscored the point: "The guys in the furniture factory are talking about refusing to work, and the hacks are taking that threat seriously."

Now I saw why Surratt was so excited. For nearly three months our "strike committee" had been doing our best to organize a protest against the conditions in the prison and had failed miserably. We'd failed to broaden our "movement" beyond our little group of so-called "hippies." Now, some of the guys in the furniture factory, mainly low riders, Blacks, and Chicanos, were becoming agitated enough to at least consider refusing to work.

"They're just talking," said Adams. "I know some of those guys. They've been complaining about one thing or another ever since we drove up to this place back in April. They complain about not being paid more. About dangerous working conditions. About not getting any breaks during the day. I'll believe a strike when I see it."

"What do you think, John?" Foots asked Surratt. "Will they strike?"

"I'm not sure," said Surratt. "It depends on what happens during the afternoon shift today. I don't think the guards will budge an inch about putting the money on the books this week. It wouldn't cost the hacks anything to put the money on the books today, but for them it's always about power and control. What the guys in the furniture factory will do in response is anybody's guess."

Cohen had been listening to the conversation intently. Now, his eyes lit up, like Surratt's.

"Maybe our group should be the spark that sets things off," he said. "I'm ready to go on strike right now. Maybe that will encourage the guys in the furniture factory to do the same."

"The key here is timing," said Surratt. "I think we should wait to see what the guys in the furniture factory do. If they strike, we can join them, support their decision, and help to build momentum. In the meantime, when we go back to work after lunch today, we need to spread the word about what's happening in the furniture factory, talk up the idea of a strike. We need to fan the flames and spread the fire."

Riding back to the farm in the truck after lunch that day, I was as excited as I had been in a long time. I knew that a moment of truth was upon me; I was on the verge of having to make an important decision. In my nearly four months at Lompoc, I had managed to maneuver myself into a position where I was doing easy time. Every time Hartman saw me talking with Surratt's group, he would tell me how foolish he thought the idea of a strike was. "All you're going to do is get thrown in the Hole and lose your good time," he would say.

From a pragmatic, individual perspective, he was probably right. Another part of me, however, was increasingly uneasy about doing nothing to resist the destructive indifference of Lompoc and the prison system in general. The same impulse that had driven me to resist the war was now driving me to push back against the prison. I could see that the war in Vietnam and Lompoc were part of the same system, and both were carelessly destroying human lives while claiming to save or rehabilitate them. It made no sense to resist the war and conform to the prison.

As our truck pulled up to the farm offices where we worked, an image flashed quickly through my mind. I saw four guards leading Foots and Surratt away from E-Unit on their way to the Hole. In my mind's eye I saw myself just sitting on my bunk, watching as they were being led away. That image made me feel as defeated and empty as I could ever remember feeling. In that instant it became clear to me that I wouldn't be able to live with myself if I stayed out on the farm, filling out Boss Bradford's forms while Surratt and Foots and the rest of our group were sitting in the Hole for refusing to work. If the guys in the furniture factory decided to strike, I would probably go with them, taking along with me as many of the guys in E-Unit as I could rally. I say *probably*, because you never really know for sure what you'll do under pressure until the moment comes to act. Talking about a strike was one thing; going on strike was another. Who knew what the afternoon would bring?

That morning I had begun to read the last of the Faulkner novels that my parents had sent to me. I read them in chronological order, starting with *The Sound and the Fury* (1929) and ending with *Intruder in the Dust* (1948). Most critics don't consider *Intruder in the Dust* to be one of Faulkner's best novels, but it is of significant historical interest, because it illuminates Faulkner's response to the incipient civil rights movement that began to emerge in the South after World War II. In the novel, Faulkner applies his characteristic modernist techniques to the detective genre. The plot revolves around Lucas Beauchamp, a proud, strong-willed Black man who is wrongly accused of murdering a White man; it chronicles the attempts of ethical White Southerners (among them a liberal lawyer in the Atticus Finch mold) to find the real killer and set Beauchamp free. Despite Faulkner's reservations about northern civil rights workers (he calls them "outlanders") intruding into Southern culture, I was enjoying the novel and was looking forward to finishing it that afternoon. Without warning, Boss Bradford

Intruder in the Dust, **William Faulkner, published in 1948.**

walked into the office a little after two o'clock and announced that we were done for the day.

"We're stopping early today," he said to me and the other clerk, a quiet guy from Seattle who liked to do crossword puzzles to pass the time. "The truck leaves in five minutes. Be ready to go."

"Why the short day, Boss?" I asked him. In the four months I had been at Lompoc this was the first time a workday had been cut short. I was curious to find out if this change in routine was connected in any way with the trouble brewing in the furniture factory.

"I'm just following orders from upstairs," Boss Bradford said. "When Warden Keimer says work is over for the day, it's over."

All eight clerks assigned to the farm piled into the back of a pickup truck and returned to the prison. Ahead of us on the dirt road I could see four other similar trucks filled with the inmates who'd been picking crops. As our truck followed the road around to one of the back entrances to the main building, I noticed that the yard was empty. Clearly, something was up. I had never seen the yard this deserted before.

"Report to your units for count," Boss Bradford told us as we shuffled inside. I began to wonder if perhaps someone had escaped, and the guards were trying to figure out who it was. Inside E-Unit I saw several inmates gathered around the windows, looking out at the yard and at the adjoining units on either side of ours. In the center of E-unit I saw Surratt surrounded by a cluster of inmates, engaged in heated discussion. He looked up when he saw me coming.

"It's happening, Eric," he said. "The guys in the furniture factory are out on strike. They shut down their machines and refused to work, right after lunch. No riot. No violence. They just refused to work unless they're paid tomorrow so they can go to the Commissary over the weekend."

I thought about how ineffective I had been in all my feeble attempts at organizing. All my arguments had fallen on deaf ears. What ultimately moved people to strike that summer at Lompoc had little or nothing to do with human rights or abstract principles. What moved people to act was the prospect of missing out on their zu zus and wham whams—cigarettes, candy bars, and other items from the commissary.

"What happens next?" asked Cohen.

"I'll tell you what happens next," said Chuy, who had just joined the clump of men gathered around Surratt. "The hacks won't want anything to spread beyond the furniture factory. They'll probably put the whole prison on lockdown until the guys in the furniture factory go back to work. They'll try to figure out who the ringleaders are, and when they do, they'll throw them in the Hole for a while. I did three years at Macalester in Oklahoma, and that's what they did there when some guys in the laundry room refused to work."

"Chuy's right," said Surratt. "That *is* what the hacks are going to do. They'll try to break up any strike before it has a chance to spread. They'll try to nip it in the bud. The real question, now, is, what are we going to do?"

"I know what we *should* do," said Cohen. "We should support the guys in the furniture factory and go on strike ourselves. We should shut this entire motherfucking prison down. Let the pigs mop the floors. Let the pigs serve the food. Let Keimer and Keith pick the crops out on the farm. It's their prison. Let them run it."

Most people nodded their heads in agreement with Cohen. Shouts of "right on" filled the air. A group of inmates over by the window started shouting through the bars to other units to the right and left of E-Unit.

Chapter 4. Mainline

"On strike, shut it down! On strike, shut it down!" Quickly, nearly everyone in the room took up the chant. Word about the strike in the furniture factory spread like a brush fire in dry grass, fanned by a warm, Santa Ana wind. We began to hear shouts to our left, coming from D-Unit, and from F-Unit to our right. "On strike, shut it down! On strike, shut it down!"

I was amazed. Two or three weeks earlier, I would have told anyone that there was no way something like this could happen at Lompoc. But suddenly things had come to a head. Some sort of tipping point had been reached, and the shifting momentum touched nearly everyone.

"Look at that, over there!" shouted Chuy. In F-Unit, inmates were lowering something slowly and carefully out of their barred windows. I looked and saw that it was a cotton bed sheet on which someone had printed, in large black letters, the word "STRIKE." Our unit erupted when we saw what was written on the sheet and the chant became even louder. "On strike, shut it down! On strike, shut it down!" The chant spread like a contagion around the prison until shouts and cheers were coming from every unit up and down the main corridor.

Amid this chaos, I tried to stay calm and think clearly about what I should do. I knew what I had to lose, because Hartman reminded me of the downside of resisting virtually every time we talked. I would lose my job out on the farm, which meant I'd lose the opportunity to read for the next year and a half; that, in turn, might cost me something if I decided to go on to graduate school. I'd lose the chance to accumulate the "good time" that would shorten my sentence from twenty-four months to about seventeen or eighteen. I'd be returned to M-unit and sent back to the mop detail where I'd have to deal, once again, with Boss Redburn's bullshit.

"Why would you want to do hard time when you can do easy time?" Hartman had asked me repeatedly, out in the yard. Initially I didn't really have a clear answer for him because I was still ambivalent. Once the guys in the furniture factory refused to work and a strike seemed possible, my ambivalence vanished: I knew the answer to his question. Easy time is just an empty prison dream, a carrot the man dangles in front of you to keep you in line. In the end, all you've done with easy time is keep the man's prison running for him. *Fuck easy time*, I thought, amid the shouting. *Let the chips fall where they may. I have to say "no" to everything this prison stands for.* I turned and joined in with the others, yelling, "On strike, shut it down! On strike, shut it down!" as loudly as I could. We chanted all afternoon until we were hoarse.

§

I looked around E-Unit and saw that nearly everyone was joining in. Low riders and hippies were chanting together. Chuy and several other Latinos who were part of his egg-stealing operation were there. Even Crow and Bubba and several other brothers had joined in the chanting, once it got started.

"This is amazing," said Foots as he looked around him. "Who would have thought something like this could happen? I just didn't see it coming."

Surratt walked over to us, a big smile on his face. "No race riot this summer guys," he said. "We're going to have a real, Depression-style sit-down strike."

At 4:30 the buzzer went off as it normally did, announcing that it was time for the afternoon count. We all stopped chanting and either sat or lay down on our bunks. The officer in charge of E-Unit that afternoon was a Latino named Martinez. Boss Martinez had always seemed like a decent guy as guards go. He never hassled us unnecessarily or maliciously. He came to work, did his job, and went home at the end of his shift. That Thursday afternoon when he took the count, he looked nervous. He walked quickly up and down the aisles counting heads, and then he returned to his small cubicle at the front of the unit. Through the glass partition we could see him talking with someone on the telephone. After ten minutes or so, he hung up, walked to the front of the unit, and asked for our attention.

"I have an announcement to make," he said. "Due to a disturbance in another part of the institution, we'll be having dinner tonight in shifts, four units at a time. E-Unit will eat dinner about sixty minutes from now in the second shift. I'll call you when it's our turn to go to the Chow Hall."

"These mother fuckers are scared," Crow said. "What goes around comes around. The bulls know they don't treat us right. Now they scared it's payback time."

An excited buzzing filled the unit. I saw Surratt talking with Foots for a while. When he was done, he handed Foots a manila folder with some papers in it. Then he came walking down the aisle toward my bunk.

"I think it's going to happen, Newhall," he said excitedly. "I really think it's going to happen."

"It sounded that way a few minutes ago," I said. "It's not just our unit; it's growing. It feels like it's alive."

"Are you still in?" he asked me, looking me straight in the eye.

"I'm in," I said. "Fuck 'easy time.'" This time when I said it, I felt no ambivalence tugging me in another direction—none whatsoever.

Surratt grinned. Then he handed me a manila folder like the one he'd handed Foots. "Here," he said. "Take these. Keep them in a safe place. You'll know what to do with them when you look at them."

Just as he said this, Boss Martinez came out of his office and walked to the front of our unit. The Associate Warden, Boss Keith, was with him. At first, I thought they were going to tell us that it was time for dinner, but I was wrong. Boss Keith looked up and down the aisles. He did not look happy.

"Inmate Surratt," he called out.

Surratt stood up. "Right here, Boss," he said in a firm voice.

"The warden wants to talk with you," Boss Keith said.

At that moment E-unit fell so silent that I could hear the guns rumbling at the air force base. Surratt walked up to the front of the unit and followed Associate Warden Keith out into the corridor. Through the glass at the front of the unit we watched them walk down the corridor toward the warden's office.

Foots came down to my bunk. "What's that about?" he asked.

"I don't know," I said. "Let's see what Crow and Bubba make of it."

We walked over to Crow's bunk where he and Bubba were talking quietly.

"What do you think that's about?" Foots asked them.

"I think that's about the Man showing us that he's not afraid of us," said Crow. "He's showing us that he can walk in here where there's eighty of us and only one of him, and he can take one of us out of here without anyone laying a hand on him."

"Why did he want Surratt?" asked Foots.

"Because someone done snitched Surratt off," said Bubba. "There's snitches all over this joint. They'll sell you out for a pack of cigarettes or some bonneroos from the laundry room. Some of them will snitch you off just because it makes them feel big to talk to the warden." ("Bonneroos" was prison slang for tailored khaki pants that were snugger fitting than the floppy "Cadillacs" inmates were given when they arrived. They could be acquired from the laundry room if you had an inside connection or purchased with packs of cigarettes.)

"That's right," said Crow. "Surratt and you guys have been talking about a strike for at least three months now. Everybody knows that. You'd better believe that Keimer and Keith know that. In fact, it won't surprise me if all of you hippie dudes have been snitched off. Now they're going to pressure Surratt to see if he'll give anyone else up. That's how they operate. They try to divide us against each other."

"Surratt won't give anyone up," I said. "He's solid."

"We'll see," said Crow.

"What's in the folders he gave us?" I asked Foots. I hadn't yet looked at the contents of the folder Surratt had handed to me earlier.

"It's a list of demands," said Foots. "Surratt must have run them off right before lunch, after he heard about the strike in the furniture factory. He's the only one I know who has access to a mimeograph machine."

"Why do you think he ran them off this morning?" I asked. "We put that list of demands together two months ago, that day when we were talking out in the yard."

"We started it two months ago in the yard," said Foots, "but Surratt finished it right before he went to lunch today. Check it out."

I took the manila folder out from underneath my mattress and pulled out one of the lists. Reading quickly, I saw that it included all the concerns our group had originally come up with that day in the yard, but Surratt had added one additional item: "All wages will be posted on the books each Friday so that inmates can go to Commissary over the following weekend." Clearly that item had been added just that morning. It was intended to build on the anger of the men in the furniture factory and to support their demand that they be paid in time to purchase zu zus and wham whams for the weekend. Surratt's final list of demands included a little something for every group in the joint.

"Surratt wants us to spread these lists around to as many units as possible," said Foots. "We should take some to dinner with us and give them to guys in other units. We need to pass them around without letting the hacks see us do it."

"That makes sense," I said. I folded up about ten of the sheets and put them into my pants pocket. Then I put the manila folder back under my mattress. That was, of course, one of the first places anyone doing even a cursory search would look, but at least the folder was out of sight for the time being.

I looked around E-Unit to see if I recognized anyone who worked in the furniture factory, but I didn't see anyone. I knew that Martin Winters worked down there, but he had not requested a move into E-Unit when the rest of us did. He preferred the privacy and security of a single cell to the more open dormitory arrangement in E-Unit. In addition, some of his biker friends lived in N-Unit, and he felt more comfortable staying where he was.

"I wish Martin were here," I said to Foots. "He could tell us what's happening down in the furniture factory."

"Maybe we'll see him in the Chow Hall when we go to dinner," Foots replied. "Sooner or later, they have to feed all of us."

Just then, as if on cue, Boss Martinez called for attention and announced that it was "chow time" for E-Unit. As we bunched together to move out into the corridor, both Foots and I took the opportunity to pass out a few sheets of the strike demands to inmates who weren't part of our immediate group.

"Read these and pass them on in the Mess Hall," we told everyone as we as we moved into the corridor.

Chapter 4. Mainline

Inside the mess hall there were fewer inmates than normal and more than twice the normal number of guards. Clearly the warden was preparing for trouble. Foots and I got our food and looked around for a place to sit. We noticed Crow and Bubba sitting by themselves on the far side of the room.

"Shall we sit with Crow and Bubba?" asked Foots.

"That's a good idea," I said.

We walked over to where Crow and Bubba were sitting.

"Can we sit with you guys?" asked Foots.

Crow and Bubba looked at each other.

"Sure," said Crow. "Have a seat."

Around the mess hall, people were watching us—inmates and guards alike. Years later, I could see that this was a small but significant moment in the strike. It sent the message that our group had been trying to send all summer: There are two groups at Lompoc—the keepers and the kept. We weren't going to have a race riot. We were going to have a non-violent work stoppage to insist that even the lives of "throwaway people" (Toni Morrison's term, from her novel *Beloved*) have value and should not be treated with indifference. Around the chow hall, everyone buzzed at the sight of four inmates rejecting the color line. The guards were visibly threatened by the growing solidarity that had begun in the yard on the basketball court and was spreading throughout the prison. They patrolled the Chow Hall in grim-faced pairs. Ignoring us, they spoke only to each other.

"What would Malcolm X say about this?" I asked Crow.

"He'd say that the hacks are a bunch of no-good punk ass motherfuckers," said Crow.

"No, no." I said. "I'm talking about the integrated eating arrangements. You guys are sitting here in a federal prison eating lunch with a couple of White devils. What would Malcolm say about that?"

"Hold on now, White boy," said Crow. "You ain't the only one in here who can read books. I read that book you gave me from cover to cover. If he were here today Brother Malcolm would say that you discover truth in prison. That's what he did. In prison all the bullshit that distracts us out on the streets is stripped away. In here we can discover truth if we pay attention. That's what Malcolm would say if he were here today."

"And what sort of truth are you discovering?" Foots asked him.

"You already know this," said Crow. "Near the end of his life Malcolm took a trip to Mecca. He discovered that not all White people are devils."

Bubba and Crow shared a glance.

"Don't get us wrong," said Bubba. "Most White people really *are* motherfuckers. Most, but not all. Crow and me think you and New are two righteous White boys. We've been talking about it. You guys are the onliest White boys Crow and me have ever trusted. Big Frank feels the same way. Big Frank thinks you guys are solid, and he don't say that about very many people."

In my forty-four years teaching at Occidental, I've never received a compliment that made me feel more honored than what Crow and Bubba said to Foots and me in the Chow Hall that day. That's why I like the word "onliest" as much as I do. That's why I occasionally slip it into a conversation with Angela, even though she eye-rolls when I do ("stop trying to talk *inner city*"). "Onliest" reminds me of the powerful sense of solidarity and trust we all felt during the strike.

Foots asked Crow and Bubba to pass some lists of demands along to people they knew in other units, especially the brothers. They agreed to circulate Surratt's handouts and to spread news of the strike demands by word-of-mouth every chance they got. Ten minutes later a buzzer sounded and one of the guards shouted out that chow time was over and that we should all return to our units. There would be no free time in the yard today.

I watched as Crow and Bubba mixed in with the inmates from M-unit and N-Unit who were entering the mess hall as we were leaving. I saw them surreptitiously passing the strike demands to other Black inmates as they made their way out into the main corridor.

I spent the rest of that evening until lights out reading, writing a letter home, and talking with inmates I didn't know about supporting the strike the next morning if the guys in the furniture factory still refused to work. I handed the list of strike demands to a couple of guys who seemed more interested than most and watched them read down the sheet.

"Right on," said one of them to me. "You're damn right we ought to get paid before the weekend. Have you ever wanted a smoke and had to wait for two days until you could get one? That's just bullshit."

"There's a clear message here," said Foots.

"What's that?" I asked him.

"Don't mess with people's zu-zus and wham whams," he said.

I woke up early the next morning, eager to see what Friday would bring. The sun was up, already promising that the day would be clear and hot. Surratt was still gone; everyone assumed he was in the Hole. I wondered what the warden had said to him during their meeting.

The prison was now officially on lockdown mode. In the mess hall, Foots and I sat by ourselves and had just started eating our oatmeal and drinking coffee when Crow and Bubba walked up to our table.

"Do you two white devils mind if two righteous brothers join you for breakfast?" said Crow, with the hint of a smile.

"Have a seat," said Foots.

Chapter 4. Mainline

We ate in silence for a while. I could tell that Crow had something on his mind, so I just waited.

"So, you guys are really serious about this strike?" he asked, at last.

"Very serious," said Foots. "If the furniture factory strikes this morning after breakfast, I'm going on strike with them. I hope you guys refuse to work, too. We're all in the same boat in here."

"Some of the brothers are talking about it," said Bubba. "Big Frank's telling some of the brothers in N-unit where he is that Malcolm would strike if he were here today. Malcolm would never put up with the bullshit they're layin' on all of us in this here joint. He'd just do his time in the Hole where they couldn't fuck with him no more. I don't think Big Frank's going to work today, no matter what the guys in the furniture factory do."

"Are you guys going to see Big Frank today?" I asked them.

"Not if we're still on lockdown," Crow said. "I might be able to get a message to him, though, through one of the trustees who delivers the mail."

"Ask the trustee to give him this," I said, reaching under the table and handing Crow a copy of the list of demands Surratt had drawn up. "Ask Big Frank to share it with the rest of the guys in N-unit."

Boss Martinez was walking past us just then, so we quickly changed the subject to basketball. At 9 a.m. the work buzzer went off. When it did, inmates in F-Unit to our right and N-Unit to our left began shouting, just as they had the day before. "On strike, shut it down! On strike, shut it down!" I couldn't see faces but I could see fists pumping to the beat of the chants. Two rough banners, sheets with writing in bright red letters, unfurled from the windows of both units. Both banners proclaimed, "On Strike."

Almost instantly the chant started up in E-unit, and Foots, Crow, Bubba, and I all joined in. I saw Cohen, Denham, and even red-haired Breintnall shouting, over in the next aisle of bunks. On a normal day, most of the fish from A and O would be filtering outside after breakfast to enjoy some free time in the yard. Other inmates would be heading down to the machine shop, the garment factory, or the furniture factory to work their morning shifts. Workers assigned to the farm would be on route to the trucks that would drive them to the fields. On this morning, Friday, August 26, I could see only five or six people moving slowly across the yard toward their work assignments. I didn't recognize any of them.

A big low rider whose bunk was in another aisle recognized one of the inmates in the yard and began to shout angrily at him. This low rider seemed vaguely familiar to me, but I couldn't place him at first. Then I remembered that his name was Dusty and that he was one of the bikers Foots and I had played basketball with when we were still in A and O.

"You weak, punk ass motherfuckers!" Dusty shouted out the window at the six guys in the yard. They looked up to see who was shouting at them, then kept walking. "We're going to cut every punk ass motherfucking one of you!" Dusty shouted angrily. "Every last one of you is dead."

Dusty's threats made me uneasy. Our strike committee had in mind a non-violent strike. *This is getting out of control*, I thought. *Should I say something to Dusty? No, not now. Nothing's going to happen while we're on lockdown. Let Dusty cool off, and then talk to him about what the goal of the strike is. There's no need for anyone to get hurt.*

Just as Foots and I were starting to talk about how to deal with inmates who didn't want to join the strike, Boss Martinez and Associate Warden Keith walked up to the front of E-unit. "I'm going to give you men one last chance to go to work," said Keith. "You're making a big mistake. You're going to lose any good time you have accumulated—for some of you, that's more than a year. You're also going to forfeit any chance you might have for parole. Breaking prison rules and regulations by refusing to work isn't likely to persuade the Parole Board that you've been rehabilitated."

Boss Keith's statement did not persuade anyone in E-Unit to go to work that day. In fact, his presence seemed to have the opposite effect.

"Fuck you, Keith," came a loud shout from the back of the unit. Martinez and Keith were standing up at the front of E-unit. All of us were crowded together in a pack near the back. There is strength in numbers—and anonymity in a crowd. I couldn't tell who had shouted at Keith and neither could Keith.

"You men are making a mistake," he repeated. "Twenty years from now you'll regret the decision you're making here today." He looked at us steadily. He had cold blue eyes, an erect posture, and gray hair, cut short in a military-style crew cut. I thought he'd said what he had to say, but he wasn't done.

"Inmates Morrill and Newhall, Warden Keimer would like to speak to you boys," he said.

I had not even laid eyes on Warden Keimer since arriving at Lompoc. I was curious to see him and to question him about some of the prison policies. I wanted to "speak truth to power," as we used to say in those days. I wanted to tell him, to his face, that his prison wasn't helping anyone and that it was damaging, to one degree or another, everyone who spent any significant amount of time in it—that it was, as Lompoc's lone psychiatrist put it, an "anti-therapeutic environment."

Foots and I looked at each other and started to move toward the front of the unit. As we began walking up the aisle, inmates grabbed our arms and shouted that we shouldn't obey Keith's order.

"Don't go, don't go, don't go!" It became a chant, and it got louder and louder.

"Stay here," shouted several voices. "We'll protect you." "Yeah, we'll fight the motherfuckers." The last voice I recognized as Dusty's. Dusty, it turned out, had a low boiling point, and he loved a good brawl. He was ready to fight anyone, any time, at the drop of a hat.

"Stay cool," Foots said. "New and I will go talk with the warden and see if we can persuade him to make some of the changes we're asking for."

"That's right," I chimed in. "We don't want violence here. We don't want a riot. We want some changes in prison policy. We want money on the books for zu zus and wham whams."

"Hell yes!" I heard Cohen shout. "Zu zus and wham whams today!"

The whole of E-Unit took it up. "Zu zus and wham whams today! Zu zus and wham whams today!" The atmosphere in E-Unit was emotionally charged and increasingly unpredictable. That Friday morning and the following eight days would produce a sense of community and solidarity more powerful than anything I've experienced since that time. That sense of community is something I've tried—with partial success at Occidental—to recapture in my life since leaving Lompoc.

We walked down the main corridor, Boss Keith leading the way, two burly guards bringing up the rear. As we walked, I rehearsed some of the questions I wanted to ask the warden when I had my chance to speak truth to power. *Why do so many inmates return to prison multiple times after you release them? Doesn't that suggest that locking all these people up is failing as a policy? Why do you have inmates who don't know how to read pushing a broom for eight hours every day rather than spending the day learning to read?* Most important, *why are so many of the inmates here at Lompoc Black or Latino?*

When we reached the sign that said "Warden," Boss Keith didn't break stride, didn't even glance in the direction of the warden's office. He simply kept walking down the corridor in the direction of the mess hall.

"Hold on," said Foots, as we walked past the door to the warden's office. "I thought you said the warden wanted to speak with us."

Keith turned and looked at us for a moment, and for the first time I could see how angry he was. His face turned red, and he stared at Dwight and me, his contempt for us visible. His voice was seething with anger. "You'll go wherever I tell you to go," he growled. He struck me as a man who was used to giving orders and having them obeyed promptly. I'm sure he saw Dwight and me as evidence of the cultural decline of the United States. Self-indulgent youth. No respect for authority. No discipline. Good for nothing. The barbarians at the gates.

We continued walking down the corridor. Two doors past the mess hall, we stopped in front of the unit prison officials refer to as "Administrative Segregation" or, more simply, "Segregation."

"We're going to the Hole," I said to Foots.

Boss Keith opened the door to the Hole, and we followed him inside along with the two guards who had served as our escort. I was somewhat surprised to discover that what inmates referred to ominously as "the Hole," looked no different from most of the other units at Lompoc. Three tiers of single cells stacked on top of one another like children's blocks. The dimensions of the cells were identical to those in M-unit, as were their furnishings. Boss Keith lead us over to a small cubicle with glass windows that seemed to serve as an office for whichever guard oversaw the Hole at any given time. Today was different, however, because we were on lockdown. Four guards were seated in chairs just outside the cubicle. I recognized Boss Schwartz from A & O, but the other guards were new to me. Schwartz and I made eye contact briefly, and he just shook his head disgustedly.

"Process these two," said Keith curtly to the four guards. Then he turned on his heel and left without so much as glancing at us.

"What are you guys thinking?" said Boss Schwartz. "Both of you have good work assignments out on the farm. Don't you know that now you'll lose all the good time you might have earned?" His tone surprised me. I thought I heard an element of genuine disappointment in his voice.

"Strip down boys," said the guard, Boss Thompson, who seemed to oversee the Hole that morning. "We have to make sure neither one of you is carrying a weapon." When the guard was satisfied we were not bringing anything dangerous or illegal into the Hole, he handed each of us a set of clean clothes.

"Pick up your shoes and follow me," he ordered. We climbed the stairs to the second tier. "You," he said, pointing to me. "Second tier." Over my shoulder I saw Foots going up the metal stairs to the third tier, escorted by Boss Thompson. I walked down the second tier, followed by one of the guards, until I came to an empty cell. As I passed the cell next to mine, I noticed an inmate sleeping on his bunk, a sheet covering his face. The guard motioned me inside my cell, and then walked back to the end of the tier, pulled a lever, and my cell door slammed shut.

Chapter 5

The Hole

I lay back on my bunk, straining to hear what I could of the chatter flying back and forth around the tiers. The entire unit was crackling with nervous energy. I was pretty agitated myself, worried about what might come next. I took several deep breaths. *Well, here I am in the belly of the beast. What have I gotten myself into? What happens next? Be calm. Regardless of what happens next, supporting the strike is the right way to go. It was tempting to flatten out my sentence on the farm and walk away, but that just didn't feel right. It felt like selling out to help the man run a prison that is quietly damaging so many lives. It felt like surrender. What happens next?*

"Odom, you motherfucker. You gonna be in some deep shit if you don't get me those cigarettes you owe me," someone shouted, down on the bottom tier to my right. "You tell your homies that if I don't have my cigarettes by next week, I'm gonna beat you like a rug."

"Fuck you, Darnell," came the reply, which I assumed came from Odom. "You'll get your fuckin' cigarettes."

As I listened to the shouts flying back and forth around the unit, I noticed that I could hear the thunder of the guns from the Air Force base up the coast. Every week, Monday through Saturday, they reminded us of their presence and their power—and of our weakness and inability to silence them.

I-Block—the Hole, by any other name—was charged with nervous excitement that morning. Everyone was on edge, including the guards. No one knew exactly what was going on or what to expect. On top of that nerve-jangling tension, there was the surreal nature of my situation: I couldn't see anyone else in the unit, but I could hear people shouting up and down my tier and the tiers above and below me. Disembodied voices. From a cell below me, on the first tier, a voice called out, "Hey Jefferson, you awake?" From above me on the third tier, down to my right, Jefferson hollered back. "Yeah, Munson, I'm awake. What's up?"

"Get your ass down here on the double. I'm lonely. I want you to suck my dick again, just like you did yesterday. It was so good."

All over the unit people chuckled at this exchange. Others chimed in, adding their two bits. "Say, Munson," someone shouted. "When he's done with you, send him down to my cell. I'm feeling lonely, too."

"Fuck all you guys. You nothing but a bunch of no good, cum-drunk, punk-ass, poo-butt motherfuckers."

This comeback was applauded by raucous laughter from all over the unit. "Get on, Jefferson," someone yelled. "You tell that weak motherfucker where to get off."

This sort of jailhouse banter went on for the next ten or fifteen minutes, with people verbally challenging each other's manhood and sexual identity or defending their own. It was just the sort of needling you'd hear in all-male environments like the military, men's locker rooms, and fraternities. Occasionally, when someone went too far and slandered another inmate's mother, sister, or girlfriend, the tone changed and quickly became more serious, more hostile, more potentially violent.

After I had been in my cell for about thirty minutes, I heard the toilet in the cell to the right of mine flush. I heard my neighbor walking around. Then I heard the occupant of the cell call out. "Hartman," said a voice I recognized immediately as Surratt's. "Hartman, are you still down there?" "Yeah," said another voice that I recognized as Hartman's. "I'm still down here on the bottom tier."

I was stunned. I had guessed that they had taken Surratt to the Hole on Thursday when Boss Keith had called him out of E-unit, but I was shocked to learn that Hartman was here as well. I was curious to hear if Surratt knew anything about events in the furniture factory. I was also eager to hear how and why Hartman wound up in the Hole. Foots was curious too. From up on the third tier, he called out: "Hartman, is that you?"

"Yeah, it's me. Who's that up there?"

"It's Foots," said Dwight. "The whole joint's on lockdown now because just about everybody has refused to work. What the hell happened in the furniture factory? And what are you doing here anyway? We thought you wouldn't join a strike."

"Well," Hartman said. "Two things happened yesterday since I last talked with you guys."

"What happened?" said Foots. "What two things?"

"Yesterday morning Boss Cutler told me to serve as lookout for him while he took this queen everyone calls 'Miss Lucy' into the back room in the kitchen. She gives him a blowjob, and he gets her things from the commissary that she wants. I told him that I wouldn't do it. I don't want to be any part of his little sex club in the kitchen."

"What did he do when you refused to do what he said?" I asked.

"He wrote me up on the spot for insubordination and took me down to the warden's office. He told the warden that I wasn't working out in the kitchen and that I should be assigned to some other job. The warden told me to go back to N-Unit until lunch and after lunch to report for work in the furniture factory."

"What happened after lunch when you reported to the furniture factory?" asked Dwight.

"That's the second part of the story," Hartman said. "I was pissed off already when I walked into the furniture factory, because I want to be a short order cook when I get out of here. Working in the furniture factory isn't going to teach me anything I can use on the streets. When I got to the furniture factory, everyone there was even more pissed off than I was. The hacks wouldn't put their money on the books so they could go to commissary over the weekend."

"We heard about that yesterday," said Foots. "We were wondering if the guys in the furniture factory would refuse to work. What happened down there?"

"Guys kept talking about needing their money for the weekend to buy zu zus and wham whams, and they slowed down the work they were doing. In fact, work almost stopped, but people didn't stop talking about their money. Dusty told Boss Williams that it wouldn't cost him a dime to post our money for the weekend. Dusty was pissed off."

"You're damn right I was pissed off," Dusty interjected from the bottom tier. "It wouldn't cost him anything to give us our money today. Not a cent. But the motherfucker wouldn't do it."

"After Dusty yelled at him, Boss Williams just about lost it," said Hartman. "He told everyone to pick up the pace and get back to work, or he was going to write up every single one of us. I guess I just lost it myself at that point. I was already pissed off at being moved out of the kitchen. When Boss Williams threatened to write up everyone in the factory it was just more than I could take. I walked over to the main control panel and threw all the switches. Everything in the furniture factory shut down, even the lights. A lot of shit can happen when the lights are off. About five minutes later, four hacks showed up; they cuffed Dusty and me and brought us here. There goes my good time, but I don't give a damn."

"I'll be damned," said Foots from up on the third tier. "It was Hartman who got this whole thing started. For the last three months you've been telling us that you didn't want any part of a strike, and here you are in the Hole—even before New and I got here. I'm shocked."

"I'm surprised too," I said. "You've been telling us for three months you thought we were nuts."

"I'm about as surprised as you are," said Hartman, "but here we are. I just got to the point that I couldn't take it anymore."

"You know, Dale," said Surratt. "I'm not really that surprised you're here. You didn't like the idea of a strike in theory whenever we discussed it in the yard. It didn't seem practical to you. But when push came to shove with Mama Cutler, I think you like the idea of being used and disrespected even less. That's why you're here right now. Mama Cutler wanted to use you and the other guys in the kitchen as things, and you want to be respected as a human being. That's basically what this whole strike is about."

Apparently, Dusty was listening because he shouted, in his loud, raspy voice, "That's the god damned truth! These hacks don't give us no respect. When my buddy, Woodworth, was released a couple of weeks ago, two of the hacks in the machine shop shook his hand and said they'd look forward to seeing him back in three or four weeks. They were joking about it. It's like they don't *want* us to succeed. That's some of what this is about. It ain't all about zu zus and wham whams. Like that hippie dude up there just said, it's about respect."

When Dusty finished talking, spontaneous cheers went up around the three tiers. People shouted their agreement. "Right on, Dusty," yelled a voice from below me. "Tell it brother," said another voice from up near the front of the unit. There was general agreement around the Hole that Dusty and Hartman had acquitted themselves well in their respective confrontations with the Man. After that, the talk died down, and people settled back on their bunks, waiting to see what would happen next. I spent the rest of the afternoon talking quietly with Surratt, Foots, and Hartman.

At about five thirty the relative quiet was interrupted by a loud shout from the far end of the tier. "Chow time," called an unfamiliar voice. "Time for dinner." During lockdown, inmates in the Hole are fed in their cells rather than in the mess hall. Inmates known as "trustees" moved up and down all three tiers with metal carts containing our dinner for the day: Grilled cheese sandwiches, cold French fries, and an apple, with some sort of Kool-Aid to drink.

"Man, this is some sorry food," complained Hartman from below.

"You should have thought of that before you got into it with Mama Cutler," called an inmate named Little Joe. "You want to be a hero, you're going to pay a price."

"Eric," said Surratt. "How did you and Foots get busted? What happened after I left yesterday?"

"I'm not exactly sure," I said. "Right after lunch today, Boss Keith came into E-Unit and gave us all one last chance to go to work. No one in E-Unit took him up on his offer, absolutely no one. Right after that, he called for Foots and me to follow him. He said he was taking us to talk to the warden, but he brought us down here."

"Somebody must have snitched you off," said Surratt. "That's what happened to me. Somebody snitched me off. Keith already knew I had been talking to people about going on strike. Somebody must have told him about the list of demands that I typed up. Only a few inmates in the joint have access to one of the mimeograph machines. I think they figured out it was me by a process of elimination."

"You did a really good thing," I said. "That list helped to pull people together. It gave everyone something concrete to unite behind."

We didn't know it then, but some of us were destined to spend the next three weeks in the Hole. The food was bad, the air was stale with the smell of sweat and excrement, and we were allowed only one hour per week out of our cells to shower and exercise, walking up and down the tier. Yet, the miserable conditions notwithstanding, I felt the same sense of inner peace in the Hole that I'd felt on the day I refused induction. As uncomfortable as it was in the Hole, being there felt right.

After the trustees circulated up and down the tiers clearing away the dinner trays, a calm settled over I–Block. The excited chatter of the morning and afternoon softened into a dull buzzing until someone down on the bottom tier began to call for a "talent show." Immediately, other voices around the unit picked up the chant: "Ta-lent Show, Ta-lent Show." Surprising, even silly, as it may sound, talent shows were popular in the Hole that summer. People don't generally associate talent shows with penitentiaries; they're a fixture of elementary school, summer camp, and sometimes high school. But we had a talent show in the Hole at Lompoc that Friday evening, and every evening for the next week.

The show began when someone on the bottom tier requested a specific song. "Sweet Pool," someone shouted. "Pool. Are you awake up there?"

"Yeah," came the answer from down to my left. "I'm awake. Whachoo want?"

"I want to hear that song you sang the other day. That song about the blue birds and the white cliffs."

"I don't feel like singing no song today," said Pool. I learned over the next few days that Sweet Pool's real name was James Pullen, and that he was from San Diego. By nature, he was quiet and reserved, but when he had an audience, he cut loose. In the joint he liked to be called "Sweet Pool" or just "Pool" for short.

The voice from the bottom tier was persistent. "Come *on*, Pool. We got nothing to do here in the Hole. We got to have some music to help us pass the time. Sing that white cliffs song one more time. You sing it real good."

It was a strange experience there in the Hole, listening to the disembodied voices of people, some of whom I knew and some of whom I knew nothing about other than what I could deduce from what they said and the tone of their voices. Around the unit, people began to get into the spirit. "Sing it, Pool, sing it." A chorus of voices began to chant from the top tier down to the bottom. "Sing it, sing it. Sing it."

"All right, all right," said Pool, at last. "I'll sing it for you, but I'm only going to sing it once. This here song is called 'The White Cliffs of Dover.' My father used to play it on his sax when I was a kid. He was in the army during World War II. This was his favorite song."

"That's the one," came the persistent voice from the bottom tier. "'The White Cliffs of Dover.' That's the one I want to hear again."

There was a brief silence while Pool composed himself. Then he sang it and sang it beautifully. No one among his normally raucous listeners made a sound while he sang. Right after I got out, I bought Vera Lynn's version of the song, which she recorded in 1944 for her album, *Those Were the Days*. The last lines of the song brought down the house:

> *There'll be love and laughter,*
> *And peace ever after*
> *Tomorrow, when the world is free....*
> *There'll be blue birds over the white cliffs of Dover,*
> *Tomorrow, just you wait and see.*
> (Lyrics by Nat Burton, Music by Walter Kent, 1941)

When Pool stopped singing, the entire unit roared its appreciation. We cheered and applauded so loudly that Boss Treadwell felt compelled to come out of his cubicle to tell us to keep the noise down. Needless to say, that just egged us on. "Fuck you, Treadwell!" people shouted. "We'll sing any damned song we want. Sing it again, Pool. Sing it again."

"No way," said Pool. "I told you I'd sing it once, but that's all. Somebody else gotta sing one now." And that was all it took: The talent show was on. Anyone who could halfway carry a tune and had a song he liked sang it. We heard folk songs, slave songs (as W.E.B. Du Bois called them), country western songs, Irish ballads, and even some hard rock. Dog attempted a version of the Rolling Stones song "Satisfaction" that was so horribly off key that he won us over by sheer force of spirit. We all pitched in and supported on the chorus, "I can't get no, Sa-tis-fac-tion." Foots surprised me with a crowd-pleasing version of "Maggie's Farm" by Bob Dylan. A little Irishman a few cells down from me on the second tier sang "Danny Boy" in as clear and rich a tenor as you'll ever want to hear. Most of the low riders were into country western music, particularly Johnny Cash; Dog, Dusty, and a third inmate I didn't know formed a trio and sang their versions of "Ring of Fire," "I Walk the Line," and "Folsom Prison Blues."

Chapter 5. The Hole 155

The talent show went on for nearly two hours. Everyone was affirmed and treated with respect. Just when our energy began to taper down, Surratt indicated that he wanted to sing one. This is when Surratt got his prison nickname. From this night forward, we didn't refer to him as Surratt or John; he was Little John, and only Little John. He wasn't tall in stature, but he had a big heart—and, as it turned out, a beautiful baritone voice.

"I'm going to give you one from Otis Redding," he said. "It's called 'The Dock of the Bay.'"

This was the first time I heard that song. I loved it immediately and so did the entire unit. When Little John stopped singing, the Hole exploded with shouts and applause. "*Otra, otra*," shouted someone who spoke only Spanish and wanted an encore. "Give us one more, Little John," I heard Little Joe call out.

"That's all for me," said Little John. "But let's do one more together."

"Pick one," shouted the crowd in unison. "You choose one for us all to sing."

"Let's do a Woody Guthrie song," said Little John. "'This Land Is Your Land.'"

"I can't sing that one," said Sweet Pool. "I don't know the words or the tune."

So Little John led all of I–Block through the lyrics of "This Land Is Your Land." We made the Hole rock that night. We had the volume turned all the way up. We knew that all we had was each other, so we supported each other with our songs.

As I lay there on my bunk, I thought about how ironic it was that just as our band of so called "hippies" was on the verge of giving up our efforts to organize a work stoppage, a strike had broken out in the furniture factory over "zu zus and wham whams." Not only that, but Hartman, who had earlier rejected the idea of a strike, had been one of the first to be sent to the Hole. *Hartman, of all people! Who would have thought that he'd be one of the first to wind up in the Hole?*

What I learned from Dale Hartman has served me well during my years teaching at Occidental College. Hartman taught me to take a developmental view of my students and of people in general. He taught me not to give up on people prematurely, particularly young people. Dale must have been twenty-two or twenty-three when I knew him at Lompoc. Most of my students today are between eighteen and twenty-two years old. That's way too early to give up on anyone, regardless of how limited he or she might seem during the first two or three weeks of class. People grow and mature at different rates. More generally, the strike—the fact that it happened at all—taught me to never give up hope and never to stop struggling against oppressive conditions. Things can look utterly bleak one day completely different a day or two later.

For some reason, it took me longer than most of my neighbors to drop off to sleep that night. The adrenalin was still pumping through my system from the songs and the shouting. Just as I was finally dropping off to sleep, a fragment of a song flashed through my mind, a song Janis Joplin used to sing. *"Freedom's just another word for nothing left to lose."* That bit of lyric, from "Me and Bobby McGee," caused me to reflect on what had happened in my life over the previous four months. *Up in Portland, my fellow citizens thought so little of how I was living my life that they sent me off to prison here at Lompoc. The officials here think so little of me that they toss me into the Hole. They've taken my journal and most of my possessions away from me, and now I've lost all of what the warden calls my "privileges." If "freedom's just another word for nothing left to lose,"* I thought, *I'm getting close to being free.*

§

I woke up Saturday morning to the shout of "chow time, chow time," coming from the far end of the tier. Breakfast consisted of a bowl of hot cereal, what my father used to call "mush," and a metal cup of orange juice. I grew up eating hot cereal, usually oatmeal, so this breakfast seemed fine to me. Hartman, on the other hand, was less than pleased. "What sort of shit is this?" he yelled. "I didn't order this. Take it back to the motherfucking chef."

People laughed at his outburst.

"You'd better eat this while it's hot, son," Boss Treadwell responded. "It's all you're going to get till lunchtime."

"I ordered bacon and eggs with some sourdough toast," complained Hartman. More chuckles. "I'm a big man. I need some nourishment!" He was playing to the crowd, but Boss Treadwell was having none of it.

"You need to drop a few pounds, son," he said. "A few breakfasts like this and you'll get back to your fighting weight."

Next door, Little John was talking to the trustee assigned to our tier. "Is the whole institution on lockdown today?" he asked.

"Yeah. The whole place is on lockdown," said the trustee, a guy named Locksley.

"What's going to happen on Monday morning?" Little John asked him.

"Your guess is as good as mine," said Locksley.

"What do you *think* will happen?" asked Little John. "What do you hear in your unit?"

"People are angry," said Locksley. "And the guards don't act like they think this is going to blow over soon."

"What do you think the guards are going to do?" asked Little John.

"I seen some of them out in the yard trying on some gas masks," said Locksley. "Another trustee was telling me about how he helped unload a shipment of tear gas canisters and other stuff in boxes labeled 'riot control supplies.' That was a few weeks ago. The guards have a bunch of new equipment they're just itching to try out."

"Just like a bunch of kids with some new toys to play with," Little John said.

Locksley continued down the second tier. I heard Little John muttering to himself. "This isn't over. It isn't over by a long shot."

"What's that, Little John?" I said.

"This strike's not going to end this weekend. The hacks will have to do something on Monday or Tuesday to break it up. I just don't know what they plan to do."

"I guess we just have to wait and see," I said. "You're right about that. We don't have a lot of options. The next move is theirs."

Little John and I spent the rest of the morning reading and chatting quietly about what it was like for me growing up in Portland, Oregon, and what it was like for him growing up in Tulsa, Oklahoma. I was curious about how he had become interested in political theory and how he had learned so much about political organizing; he was interested in why I was drawn to the study of literature, an academic field that he viewed as cloistered in the Ivory Tower, detached from the real world and social change.

"Literature isn't apolitical," I insisted. "It's not politics, but the study of literature does have a political dimension to it."

"The stuff you teach doesn't have much to say to the guys here in the Hole," he countered. "Maybe you can see the underlying ideology, but these guys don't know the language. You've got to learn to understand the importance of zu zus and wham whams, Eric. You can't reach the people with books. You reach them with bread-and-butter issues."

"So, you don't think that literature or art in general has any role to play in social change?"

"That's not what I said. I think there's a role for art, but it's just not as big a role as you seem to think."

"Do you think I'm an escapist?"

"If you were an escapist, we wouldn't be here in the Hole, having this conversation. Actually, I think you'll be one of us some day."

"What do you mean by 'one of us?'"

"Part of the movement. Sooner or later, I think you'll be part of the movement for real democracy."

A little before noon, Locksley returned with his cart, carrying lunch for our tier. He passed my lunch through the bars.

"I got something else for you, too," he said, handing me a copy of Joseph Heller's *Catch-22*. "Barber said to tell you that he didn't want you to get bored in the Hole."

"Tell Barber that I owe him one," I said. "Tell him I said thanks for not giving up on me. He'll know what that means." I spent the rest of the afternoon reading *Catch-22* and talking with Ratliff about Nixon's "secret plan" to end the war.

At about 5:30, I heard a voice shout out "Chow Time! Time for Dinner!" I heard the metal cart slowly moving along the second tier. When it stopped in front of my cell, I was surprised to see that it was being pushed by Boss Schwartz, the head guard from A&O. He looked at me and slowly shook his head.

"What are you doing here, Newhall?"

"I know what I'm doing in here," I said. "What are you doing out there?"

"You can't even stay out of trouble in prison," he said in a frustrated tone. "I guess I was wrong about you. I thought you were going to get with the program."

As Boss Schwartz continued to work his way down the second tier, I heard a shout from the ground floor.

"God damn, I like what I'm looking at this evening," Little Joe called out.

"What's that, Little Joe? What's that you like looking at?" It was Dog, sounding like he was still half asleep.

"I like seeing pigs at work," said Little Joe. "Look at Boss Harden here, sweating like a pig. How does it feel to do some real work, Harden? I'll bet you never worked a day in your life until now. If you worked more, you wouldn't have to drag that beer belly of yours up and down this tier."

Shouts came from all over the unit in the wake of Little Joe's outburst. I didn't join in; I could still hear my father's admonition to "Hate the deed, not the doer." If your goal is to change a person's mind, reducing him or her to a type—a thing—is not an effective strategy. But I was in the minority, that day; the place erupted into a storm of slurs and taunts.

"Work, swine!" I heard Little Joe yell. "Work until you sweat blood, you motherfuckers."

People shouted and rattled the metal bars of their cells. It was utter pandemonium.

"Joe," I heard Dog call out, in a voice loud enough to be heard above the uproar. "Joe, can you hear me?"

"Yeah, Dog, I can hear you fine. What's up?"

Chapter 5. The Hole

"You know what I would love to have for breakfast tomorrow?" asked Dog.

"No, what's that Dog?" replied Little Joe.

"Down in Bakersfield where I'm from, there's a little coffee shop near where I lived before I was busted. I used to love to go in there and order their eggs and swine omelet." Again, the entire unit erupted.

To their credit, the guards simply finished serving breakfast and took the carts back to the mess hall. No doubt they were angry, probably outraged, because they were not accustomed to this level of overt disrespect, but there was nothing they could do to control the situation. Yet. Up and down the tiers people rattled the bars of their cells, shouted curses at the guards, and began to suggest other orders they planned to place at their own favorite restaurants back home.

"I'll have to try that sometime if they ever let me out of this motherfucker," said Dog. "An egg and swine omelet. Chopped swine."

"I just like that old stand-by," said a voice I didn't recognize.

"What's that?" shouted Little Joe.

"A swine and cheese sandwich on wheat bread with mustard and mayo. You give me a good swine and cheese with some chips and a coke, and I'm as happy as a pig in shit."

Again, the whole place erupted and everyone, me included, rattled the bars of our cells. Months, in some cases years, of frustration and fury were spinning out of control.

"Fuck the pigs!" shouted someone up above, on the third tier. "Death to all pigs!" shouted another voice, from down below. "Three little pigs, three little pigs," shouted someone up on the third tier, and immediately everyone began to chant in unison: "Three little pigs, three little pigs!" The raw emotion that was suppressed on a typical day was bubbling to the surface and boiling over.

"This isn't exactly what I had in mind," I said quietly to Surratt when the noise died down. "This isn't what I had in mind at all."

"You can't make an omelet without breaking a few eggs," said Little John.

After dinner that evening, Boss Schwartz walked up and down our tier, picking up the empty trays and delivering mail. The guards had been ordered to serve the meals and deliver the mail because the warden and associate warden had lost confidence in the trustees. Apparently, some of the trustees had been delivering messages and contraband, from candy bars to marijuana, up and down the tiers in the Hole and from unit to unit around the institution. Some of the trustees had been sent back to their units; others had been put in the Hole along with us. At Lompoc, there was no middle ground anymore. Either you were one of the keepers or one of the kept. Them or us. The big house was a house divided.

When Boss Schwartz reached my cell, he handed an official-looking letter through the bars. It was, of all things, a jury summons. The irony was not lost on me: I'm sitting in the Hole at Lompoc and Boss Schwartz hands me a jury summons from the Superior Court in Portland, Oregon. Jury service was mandatory, the letter admonished, warning me that I would be subject to a substantial fine if I did not respond to the summons within ten days. The absurdity of my situation made me laugh.

"Boss Schwartz," I said. "I need your help with something here."

"What's that?" he said, giving me a skeptical look.

"Look at this," I said to him, extending the summons through the bars. "First they sentence me to two years; then they threaten me with a fine if I don't report to the Superior Court in Portland on September 25th at 7:30 a.m."

Boss Schwartz read the summons but saw no humor in it. "Just tear it up, Newhall. They won't fine you once they figure out you're locked up. And I can tell you for damn sure that we aren't going to let you out early to get up to court. You're stuck here for the full two years. Just tear that letter up."

He shook his head again and gave me a look that seemed to contain a measure of authentic disappointment. He took a few steps on down the tier, and then did an about-face and walked back to my cell.

"You know, Newhall," he said. "When you were getting ready to leave A & O back in May, I wrote you a good report. I expected you to be a model inmate. I even recommended you for a position out on the farm as a clerk. I thought you'd do some easy time out on the farm and then get out of here."

"That's what I thought, too, Boss—for a while. But then I came to see that easy time is part of the problem. There are too many people in this country right now trying to do easy time instead of doing the right thing. Easy time is like a drug. It's habit forming."

Boss Schwartz looked incredulous and more than a little disgusted. He was just putting in his own time, earning money to support his wife and children. He couldn't fathom why I would go on strike and risk getting thrown in the Hole. Nor could he see anything wrong with the way Lompoc was being run. He was just doing his job.

"Do you want to know why you're sitting here in the Hole?" he asked me. "Do you want to know when all this mess started?"

"Yeah, Boss," I said. "I've spent a lot of time thinking about how and why I wound up here."

Little John had been listening to our conversation, and he inserted himself at this point.

"I'd like to hear too, Boss," he said. "Why *are* we in here?"

"I was in Korea with MacArthur in 1950," said Schwartz. "That's when

Chapter 5. The Hole

all this mess really began if you understand a little history. I don't think you young guys today know enough history. All this confusion began when they stopped us at the Yalu River and wouldn't let us finish the fucking job. We had the commies on the run, and the politicians made us stop. I'll bet you never heard of the Yalu River before, have you?"

"Sure, I've heard of it," said Surratt. "It's a river that divides North Korea and China. During the Korean War, the UN troops pushed up into North Korea. In November of 1950 about 200,000 Chinese troops came across the Yalu and drove the UN troops back to the south. Truman didn't want to get involved in a land war with China."

"Well, I'll be damned," said Schwartz, sounding genuinely surprised. "Most guys your age have never heard of the Yalu. You have it just about right, except you left out the part about Truman being a chicken shit. He told MacArthur to cut and run. If he'd let us finish the job, we wouldn't be here having this conversation."

"If Truman, Eisenhower, Kennedy, and LBJ understood Vietnam a little better, we wouldn't be sitting here," said Little John.

"Little John's right," I said. "The Vietnamese just want foreigners—Chinese, Japanese, French, and Americans—out of their country. I'm here in the Hole because I agree with the Vietnamese that they should have the right to determine how to run their own country."

"You guys are ruining your lives," Boss Schwartz said, wearily. "You've been misled by the same fool politicians who made us stop at the Yalu when we were in Korea. Now you won't be able to vote. And you won't be allowed to buy a gun to protect yourselves."

Boss Schwartz continued down the tier with an air of resignation—shaking his head.

"These guys will never see the light," said Little John.

"It seems that way," I said. "Most of that generation doesn't see any real difference between World War II, Korea, and Vietnam. I think they're the ones who need to read more history."

"It's not enough just to read history," said Little John. "You have to read it, but you also have to understand it. Boss Schwartz had the experience, but he missed the meaning."

About an hour later I was dozing on my bunk when I heard shouting coming from the entrance to the Hole. After a few minutes, Boss Schwartz walked past my cell escorting three naked inmates, one of whom walked with a pronounced limp, to cells just past mine on the second tier. Boss Schwartz put the limping inmate, a guy named Sonny Stark, into the cell next to mine.

Remembering the angry expression on Sonny's face when Schwartz took him to his cell, I decided to leave my neighbor alone, at least for the time being. I lay on my bunk reading Joseph Heller's absurdist novel *Catch-22*.

For years I included *Catch-22* in my course on American Fiction Since World War II. Today it strikes me as somewhat longer than it needs to be, but when I read it for the first time, there in the Hole, I hoped it would never end. It took my mind off the numbing tedium of being locked in a small cell day after day. I identified with Yossarian's sense of being in conflict with a system gone mad.

A few years ago, I dropped *Catch-22* from my syllabus and replaced it with *The Things They Carried*, Tim O'Brien's collection of linked short stories about a platoon of American soldiers fighting in the Vietnam War. Blurring the line between fact and fiction, *The Things They Carried* illuminates, better than *Catch-22*, the current rancorous division in our country between blue states and red states. O'Brien's book helps to explain the difference in perspective between cold warriors like Boss Schwartz and dissenters like Foots and me. As much as I love *Catch-22*, *The Things They Carried* does more to help my current students understand the country in which they are coming of age.

Catch-22, Joseph Heller, published in 1961.

Around 8:00 p.m. the unit began to buzz again. Something about evening in the Hole with no possibility of going anywhere or doing anything energized everybody, turned up the voltage in an atmosphere already crackling with pent-up anger. Inmates shouted insults—at the guards, at the warden and associate warden, at each other. Everyone's manhood was called into question in a variety of creative ways; everyone defended his manhood with colorful ingenuity.

This hyper-masculine banter was followed by a long discussion (about two hours) of how to commit different sorts of crimes without getting busted. Most of this two-hour "crime workshop" was devoted to what would be referred to in academic circles as "best practices."

Those inmates sentenced for car theft all agreed that if you steal a car, you should be sure to take it across a state line. Taking a stolen car across a state line means that if you are apprehended, you will do time in a federal rather than a state prison—a much less dangerous way to do time. Con artists of various sorts (particularly "shortchange artists") suggested numerous ways to separate unwitting victims from their money; they warned against getting greedy. In their view, multiple small stings were the smartest way to earn a good living without winding up in the joint. The pimps changed my view of prostitution that evening. Judging from TV shows and movies I'd seen, I'd always assumed that women who became prostitutes had at least some degree of choice in the matter. Five pimps from Los Angeles persuaded me very quickly that prostitution is coercive—brutal, violent, and degrading, a form of slavery that is as despicable as any other form of slavery. The evening closed with a discussion of home burglary. The "takeaway," emphasized by all speakers, was that you should spend most of your time on the preparation (planning) and very little inside the home you rob.

After about two hours, the discussion of criminal techniques seemed to have run its course. Little John, ever the organizer, raised the call for another songfest. He may have had reservations about literature's role in social change, but he understood the power of music to bring a group of people together. His call for another talent show quickly turned into a chant that swept like a wave around the tiers and reenergized everyone in the Hole. "Tal-ent show! Tal-ent show! Tal-ent show!"

Many of the songs and the singers were the same as they'd been the night before, but the repetition didn't seem to bother anyone. By popular demand, Sweet Pool opened the festivities again with "The White Cliffs of Dover"; he remained the opening act for every talent show that took place during the strike. Among everyone in I-Block, Pool had the purest voice, a voice that might have led to a professional career had circumstances been different.

A couple of the recent arrivals from earlier that day contributed new songs. One of them was Sonny Stark.

"Sonny," I heard a voice call out from down to my right on the second tier. "I know you're over there, cause I saw you walk by my cell butt-ass naked earlier today. Are you awake?"

"Who is that?" a voice in the cell to my left responded. "Who's that calling me?"

"It's Lawson," came the reply. "I saw you walk past this morning, but you looked so pissed off I didn't say anything. What's happening?"

"Ain't nothing happening," said my neighbor. "They busted me because I wouldn't go back to work down in the furniture factory. Boss Chillington says I have a bad attitude. Shit! *Bad attitude*? He don't even know the half of it."

"Sonny," said Lawson. "Sing that song you used to sing out in the yard when you still had your guitar. Sing 'The Green, Green Grass of Home.'"

Shouts of encouragement went up. Other inmates had also heard Sonny sing this song out in the yard, apparently, and they approved of Lawson's suggestion. After a good deal of verbal nudging, Sonny sang "The Green, Green Grass of Home," a country western ballad, and the crowd went wild. There were a lot of country fans at Lompoc that summer, particularly among the bikers, and Sonny had a voice that spoke to some common element in our hearts and, temporarily, set us free from the bars that held us.

§

It wasn't all singing down in the Hole during that second half of August. There was a lot of deep-down, serious talk as well. It turned out that Sonny had enlisted in the Marines about a year after he graduated from high school. He had been fired from a minimum wage job at a gas station and had difficulty finding any other regular work in Houston. Vietnam sounded exciting to him; he had never travelled outside the United States before. Becoming a Marine sounded like a manly and mature thing to do. Then, too, he needed a way to make some money to help out his mother.

Shortly after arriving in Vietnam in January of 1967, Sonny was badly wounded in both legs the first time he left the base. Despite two surgeries, his left knee never fully healed, leaving him with the limping gait I'd noticed when he passed by my cell.

During the months he spent recovering in a military hospital near Hue, Sonny fell in love with the nurse who took care of him. She was impressed with him, and with the Purple Heart he was awarded. Listening to him tell his story, I was reminded of Hemingway's *A Farewell to Arms*. Soldier wounded in World War I falls in love with attending nurse and makes a separate peace with the war.

Ultimately, the military shipped Sonny home to finish his two-year stint at a desk job in Houston. Before he left Vietnam, he gave his nurse

Chapter 5. The Hole

a two-pound package of some very strong Vietnamese marijuana and asked her to send it to him at his mother's address. He was busted the day it arrived, charged with possession with intent to sell an illegal substance, and sentenced to a "zip-six." Sonny was one very angry young man when he walked into the Hole at Lompoc.

"It's bullshit, is what it is," he said repeatedly during the days we were neighbors. "I bled for my country. I can't walk right anymore. My legs hurt anytime I have to walk more than across the street. And they go and lock me up in this motherfucker because I have possession of a plant."

I sympathized with Sonny. But I couldn't help wondering, as I fell asleep that Saturday night, how he'd react when he discovered that he was living next to a draft resister.

§

The next day, Sunday, was one of the high points of the strike. It was my third day in a row with no exercise out in the yard, and I was already sleeping less soundly and waking up early, with the sun. Most people were still sleeping, and the Hole was quiet, as was the Air Force base; because it was Sunday, the guns were silent.

I pulled my copy of *Catch-22* out from beneath my mattress where I kept it hidden. Reading that novel in the joint was one of the more powerful reading experiences I've ever had in my life. Heller's take on the military bureaucracy coincided neatly with my growing understanding of what happens to individuals in the prison system. The "correctional system," as they call it, is madness masquerading as a rational system; the notion that people can be "rehabilitated" by spending time in cages is a grotesque travesty.

After I'd been reading for half an hour or so, a voice called from the cell to my left.

"Neighbor, is there anyone awake over there?"

"Are you talking to me?" I responded.

"Yes," my neighbor replied. "I don't think there's anybody in the cell on the other side of me. I'm Sonny. Sonny Stark. What's your name? How long you been here in the Hole?"

"My name's Eric Newhall," I said. "I got here Friday afternoon. Day before yesterday. I saw you walk past when they brought you in yesterday. I heard what you said about being busted for possession of a plant. I don't smoke weed, but I agree with you that it doesn't make sense to lock people up in a place like this because they like to smoke it."

"What'd they put you here in the Hole for?" he asked.

"I'm not exactly sure," I said. "Nobody's said anything to me about it. Boss Keith just came into E-Unit after lunch on Friday and called my buddy Foots and me out. They brought us down here on Friday afternoon. I think they think we had something to do with the strike in the furniture factory."

At this point I decided that since Sonny asked me about why I was in the Hole, it would be all right if I asked him the same question.

"How'd you end up in the Hole?" I asked him.

"I'm not sure either," he said. "I was out in the furniture factory, and I refused to go back to work. But so did everybody else. I really don't know why they busted me and not everybody else who refused to work, too."

"Sonny, is that you up there?" I heard Hartman call from the bottom tier.

"Yeah, it's me," said Sonny. "Is that you, Dale?"

"Yeah, it's me," said Dale. "I thought I recognized your voice. I think they busted you because you and I sometimes hang out in the yard together, and I also hang out with some of the hippies who have been talking about a strike for a few months. They think you and I are part of some hippie plot to shut the prison down. Somebody must have snitched you off."

"I ain't part of no plot," said Sonny. "I ain't no hippie flowerchild either."

"I'm not part of any plot either," said Hartman, "but I'd do the same thing if I had it to do over again. Is that Newhall you're talking to up there?"

"Yeah," said Sonny.

"He's solid," said Hartman. "You can trust him and his crime partner, the guy they call Bigfoot."

Dwight and I had been sentenced on the same day for the same offense in the same courtroom in Portland. In the joint that made us "crime partners."

Having introduced ourselves to each other, Sonny and I started a conversation that went on for a couple of hours. Sonny told me why he enlisted in the Marines, what training camp was like at Parris Island, and what happened to him on his first search-and-destroy mission in Vietnam.

"It wasn't anything like the recruiters told me it would be," he said. "It wasn't about freedom or democracy for the people of Vietnam. The lifers were just trying to get their medals and get their twenty years in so they could pick up their pensions, and the enlisted guys like me were just trying to make it through alive. For me the worst thing was when I came to see that most of the Vietnamese people didn't really want us to be there. I nearly lose one of my legs fighting for freedom for the Vietnamese people, and most of them didn't even want me to be there. They see us as invaders.

You could see it in their eyes, regardless of what some fucking politician says about us being liberators."

I thought about how I should respond to what Sonny was saying. Should I talk politics with this angry, wounded vet, or should I simply mumble some sympathetic words about his being wounded and move on to some other, safer subject? I had mixed feelings about this, but I remember thinking to myself that Sonny had been lied to enough in his life already; I didn't want my name on the list of people who had lied to him.

"Can I be straight with you?" I asked him.

"Sure," he said. "I've heard enough bullshit in the last two years to last me for a lifetime. What's on your mind?"

"Everything you just said is why I told them I wouldn't go into the army."

"Say what?" he asked.

"I said that everything you just said is why I refused induction into the army. That's why I'm here at Lompoc in the first place."

"You're a draft dodger?" he asked.

"No, I'm not a draft dodger," I said. "I didn't dodge anything. I'm a draft resister. I told them I wouldn't have any part of their war. I told them that the Vietnamese don't see us as liberators. They see us as another foreign power invading their country, like the Chinese, the Japanese, and the French."

There was a long silence as Sonny took all this in. I've talked with a good number of Vietnam vets in the fifty years since that summer, but at the time Sonny was the first vet I'd spoken to in person since my trial. I wasn't at all sure how he would react to what I was saying.

"No shit," he said. "They sent you a draft notice, and you just tore it up?"

"Not exactly," I said. "They sent me a draft notice, and I showed up on the appointed day. I just didn't step forward when they called my name."

Again, a long silence followed my statement. I could almost feel him mulling over what he had heard.

"You know," he said finally. "You're being straight with me, so I'll be straight with you. If you had told me all that a couple of years ago, I might have tried to pick a fight with you. I was gung-ho before I went to Nam. In basic training, they told us that guys like you were yellow sons of bitches, disloyal to our country, probably communists. That's what I would have thought before I went to Nam. But not now. I know more now, and I've seen Nam with my own eyes. My buddies are still dying over there for no good reason. They're still over there dying for a mistake. I've never said this before, but if I had it to do over again, I'm not sure I'd go, either. I'm not sure if I'd go to Canada or to the joint, but I don't think I'd go to Nam again, knowing what I know now. My neighbors in Houston would have hated me if I had refused to be drafted, and I think my mother and all my relatives would have been ashamed. It's like you and me was raised in totally different countries. But if I knew then what I know today, I think I would have refused to go too."

"Shake my hand, you hippie motherfucker," he said, reaching through the bars as far in the direction of my cell as he could. I reached as far as I could in the direction of his cell, and we shook hands through the bars.

Today when I teach about the Vietnam War, I still see it as a tragedy for virtually everyone involved and one of the worst foreign policy decisions ever made by our political leaders. Martin Luther King was right about the Vietnam War, and he paid a terrible price for being right. Conversations with Sonny Stark and later with another veteran, a friend who taught at Occidental for several years in the 1980s, have sharpened my thinking about who was to blame for that disastrous war. Most of my remaining anger today is directed at our leaders, in particular those leaders who lied to us about what they were doing in Vietnam.

I continue to think that our troops were engaged in an immoral war, but today I have a better understanding of why young men like Sonny went to war. I was privileged, fortunate enough to have had access to the people, books, and articles that opened my eyes, and deepened my understanding of the war. Sonny didn't have the same sort of support and information in Houston that I received at home and in college when I decided to resist.

At around 8:30 p.m., with no official announcement, everyone seemed to sense that it was time for the singing to begin once again. Three days together in the Hole, and we all seemed to be in the same rhythm, making decisions with a collective mind. Calls went up for Sweet Pool to get us started.

"You on, Pool! It's show time! You up! Sing that song about the bluebirds and the white cliffs." Someone started a chant to give Pool some encouragement to get us started. "We want Pool, we want Pool." The chant went on for thirty seconds or so and then stopped. And then Pool sang it. That Sunday evening, he sang it with even more soul than he had before. His singing set the tone for the next two hours. Everyone felt it. When Pool sang, I almost forgot that I was locked up.

Other songs followed, many of which we had heard before, but they all seemed fresh and alive that Sunday evening. It didn't really matter what people sang; what mattered was that we were singing. Foots sang a Woody Guthrie song called "Crawdad Hole" that went over well. Sonny repeated his version of "The Green, Green Grass of Home." Chuy added some cultural variety with a mariachi song in Spanish, "El Rey." Shorty, a talented con man, surprised everyone with a soulful rendering of "Amazing Grace."

A young biker from Bakersfield named Eddie Pennington sang a song by Merle Haggard called "Mama Tried" that drew cheers from around the Hole. Someone sang a rousing version of "Folsom Prison Blues"; someone else followed with a less melodious rendering of "I Walk the Line." Johnny Cash was already a folk hero to most of the bikers at Lompoc that summer.

Between songs, people shouted out whatever was on their minds and received cheers of affirmation in return. People cursed the guards, the parole board that had turned down their petition to be released, and the judges who had originally sentenced them. Black inmates cursed every White prison official who had ever told them they "had a bad attitude" and "needed to get their head right before they could be released." People cursed the wives and girlfriends whom they suspected of cheating on them back home. They cursed the crime partners who "ran faster than they did" and beat them to the prosecutor's office to "cop a plea" and cut a deal for a shorter sentence by selling them out.

After about two hours, all of us sensed that it was time for Little John's finale. The shouting and cursing gradually gave way to calls for "Dock of the Bay." Again, a rhythmic chant started—"Lit-tle John! Lit-tle John!" "Give us 'Dock of the Bay,' Little John!" someone shouted. "Right on!" someone else seconded. "'Dock of the Bay!'"

Little John rose to the occasion and gave the crowd what they wanted. No one sings that song like Otis Redding does, but that Sunday evening Little John sang it better than anyone I've ever heard, other than Otis. I still play Otis's version a couple of times every week, just because it reminds me of the sense of solidarity I felt that Sunday evening in the Hole at Lompoc fifty years ago.

After Little John sang his version of "Dock of the Bay," he led us in a rousing version of "Solidarity Forever," sung to the tune of "The Battle Hymn of the Republic." By the end, we were all on fire. Divisions of race, class, hippie/biker, gay/straight seemed to evaporate. We experienced a powerful moment of human solidarity that transcended the barriers that had previously divided us against each other. We all sensed that we were part of something special and unique. I knew, even at the time, that this Sunday evening in the Hole would stay with me for the rest of my life.

I thought we were done after the singing ended, but it turned out that we weren't. From down on the bottom tier, I heard Little Joe's voice ring out. "Fellas, this has been real nice, real nice, but we're not done yet; we got to do one more thing."

"What's that, Joe?" Dog shouted back to him, his voice hoarse from all the singing and shouting.

"What's up, Little Joe?" I heard Hartman call.

"I think we need to levitate this mother fucker."

"Say what?" Dog asked.

"You know," said Little Joe. "We need to pick this motherfucker up off the ground. We need to show the guards and Warden Keimer what we can do to their fucking prison if we want to."

I don't think that Foots believed in levitation any more than I did, so I was surprised to hear him shout out in support of Little Joe's idea. "Joe's right," yelled Foots. "Let's pick this motherfucker up! Let's show the guards and Boss Keimer what we can do anytime we want to. Let's send them a message about power."

Pandemonium broke out again, even louder than before. Everyone chanted in unison. "Le-vi-tate! Le-vi-tate!" I saw Boss Schwartz walk past the front of my cell toward the other end of the tier. The shouting was so loud that he didn't even try to get us to quiet down. He looked worried.

"Le-vi-tate, le-vi-tate." The chant grew louder, and then, just as suddenly as it began, it stopped.

Little Joe took charge of the levitation of Lompoc at that point, on the grounds that he had suggested the idea, but also because he seemed to know more about the process than anyone else.

"Be careful now," said Little Joe. "Everyone needs to calm down a little bit. We all have to be concentrating if we want to do this right. Take a few deep breaths. Breath in. Breath out. In and out. Concentrate. We don't want to break this motherfucker. That's not what we're trying to do. We just want to show the warden what we have the power to do if we want to. Be very careful."

And then he started to chant "Om, Om," the same way the poet, Allen Ginsberg, chanted it from the podium the time he gave a reading at Occidental College, right after I joined the faculty. "Om, om, om." Everyone else followed Little Joe's lead and soon the entire population of the Hole was chanting "Om." Then, just as Little Joe had directed us, we lifted the prison off its foundation. Suddenly, everyone stopped chanting; we just held Lompoc there in mid-air, eight inches or so off the ground. Most of us were pleased with ourselves at that point, but Little Joe was not yet entirely satisfied.

"Eight inches is good," he said, "but I think we can do better. Let's go for a full foot. We need to lift this motherfucker a foot off the ground. Then we can all go to sleep."

So that's what we did. At least, that's what I believe we did. The chant went up again. "Ommmmm. Ommmmm." Loud and resonating in unison. "Ommmmm. Ommmmm." Then, as if on cue, we stopped again.

"We got it!" shouted Little Joe. "One foot. We got it. Now let's set this motherfucker down *real* carefully so we don't break anything. We made our point. Now let's be responsible so we don't cost the good taxpayers of this country anything extra. Let's set this mother back down, right where we found it."

So, we did. With infinite care and precision, we set the prison down, ever so gently, on its foundation, good as new.

There were a few arguments the next day about how high we'd lifted the prison off its foundation. A couple of guys on the bottom tier claimed that we never actually got it above six inches, but they were shouted down because on the bottom tier they didn't have a clear angle of vision. The guys on the top tier claimed that they had a better view, and they swore to a man that we levitated the entire joint at least a foot off the ground. I've always deferred to the guys on the top tier on this point because they had the clearest view. One thing is certain: You won't find anyone who was there that night who will deny that we levitated Lompoc. Everyone was, and remains, in agreement about that basic fact.

After the singing ended, the unit quieted down and people started to drop off to sleep. I was beginning to doze off myself when I heard Little John's voice whispering from next door.

"Newhall," he whispered. "Are you still awake?"

"Yeah, Little John. What's up?"

"You know this can't last, don't you?"

"What do you mean?"

"You know that the warden and the guards can't afford to let this strike go on like this. They have to regain control of the prison. They have to show us and the people they report to who's in charge." As usual, Little John was several steps ahead of the rest of us.

"How are they going to do that?" I asked him.

"I'm not sure," he replied, "but I know that whatever they do, it's not going to be pretty."

On that ominous note, I nodded off to sleep, wondering what the new week would bring.

§

I woke up the next morning to the sound of the breakfast carts rattling down all three tiers and angry shouts from all over the unit. Through the windows I could see a number of inmates, maybe nine or ten, walking through the yard, toward their assigned jobs.

"Motherfucking scabs!" I heard Dog shout. "When I get out of here, you're in some deep shit."

Snarls, threats, and imprecations issued from all over the Hole, directed at the handful of inmates who had apparently decided to accept the warden's invitation to go back to work.

"Little John," I called. "You awake?"

"Yeah, I'm awake."

"What's going on?"

"The warden's trying to break the strike," he said. "Divide and conquer. I'm guessing that they're offering to let people go back to work with no loss of good time. I'm actually surprised that more people aren't accepting the offer."

The number of men walking toward their assigned jobs was only a small trickle. By all appearances, the prison officials were going to have to think of another tactic if they wanted to get the prison population back under control again. *I wonder what's going through Boss Keimer and Boss Keith's heads right now?* I thought. *Will they even consider any of the reforms we've suggested? What's their next move going to be?*

As things turned out, we didn't have to wait very long for an answer. After breakfast, I pulled out *Catch-22*, intending to read for the rest of the morning. I had just reached the mid-point in the novel, the chapter in which Colonel Cathcart instructs the Chaplain to lead the men in prayer for a tighter bomb pattern. Suddenly, the relative quiet of the Hole was broken by angry shouts out in the prison's main corridor. The shouts grew louder and louder and increasingly frenzied. I waited for them to stop or to at least diminish, but they didn't. More and more voices joined in. The Hole grew quiet, listening. We heard shouts but couldn't tell who was shouting or why. Then we began to smell the gas. The men in the cells closest to the corridor smelled it first.

"Oh, shit," I heard Dog curse from the far end of the bottom tier. "It's tear gas. Get ready, guys; it's tear gas." Tear gas was gradually spreading from the corridor through the entrance into the Hole. It moved slowly down the tier toward my cell. I heard guys down to my right coughing before I caught my first whiff of the gas. When the gas reached me, I started to cough, and then I started to gag as the gas grew thicker. I remember beginning to panic. This was the first and only time in my life that I thought that I might die.

Down the tier to my right, I heard Dog cursing. "These dumb motherfuckers don't know what they're doing," he said. "They shot too much gas. They're not even thinking about us. They don't care. We're going to suffocate in here." I heard a note of real fear in Dog's voice that I'd never heard before. The whole unit went crazy at that point, because all of us sensed that Dog might be right. We could feel it. The gas was getting thicker and thicker, and nearly everyone was coughing and struggling to breathe.

"Let us out," people began to shout. "Schwartz, you dog motherfucker. Open the cells. Open the cells so we can get out into the corridor. We need some air. We can't breathe. We can't breathe." All around me,

Chapter 5. The Hole

I heard the sounds of panicky men coughing and gasping for air. It was complete chaos, and no one seemed to be in charge. *These careless fools have shot too much gas*, I thought. *Is this how it's all going to end?*

Looking back, I can see that there was no way in hell Boss Schwartz was going to open the doors to our cells and face the collective anger of the men in the Hole. Adrenalin was flowing; people were enraged and damn near out of control. I honestly think that if Boss Schwartz had let us out that morning, he might have been killed. I'm not sure what I would have done if I'd had a gun in my hand. I now understand the uncontrolled rage that triggers wartime atrocities. Rage doesn't justify atrocities, but it sure as hell helps explain them.

Amid all the chaos, I heard a calm voice coming from the cell on my left.

"Newhall, are you all right? Are you OK over there?" It was Sonny.

"Not really," I gasped. "This gas is some bullshit."

"Listen to me," Sonny said. "Tear off a piece of your sheet and run some water on it. Then hold it over your nose and mouth and breathe through it. It'll let the air through and filter out most of the gas. And another thing. If you really need air, put your head down into your toilet bowl and flush it. That'll create a vacuum, and you'll have some air with no gas in it."

I did as Sonny suggested, and immediately I got more oxygen. I could still smell the gas, and tears were streaming down my face, nearly blinding me, but I could now breathe more easily. I flushed the toilet several times and gradually stopped coughing and gasping for air.

"Little John!" I called.

"Yeah," came the answer. I gave him the same instructions that Sonny had given to me, and within a few minutes word spread around the unit, and everyone was breathing through wet fabric of some kind and flushing their toilets and breathing air from the vacuum. Sheets seemed to work best, but some people tore up their blankets. Others used socks, underwear, or T-shirts. But everyone survived and made it through the tear gas.

Out in the corridor, things were not going as well. I heard people running and shouting. Then the tone of the shouts changed from anger to panic and pain.

"People are being beaten out there in the corridor," I heard Dog shout from his cell on the bottom tier. "They're beating the shit out of them with their Billy clubs."

Twenty minutes later, it was all over. The Hole was as quiet as a tomb. People closest to the entrance to I-Block tried their best to hear what was going on, but the corridor was quiet now, and there were no trustees available to tell us what was happening.

"Little John," I said. "Can you tell what's going on?"

"I'm not sure," he said. "I'm guessing that they have people back on lockdown again, but I can't tell for sure."

After the noise in the corridor subsided, the Hole slowly began to buzz again with people speculating about what they had heard. Rumors were rampant. A while later, we heard shouts coming once again from the entrance to the Hole. The shouts weren't as loud as they had been earlier, and they seemed to be coming from fewer people. More inmates were being brought to the Hole. Down on the first tier, guards were leading newly arrived inmates into cells on that level. A few minutes later, I heard people walking down toward my end of the second tier. I saw Big Frank walk past my cell, naked as a jaybird, with a guard holding onto each of his massive arms. He was followed by Crow and two White inmates I had never seen before. I heard cell doors creak open and clang shut. Then I heard more inmates being put into cells up above me on the third tier. I waited until all the guards walked back to the front of the unit, and then I called to Frank and Crow, down to my left.

"Fellas! What's going on out there? What the hell happened?"

"Who's that?" asked Crow.

"It's Newhall," I said. "I just saw you and Big Frank walk by my cell. I'm down here to your right on the second tier. What happened out in the corridor?"

Big Frank told about what had happened, with Crow adding a detail now and then when he thought Frank had left out something of significance.

"The warden and the guards thought that the strike was over last Friday, and that people would go back to work this morning," Frank said, loud enough that the whole unit could hear. "The warden thought that he had all the so-called leaders of the strike in the Hole by the end of the day on Saturday. He let things cool off some more on lockdown yesterday, and then this morning an announcement came out over the loudspeaker that the lockdown was over, and we should all return to the regular work schedule. Six units would be released at a time for breakfast. After breakfast, people were supposed to get on to their assigned jobs. The warden wanted to return to business as usual."

"But that's not what happened," said Crow. "Tell 'em what happened instead."

"It seemed like some people were ready to go back to work after breakfast," Frank said. "Truth be known, lockdown ain't no picnic. It gets damned boring being stuck there in your cell or your unit for the whole day. No exercise, no fresh air, you can't talk with anyone outside your unit. Some people were getting antsy and were ready to go back to work, but even more of us wanted to stay on strike. The guys in the furniture factory weren't the only ones pissed off, it turns out. We were just the spark that set things off."

"So, what did they do?" I asked. "Did people just go back to their cells after breakfast?"

"No," said Frank. "We didn't go back to our cells. After breakfast we just sat down in the hallway in front of our units and wouldn't move. You had about three hundred people sitting down in the hallway and another three or four hundred being let out of their units for the second breakfast shift. The second shift saw what was happening, and half of them just sat down in the corridor too."

"An old-style 'sit down' strike," said Little John.

"Just like back in the thirties during the Depression. No violence, at least not at first. People just sat down and wouldn't move." "That's what it was, all right," said Frank. "A regular sit-down strike. Crow and I were sitting there in the hallway along with everyone else. Even the Indians were there with us. David Running Wolf and Snuffy were both out there. Those two dudes have some righteous heart."

"How long did this go on?" Little John wanted to know.

"About half an hour, maybe forty minutes," said Frank. "I don't have a watch. I don't want one. Watches make the time go by too slow. Anyway, we was just sitting there in the main corridor talking when I heard someone shout, 'Heads up!' I stood up and looked down to the far end of the corridor, down by A&O. There were about fifty hacks down there walking down the corridor toward this end. There were about four hundred of us sitting out there in the corridor, bunched together. We had them outnumbered, but the hacks had tear gas, Billy-clubs, gas masks, and I don't know what else."

"This didn't have to happen," said Crow. "It didn't have to come down like this. All the hacks needed to do was to put people's earnings on the books for them so they could buy some fucking cigarettes and candy bars for the weekend. That don't seem like much to ask."

Surratt had been listening to what Frank and Crow were saying.

"It's not much to ask," he said. "But this is bigger than 'zu zus and wham whams' for the weekend. This is about control and power. They needed to show us who's boss."

"That's right," said Crow. "They needed to show us who's boss. They also had some new equipment they wanted to try out, like a bunch of little kids with new toys. Coming down the corridor toward us with their gas masks, they looked like something from another fucking planet."

"Anyway," said Frank. "They got about a third of the way down the corridor and stopped. We saw they had tear gas, so we backed up down here toward the Chow Hall and I–Block. Four hundred or so guys were packed into this end of the corridor. When they shot the first few canisters of gas, all hell broke loose. People were yelling, scrambling to get away from the gas. I'm a big man, and I was almost knocked down. I thought some of the little dudes might get trampled in the rush."

Crow chimed in again. "Dudes were running up and down trying to get into one of the living units, any unit, to get away from the tear gas. Some of the doors were open, and some were locked. I tried to get into M-unit, but the door was locked. I'd say that about three-quarters of the guys managed to escape into one unit or another, but that still left over a hundred of us in the hallway. People were gasping for air. Some guys were lying on the ground and getting stepped on. The hacks kept coming forward, and they beat the living shit out of everyone in their way. That's what you guys heard in here. The beating only lasted about ten minutes or so, but it seemed like a whole lot longer. After they made their point, the hacks backed off down the corridor."

"What happened then?" Foots asked from up on the third tier.

"Then we heard the warden's voice over the loudspeaker," said Frank. "He ordered everyone in the hallway to return to their assigned units. The doors to all the units were opened, and people did as they were told. The corridor was cleared, and most people were put on lockdown again in their cells. A few of us were brought down here, two or three at a time."

"Why did they single out you and Crow?" asked Surratt.

"Snitches," said Big Frank. "After people were back in their cells, the snitches went to work. It seems like any brother who was ever seen talking to any of you hippies was pulled out of his unit and put in the Hole here. They were talking to Bubba right after they called Crow and me out of our units. I saw them talking to Bubba and Eddie Jones. They'll probably come walking through that door pretty soon. It's funny. All they're guilty of is playing basketball out in the yard with a couple of White dudes."

That Monday morning, when the guards shot the gas, was the beginning of the end of the strike. It was the moment when the tide turned. The entire prison remained on lockdown until Friday of that week. Every night there was chanting and singing in virtually every unit. "On strike, shut it down! On strike, shut it down!" A few scabs gradually began to drift back to work on Wednesday and Thursday, but not enough to make a real difference. From the Friday when the guys in the furniture factory refused to work through the following Friday, the warden and the guards had to run their own prison. We weren't going to run it for them. We shut it down, and we yelled, chanted, and sang until we were hoarse. They tried to stop our singing in the evening, but they couldn't do it. Whenever they silenced one tier, the other two tiers would break out into song, even louder than before.

We learned later from an inmate whose mother happened to visit him that second Friday, the last day of the strike, that the local paper in the nearby town where most of the guards lived ran several stories about the "unrest at Lompoc." No inmate, of course, was allowed to speak with the press, but Warden Keimer was quoted at length. The "official version" of the strike provided by Warden Keimer assured the public that "everything was under control at the institution," and that the inmates were demanding color televisions for every unit and a swimming pool for the yard. "You can just imagine how difficult it would be to prevent violence at Lompoc if we let fifty or sixty of these individuals into a swimming pool at the same time. As for color televisions, I don't really have a comment other than to say that I don't believe the public wants us to coddle the prisoners. This is a prison, not summer camp. We don't want them to be too comfortable."

There was no mention in the article of "zu zus and wham whams." There was no mention of inadequate medical care or of the fact that one psychiatrist and two psychologists were expected to meet the psychological needs of the around twelve hundred inmates. No mention of "job training programs" that didn't prepare anyone for real jobs out on the streets. Whenever I teach Melville's *Billy Budd*, I call my students' attention to the subtitle of the tale, "An Inside Narrative," and I ask them what the subtitle means. We always have interesting discussions of "inside narratives" in contrast to "official narratives." There are always more than enough examples of "official narratives" in that day's newspaper to keep the discussion lively.

We remained on lockdown through Friday of that second week—for a total of eight days. Through the windows that looked out into the yard we could see that a growing number of inmates were gradually going back to work. What had been a small trickle of workers on Tuesday became a medium sized trickle on Wednesday, and by the end of the day on Friday, lockdown was over, and it was business as usual.

That second Friday, the end of my first full week in the Hole, the warden began to move selected inmates back to their "home units." Every hour or so someone would be let out of his cell and called up to the front of I-Block. Associate Warden Keith seemed to be in charge of implementing the process. He had brief conversations with selected inmates, during which he asked them if they were ready to return to work. Without exception the inmates with whom he spoke answered that they were ready to leave the Hole and go back to work.

Boss Keith never called the name of anyone who was part of our original organizing committee of ten, nor did he call Hartman, Little Joe, Dog, Dusty, or any of the guys from the furniture factory who got the strike going in the first place. The eighteen so-called "instigators" all spent nearly three more weeks in the Hole (almost a month, in total), and then, two by two, most of us were shipped out to different prisons all over the country, no more than two "troublemakers" per prison.

By that second Friday evening after dinner, our ranks were considerably depleted. Foots tried to get some singing started, but Sweet Pool had returned to his unit and wasn't there to start things off. Sonny Stark didn't feel like singing that night, so Dog sang his own version of "The Green, Green Grass of Home." His voice was not as good as Sonny's, but he sang with such gusto that he won the crowd over and received a nice round of applause when he finished. Nevertheless, we could all sense that something was missing. A number of cells were empty now, and the volume was noticeably weaker. We could all hear it and feel it. We had experienced a beautiful moment of solidarity on Sunday, and now, five days later, that moment was gone. Little John did his best to lift the mood with another rendition of "Dock of the Bay," but it just wasn't the same. We gave it one last shot with "Solidarity Forever." We shouted more than sang it at the top of our lungs, but this time the guards didn't even bother to come out into the unit to quiet us down. They knew the strike was over and that they were back in control.

By the end of the day on Friday of that second week, the warden had returned all but eighteen of us to our original units. The strike had run its course in about eight days, and the mood among the men remaining in the Hole was increasingly subdued. That second Friday evening, after we tried and failed to generate one last songfest, I had a conversation with Sonny that has stayed with me all these years. He, Little John, and I had been talking with each other throughout the week about a range of topics, some political, some personal. We had gotten to the point where the three of us felt comfortable with each other, even when we disagreed about a small issue here or there. A level of trust developed there in the Hole that enabled us to talk about subjects we probably would have avoided out on the streets.

"Sonny," I remember saying to him ten minutes or so after the guards turned out the lights that second Friday night. "Sonny, are you still awake?"

"Yeah, New. I'm still awake. What's up?"

"Would you mind if I ask you a question about something I've been thinking about for a while? It's kind of personal."

"Well," said Sonny, "that depends on what the question's about. What's on your mind?"

"It's about Vietnam," I said. "It's about fighting in Vietnam. It's something I've been thinking about for a while."

"Fire away," he said. "People are always asking me about Nam, and did I see this and did I do that. If I don't like a question, I just don't answer it. What's your question?"

"Were you ever ordered to go into one of those tunnels I keep reading about?" I asked him. "You know, those tunnels where they went to escape the bombs and the napalm we were dropping? Were you ever ordered to go down into one of those tunnels?"

There was a brief silence before he responded. "Yeah," he said, eventually. "I wasn't one of the 'tunnel rats,' guys who specialized in blowing tunnels, but I did some of that. I did my share of that. When we had to check out a tunnel, the platoon would get together and draw straws. The man with the short straw crawled the tunnel. After a guy took his turn, he didn't have to draw a straw again until everyone else had gone once. We rotated tunnel duty. Why do you ask?"

"Ever since I heard about the tunnels, I've wondered if I could have done what you had to do," I said. "I'm kind of claustrophobic. I've read that the Viet Cong put poisonous snakes in some of the tunnels. I've also read that they booby-trapped some of the tunnels with mines. That's a lot of pressure—wondering every move you make if you're going to blow yourself up. I guess I'm asking you about the tunnels because I've always wondered if I could have handled that."

"Ah, don't be so hard on yourself, New," Sonny said. "If you didn't have some sort of heart, I don't think you'd be here talking to me."

"I appreciate your saying that," I said. "But I still think those tunnels were something different."

"In Nam," said Sonny, "most people simply sucked it up and did what they needed to do. I think most people can do what they need to do when a situation arises."

"I'm not sure," I said. "I'm still not sure how I would have reacted."

"Hey, man," said Sonny. "We got to get some sleep. Let this shit about the tunnels go. No telling what these motherfucking guards will throw at us tomorrow."

Losing is never any fun and I knew that, since the tear gas, we'd been losing. In fact, we had been getting our collective asses kicked. I lay there on my bunk that Friday evening trying to go to sleep, but I couldn't stop thinking. I could hear Sonny snoring softly to my left, and I envied him, but too many thoughts were rushing through my head, preventing me from dropping off. I was trying to make sense of the last week—trying to understand what it meant, or if it meant anything at all.

"Little John," I said in a low voice, in order not to wake anyone else up.

"Are you awake?"

"Yeah, New," he answered quietly. "I'm still awake."

I didn't even know what I wanted to say or exactly what I wanted to ask him. I just knew that I wanted to hear what someone whose intelligence I respected was thinking about what had happened over the last eight days.

"They beat us," I said. "Motherfucking Keimer and Keith, and the hacks. They kicked our butts and they beat us. They're probably at home right now drinking beer, watching TV, and laughing about the ass whipping they gave those guys out in the corridor."

"They didn't beat us," Little John said, in a firm voice. "They just slowed us down. It's not over."

"What do you mean, it's not over?" I asked him. "More people went back to work today. Even more will probably go back next Monday. By the end of next week, everything will be back to normal. It will be as if nothing ever happened. We're stuck here in the Hole, and they're holding all the cards. We don't know when they're going to let us out of here, and we don't have a clue about what happens next."

Little John paused briefly before he responded. "It's not over," he said, "because no one who was any part of this strike will ever be the same again."

"What do you mean?"

"I mean that every inmate in this joint saw what can happen when ordinary people stand up and stand together. Everyone saw what can happen when we don't allow ourselves to be divided by all the things the hacks use to divide us. We didn't have the race riot the hacks were expecting, and, in fact, hoping for. For about a week the bikers, the hippies, the Blacks, the Chicanos, and even the Indians stood together as one. We rocked this prison. The guards know it and we know it. For eight days, we watched them sweat to run their prison. We had nothing except each other, and we shut this place down for an entire week. Think about it. We had no resources, and we shut this system down for eight days. You felt the power of that, and you're not ever going to be the same person again. They didn't beat us, New. They just slowed us down for a while. The point of the strike is not that it only lasted eight days. The point of the strike is that it happened at all. No one can ever take that fact away from us."

I've never forgotten Little John's optimism and courage, but I was still feeling gloomy and let down by the end of the strike and the uncertainty about what would come next. "I hope you're right," I said. "Right now, though, I'm not feeling all that optimistic. These motherfuckers have a lot of guns, and they're willing to use them. LBJ has pulled out of the election, but Humphrey and Nixon basically agree with him about the war, and it looks as though one of them is going to win in November. Nixon talks about a 'secret plan for peace,' but I don't believe a word he says. Bobby

Chapter 5. The Hole

Kennedy's dead. McCarthy's still running and criticizing the war, but he doesn't seem all that enthusiastic about the campaign. LBJ's still dropping bombs all over Southeast Asia. Every day we can hear the guns being fired up the coast a few miles from here. It all feels like David against Goliath to me. I can't get those guns out of my head."

"You just made my point for me," Little John chuckled. "Don't ever bet on Goliath. In the end, he doesn't win."

§

The next morning after breakfast, I was sitting on my bunk trying to finish *Catch-22* when Boss Schwartz came walking down the tier, delivering mail. The guards were still delivering our mail and our food in I-Block because Warden Keimer felt that some of the trustees were too supportive of the strikers.

"Surratt," called Boss Schwartz when he reached Little John's cell. "Here's a letter for you." Boss Schwartz then stopped in front of my cell. "Newhall, two letters for you today."

He handed the envelopes through the bars. I could tell from the handwriting that one was from my mother. The other was from the United States Superior Court in Portland, Oregon. The gist of the letter from the Court was that a group of judges from Oregon, Massachusetts, and one other relatively liberal state had met recently and had concluded that inmates who were incarcerated for refusing induction into the armed forces were not being treated equitably by the Federal Prison System. The letter mentioned several issues (access to reading materials, correspondence lists, adequate medical care, access to parole) but the key point was that the judges had decided to cut in half the sentences of everyone from their respective states who had been convicted of a selective service violation during the past four years. This literally meant that with the stroke of a pen, the time I had remaining to serve, counting my accumulated good time, was cut from fifteen months to about five months. Here I was sitting in the Hole, accused of "instigating a riot," and my sentence was cut in half. I was suddenly "short," as convicts say. I couldn't believe what I was reading. I was a little less than five months from being released.

"Foots," I called out. "Did you just get a letter from Belloni?"

"Yes," he called back. "I did."

"Is it a mind blower?"

"Yes, it is," he called back. Neither one of us wanted to talk openly about our good fortune within earshot of others who still had years to go on their sentences.

From that moment on, until the day I was released, my gloomy morale brightened. I could do five months "standing on my head," as Crow used to say. I could see light at the end of the tunnel.

After a few minutes, Little John whispered to me from the adjoining cell. "New, what's up? Is it anything you can talk about?"

I thought carefully about how to respond. I knew that Little John's sentence was a "zip-six" and that he could be held for up to three or four more years. But Little John was one of the people in the joint in whom I had developed complete trust. I gave him a straight answer.

"Yeah," I said quietly. "It's good news. Some judges in three states have cut the sentences of draft resisters in half on the grounds that we aren't being treated fairly or equitably. No draft resister has ever been paroled. Apparently, the Federal Judges in three states consider that fact to be evidence of discrimination. I'm short. I have about five months left to do."

There was a brief silence as Little John absorbed what I was telling him.

"That's great," he said. "That's just great."

Little John was, and I'm sure still is, a truly generous and politically committed person. Just about everyone at Lompoc was being treated badly, but he had the good grace not to point that out. He seemed genuinely happy for me.

"Say," he said after a few moments. "You have less than a year left on your sentence."

"That's right," I said. "I went from having about fourteen months to do one minute to having about five months to do the next."

"You've got less than a year to go," he said. "That means they can't keep you in a medium security joint like this one anymore. They've got to transfer you to a minimum-security facility. You can do some easy time at a minimum-security joint and finish off your sentence."

Little John knew far more than I did about the rules and regulations that govern different types of prisons. I took his word on this particular point and set myself to wait until the powers that be determined where I would be placed next to serve out the remainder of my sentence.

Hartman and Dog were the first two of the eighteen alleged "riot instigators" to be shipped out to another prison. This happened, I believe, early in our third week in the Hole. After mail was delivered one afternoon, Hartman called out to Foots and me. "Foots. New. I just got a letter informing me that I'm being transferred to a joint in Covington, Kentucky, to do the rest of my time. I leave early tomorrow morning. They're transferring me back to my hometown."

A few minutes later Dog called out from his cell on the bottom tier. "Hartman. I'm being transferred to the same joint in Kentucky—tomorrow morning. It looks like we'll be hitting the road together."

Chapter 5. The Hole

Since Dale was originally from Kentucky, he was not at all unhappy to be returning to his home state. Dog, originally from Bakersfield, was less enthusiastic, but he warmed to the idea as Hartman told him about the virtues of Kentucky. People began to say their farewells, promising to stay in touch with each other when they were released.

Dog got emotional on his final evening at Lompoc. He started telling people how pleased he was to have known them. He handed out the name and telephone number of a motorcycle shop in Bakersfield where we could find people who would always know how to get in touch with him.

"Newhall," he called out to me that last evening before he left. "Do you have a bike? Do you own a motorcycle?"

"No," I answered. "For that matter, I don't really own a car either."

"God damn, New," Crow gasped from the bottom tier. "First, I discover that you buy your clothes from Penney's. Now I hear you don't have no wheels. How the hell do you take care of business?"

"My last year in school, I had my family's old Studebaker Lark," I said. "I left it in Portland when I was sentenced."

Crow chuckled. "Studebaker Lark," he said, skeptically. "Now I'm really starting to suspect that you a slug. You sure ain't no player."

Laughter rippled around the unit. There was more laughter when Crow launched into a description of how he thought I must look driving around town in my Studebaker Lark wearing my clothes bought from Penney's.

"You guys lighten up on New," Big Frank called out, coming to my defense. "New and Foots may not be players yet, but they young, and they got plenty of potential. They players of the future."

At this point Dog surprised me, and, I believe, everyone else in the Hole. "Frank's right," Dog said to the whole unit. "New and Foots are solid. I admit that I never had no use for hippies before this. I always thought hippies were soft—weak with their long hair and their flowers and all. But New and Foots are different. They were down here in the Hole a day after I was. They were down here at the start of the strike. That shows me some heart." He paused for a few moments. "In fact," he decided, "I'm making them honorary bikers as of right now. You hear that Newhall, Foots. You guys can consider yourselves honorary bikers from now on. You can consider yourselves honorary members of the Bakersfield Chapter of the Hell's Angels."

"Damn, Dog," said Foots. "That's an honor. I really appreciate it." And then Foots apparently started to feel the power of the moment, because he surprised me too. "I thought you were just a hard ass when I saw you out in the yard for the first time," said Foots. "Down here in the Hole I can see that you're a lot more than that. I'm taking it upon myself right now to declare you an honorary hippie. And come to think of it, that includes all of you guys from the furniture factory who got this strike going in the first place. Some of us hippies were doing our best to get people to strike, but we didn't get the job done. You guys got the thing started and you deserve a lot of credit. I hereby declare all of you to be honorary hippies."

"I second that motion," I shouted out. "Foots is right. All of you guys down in the furniture factory showed us a lot of heart. You led the way. You were the spark that that started everything."

Dog was feeling the spirit now, and he surprised me again. "Fellas, I got to add one more thing."

"What's that," called out Little Joe. "You get on, Dog, you bad motherfucker. What do you want to add on your last night here in the Hole with us?"

"I want to say this right," Dog said, "so that you all understand what I mean. I never knew no Nee-groes before."

At this point Crow broke in. "All due respect, Dog," he said, "but Frank and I don't consider ourselves to be 'Negroes.' We Black."

Crow's correction did not seem to bother Dog in the least, and, in fact, he accepted it gracefully. "No disrespect intended Crow," he said. "No brothers—no Blacks—went to my high school, and we didn't let none into our motorcycle club down in Bakersfield, either. That was just the way things were in Bakersfield where I grew up. You and Big Frank are different. You're down here in the Hole with all of us, and you're both just as good a man as anyone here. I'm making you and Frank honorary bikers and members of the Bakersfield Chapter of the Hells Angels right here and now." There was a brief silence after Dog's statement, and then loud shouts went up from the bottom tier to the top.

The cheers and shouts spread around all of I-Block, and then everyone started to feel the spirit of what was happening. It was an extraordinary moment. Crow and Big Frank declared Dog and Little Joe to be honorary brothers and Dog and Little Joe, without a moment's hesitation, expressed their appreciation for the honor. Chuy, normally quiet and reserved, started making everyone present into honorary Chicanos and Brown Berets and telling all of us that one day in the future we'd all be welcome in Atzlan, the legendary Chicano homeland.

There was a general tearing down of barriers there in the Hole at Lompoc, barriers that normally divided us into hostile factions on the streets. We wanted to give each other something meaningful because of what we had been through together. All we had to give was words, so we let down our normal prison defenses and spoke to each other from the heart. There was a feeling common to everyone present: if someone had shown some heart during the strike, he belonged.

Chapter 5. The Hole

I've carried the transcendent feeling of that moment inside me from that day to the present. It was a democratic moment in the best possible sense of the word. No color line, or for that matter any other sort of line, divided us from each other. We were all equal citizens in the small community we created there in the Hole at Lompoc. That surging feeling of equality that I felt long ago still energizes me today and gives me hope for the future. It's as close to having a religious experience as I've ever come.

Amid all the emotion, I heard Little John's voice coming from the adjoining cell.

"Newhall," he said.

"Yeah," I answered.

"This is what I'm talking about," he said. "Once you've seen something, you can't un-see it. Once consciousness has been changed, you can't un-change it. The consciousness of everyone here in the Hole has been changed, to one degree or another, forever. You can hear it in this conversation. You're never going to be the same. Dog is never going to be the same person he was before this strike. They didn't beat us, Newhall. They just delayed the inevitable for a while."

During all the jubilation and reconciliation that preceded Dog and Hartman's departure for Kentucky, there was one note of skepticism, one cautionary, resisting voice. Appropriately, I thought at the time, it was David Running Wolf, descendent of Native American people who had been betrayed for centuries by the lies of White men.

Running Wolf had come into the Hole with the other guys from the furniture factory. When Dog announced that he wanted to make everyone from the furniture factory into honorary bikers, Running Wolf sounded a little dubious. His father had warned him from the time he was a boy about taking the words of White men at face value.

"Hold up," he told Dog. "Hold up. I'm not sure I can really see myself riding nowhere on a Harley with a bunch of bikers from Bakersfield. We didn't have bikers on the rez when I was growing up, at least not white ones. Let me think about this overnight. I appreciate the honor, Dog, but I want to think about it for a while."

Dog assured Running Wolf that he understood and told him to go ahead and think about it overnight. Brotherhood involves no coercion. Hartman and Dog left in the dark the next morning before any of us were awake. Running Wolf, to the best of my knowledge, never gave Dog an answer. His skepticism served as counterpoint to the overall jubilation of the evening, helping to keep us all grounded in reality.

§

By the start of our third week in the Hole, the days were really beginning to drag. The remaining strikers continued to be transferred, one or two at a time, to other joints around the country or back into the general population at Lompoc. Slowly, life returned to normal.

Near the end of that third week, Little John was shipped out to a prison in Terre Haute, Indiana. I had never heard of this prison before, but Little John had and what he had heard wasn't good.

"It's not like Lompoc," he told us. "It's not mainly for younger inmates and less hardened offenders. It's a maximum-security joint with convicts of all ages and more repeat offenders. It's a heavy place," he said. I could hear the anxiety in his voice.

Foots and I had grown close to Little John since we first met him, and we had grown even closer during our time in the Hole. We liked him personally and respected his commitment to what he always called "the people." I've known many people in my life who spout a lot of rhetoric about social justice and political change, but when push comes to shove, they aren't willing to put anything on the line. Little John was willing to put it all on the line—at significant cost to himself.

The evening before Little John left Lompoc, he, Foots, and I had a conversation. We talked for a long time about what we planned to do after we got out—our plans for the future—what we thought we'd be doing with the rest of our lives. The last thing Little John said before we went to sleep was, "One day, I think both of you guys will be one of us, part of the movement—the movement for a real democracy." Coming from Little John, that comment meant a lot to me. The next morning when I woke up, he was gone. I never saw him again. I have no idea how things turned out for him at Terre Haute.

I was shipped out to McNeil Island in Washington after spending a total of twenty-two days in the Hole. For reasons I'll never understand, Foots was kept in the Hole for two more weeks before he, too, was sent up to McNeil. That last evening before I left Lompoc, I spoke for a long time with Crow and Big Frank. We wished each other the best in the future and promised to stay in touch. "It would be great to get together, the three of us and Foots," I said, "maybe play some hoop, drink a couple of beers." We all agreed and said that we would look forward to getting together on the streets.

The next morning, before the sun was up, I was awakened by the sound of my cell door opening. A guard carrying a flashlight told me to gather my personal belongings and follow him to meet the federal marshals who would be driving two others and me back up the coast to the Pacific Northwest. I dressed quickly, threw a few photographs and letters into my pillowcase, and followed the guard down the stairs. When we got out to the main corridor, he stopped and looked at me with an odd expression on his face.

"One last thing," he said.

"What's that?" I asked.

"I need to get your signature on one more form before you can be transferred."

"What sort of form?"

"It's just a formality. It says that all your personal possessions have been returned to you. Just sign your name here, on this dotted line, and we'll be on our way." He handed me a pen and a one-page form attached to a clipboard.

The guard was clearly uneasy about something. His manner seemed odd to me, as though he were conning me in some way. I sensed that something was wrong, but it was early, and I was still waking up. I paused for a few moments, just looking at him as he nervously shifted his weight back and forth from one foot to the other. Then it hit me what was happening and why he wanted my signature on the form.

When an inmate is placed in the Hole, his personal belongings are all taken from his locker, put in a cardboard box, and held until the inmate is returned to the general population, at which point his belongings are returned to him. My belongings had not yet been returned to me, and since I was on the verge of leaving Lompoc, this was my last chance to get them back.

"But my personal belongings haven't been returned to me," I said. "They took everything from my locker when I was put in the Hole. When do I get my stuff back?"

"You'll get what you have coming to you when you get up to McNeil Island," snapped the guard.

"Does that include the journal I was keeping?" I asked him. "I started keeping that journal in County Jail up in Oregon, and I continued it once I got here. When do I get my journal back?"

At this point a little smile flickered across the guard's face, and I knew that I was right about why he wanted my signature.

"The only thing I really care about is my journal," I said. "It's my record of my time in custody; I want to be able to read it and think about it in the future. It's just words and thoughts. It's not worth anything to anyone but me."

"You've got a decision to make, Newhall," he said, "and you need to be quick about it. You can sign this form right now and get on up the coast to McNeil Island, or you can refuse to sign and go back to the Hole until you're ready to sign. It's up to you. The Marshalls are scheduled to leave in about fifteen minutes. What's it gonna be?"

I stared at the guard, weighing my options. The prison system's willingness to take my written words, thoughts, and memories from me embodies much of what I loathe about the "Correctional System": the indifference to the lives and wellbeing of the inmates who pass through it—the very inhumanity that caused us to strike in the first place. These thoughts flashed rapidly through my mind. I was angry, but I decided, I'd had enough of the Hole for a while. Little John was right: There would be more fights to fight and lines to cross—or not cross—in the future. I signed the form and never saw my journal again.

My last conversation at Lompoc ended on that sorry note. A dishonest guard stole the history of my time in custody from me, and I contributed to the travesty by signing my name on a form, endorsing a lie. No one's hands are ever completely clean. I left Lompoc in the dark that morning, hours before the sun came up, shackled to two other prisoners I had never seen before. No one else in the Hole was awake when I left. I was done doing time at Lompoc, but I was far from done thinking about it.

Epilogue

In the fifty-four years since I left the Hole at Lompoc, I've talked with only three of the men who were there with me, and I've seen only two of them in person. I had a phone call from Dale Hartman around the middle of April in 1970, a few months after he was released. He had saved my parents' phone number, and he called their house in Portland, thinking that I might be staying with them for a while. His call lifted my spirits because he seemed to have gotten his life on track.

Talking with Dale on the phone, it was hard to tell for sure about his circumstances and frame of mind. It was a lot like listening to the voices in the Hole. Only a voice. But he did seem genuinely happy.

"How are you doing?" I asked him.

"Overall, pretty well," he said. "When I got out of the joint in Covington, a cousin of mine let me stay with him until I could get my own place. I got a job working at a hamburger joint. It wasn't much of a job at first, but it was work, and not everyone will hire an ex-convict. My plan was to work here for Crystal Burgers in Covington while I looked for something better. As things turned out, our manager likes me. He's encouraged me to stay and work my way up the ladder. He's an older guy, and he plans to retire in a couple of years. He says he'll teach me the ropes and that I can probably take his position as manager at Crystal Burgers when he leaves. He says he'll recommend me to his boss."

"That sounds great," I told him. "I always noticed that you were good at providing food for the rest of us. You always had your locker filled with zu zus and wham whams."

"Damn," Dale said. "That phrase brings back a lot of memories. 'Zu zus and wham whams.' I haven't heard anybody talk about zu zus and wham whams since I got out."

"That's what got that whole strike started," I said. "Zu zus, wham whams, and you."

"That's a good memory," he said. "It's funny that one of my best memories comes from my time in the joint. I think I respect myself more now than I did before I went to prison. You'd think it would be the other way around, but for me it isn't."

"I feel the same way," I said. "That strike changed how I see a lot of things, even though it only lasted eight days. I still think about it a lot. I left prison believing that if I could resist injustice behind bars, I could resist it anywhere."

"It was a turning point for me too," he said. "It's strange, but when I think back to Lompoc, it seems to me that strike was my first step toward a better life. Something happened to me there in the Hole."

He asked me what I was up to, and I told him that I was hoping to continue in graduate school at UCLA, probably American literature.

"I think I know more about the U.S. now than I did before my time at Lompoc," I told him. "Prison has a way of clarifying things, cutting through a lot of superficial crap."

We chatted for a few minutes more—memories from Lompoc—and then hung up, promising to stay in touch.

That was the last I ever heard from Dale Hartman. I have no idea if what he was telling me was true or if he was just telling me what he thought I wanted to hear. He was a disembodied voice from the past, connected to nothing more than memories. I like to think of him working as the manager of Crystal Burgers in Covington, Kentucky, married to the woman he'd been dating when we spoke, Julie O'Leary, with two or three children by now, maybe even grandchildren. I tried to reach him the Christmas after he called, but the number he gave me had been disconnected.

I saw Crow twice after we got out. I was released from McNeil Island near the end of January 1970, having served a little over nine months; Crow was released from Lompoc in April 1970, having served four years for possession of marijuana with intent to sell. Crow called my parents' home in Portland right after he got out and asked my father to let me know that he could be reached at his mother's house in Los Angeles. He planned to stay there until he got back on his feet. My father told Crow that I was in graduate school at UCLA now and that he would pass his message along to me.

I called Crow the day after my father gave me his mother's phone number. I was eager to see him, I said, but I had a paper coming due on Friday and needed to finish it. Could we get together that Saturday to catch up? Before we hung up, we gave each other an update. At one point, I asked him how Big Frank was. "You didn't hear?" he said. "Frank's back inside. He's in County Jail down in San Diego, doing six months."

"So soon?" I asked. "He just got out! What happened?"

"He was doing pretty good for a while. Got a job as a night watchman at a furniture warehouse. He worked the graveyard shift from midnight till eight, slept most of the day and hung out with his friends at night."

"What did they bust him for?" I asked.

"Weed," said Crow. "He had about four ounces on him when he and a buddy were pulled over by a cop."

"What were they pulled over for?" I asked.

"For nothing. For being two brothers in a car driving through a white neighborhood. The cop thought they 'looked suspicious.'"

"Damn," I said. "Some things just don't seem to change." I had planned to take Big Frank and Crow up to Pauley Pavilion to play some basketball, just for old time's sake. I didn't realize quite how much I was looking forward to doing that until Crow told me that Frank was locked up again.

"You been playing any hoop since you got out?" I asked him.

"A little," he said.

"How'd you like to play a little pickup ball in Pauley Pavilion, home of the UCLA Bruins?"

There was silence at the other end of the line. A long pause. "They'll let me play in there?" he asked, incredulously.

"Sure," I told him. "There's a regular game that starts about 11:30 and ends about 1:00. It's half-court, four on four, just like we used to play at Lompoc. If you can meet me at my place in Venice this Saturday, I'll drive us up to campus and we can play some ball and get some lunch afterwards. They'll let you into Pauley as my guest."

"Sounds cool to me," he said.

§

That Saturday Crow got to my apartment a few minutes after eleven. He didn't seem to have changed at all except that now he was wearing a navy blue Adidas warm-up suit and what looked like a new pair of Adidas basketball shoes. Same old Crow. Same old smile.

"Hey, man, it's good to see you," I said. "Come on in and check out my place. It's not much, but it's home for the time being."

He looked around my apartment, quickly sizing things up. "You sure do have a lot of books," he said. "A lot of books and no music, no records."

"I've got to put the books first," I said. "The tools of the trade. You want something to drink before we go? I've got some coke and some lemonade."

"No thanks," he said. "I'm good."

"All right," I said. "We might as well head up to campus. If we leave now, we can get into the first or second game. We won't have to wait too long."

"Hold up," he said. "Hold up. There's one last thing I got to check out before we go."

"What's that?"

"I got to check your closet," he said.

I laughed because I knew what was coming. He walked over to the small closet in my bedroom and pushed open the sliding door. He smiled when he saw the pair of black Florsheim wingtips next to the worn pair of Penney's work boots on the floor of the closet.

"I'll be damned," he said. "You really did get yourself some Florsheim's. I got to let Frank and Bubba know."

We got into the old Studebaker Lark that I was still driving and took the 405 freeway north up to Westwood and the UCLA campus. I don't know for sure, but I suspect that Crow had never been on a college campus before. He looked around at the buildings, the statues on the beautifully manicured lawns, and the nicely dressed co-eds as they passed by.

We walked down the concrete steps that lead into Pauley Pavilion. As we walked through the doors that open onto the main court, I saw Crow's eyes widen.

"It's just like it looks on TV," he said. "New, this is a dream come true. I never dreamed I would play basketball in Pauley Pavilion. A dream come true."

"For me, too," I said. "Ever since I got out, I've wanted to get you, Frank, Foots, and me together to play some ball in Pauley. Someday I'd like the four of us to take on all comers, just the way we used to at Lompoc."

We played for about two hours. I was ready to leave sooner, but Crow was clearly having such a good time that I didn't want to cut it short. Games were to eleven, one point per basket. We had one run where we won five games in a row and finally lost to a team that had a very good big man. When we lost, we sat on the sidelines, talking and waiting for our next turn.

"You got any kind of job prospects?" I asked him, remembering the conversations we had had at Lompoc.

"I got a few things I'm looking into," he said.

"What kinds of things are you looking into?" I asked him.

He immediately looked down at the wooden floor of the gym, avoiding any eye contact. Clearly, he didn't want to give me any specific details. This made me uneasy, but I knew better than to press him.

"I don't want to see you back in the joint like Big Frank," I said to him. "You have a lot of years ahead of you. Find some good, legal way to earn a living and work your way up."

Epilogue

Kareem Abdul-Jabbar (then Lew Alcindor) plays offense in UCLA basketball varsity-frosh game, Pauley Pavilion, November 27, 1966. Abdul-Jabbar would go on to become not only a basketball legend but a fierce, fearless activist for social and racial justice. He was an early and outspoken opponent of American involvement in Vietnam, the only college athlete to attend the 1967 Cleveland Summit of Black athletes supporting Muhammad Ali's refusal to be drafted. Photo: Los Angeles Times *Photographic Archive, UCLA Library Special Collections. Licensed under a Creative Commons Attribution 4.0 International License.*

"You just don't get it, New," he scoffed, shaking his head, a pained expression on his face. "I told you all this before, down at Lompoc. I got things I got to have, and they cost money, more money than I can make pushing a broom or selling something. Car, clothes, a nice pad, a good stereo. I got to have them things if I want to have any kind of life."

"Just don't do something that's going to get you busted and sent back to the joint," I said.

"A man's got to do what a man's got to do," he said.

Just then, the game ahead of us ended and it was our turn to play again. Crow had a shorter man guarding him, so we worked the ball around until we could get it to him inside. Crow scored over his man, practically at will. I think he had seven of our eleven baskets in that game. I could tell he was feeling good. That's how I like to remember him—shooting the lights out and walking off the court at Pauley Pavilion with that big smile on his face.

"That's it for me, New," he said. "I like to go out on top."

"Let's find something to eat," I said. "Lunch is on me." I drove to a popular hamburger stand on Lincoln Boulevard near where I lived and pulled into an empty parking spot.

I was worried; I was pretty sure I knew what Crow was contemplating. About a fifth of the men incarcerated in the U.S. are there for some sort of drug-related offense. The prison system is prime recruiting ground for drug dealers. The big dogs who make most of the money are the guys at the top of the food chain. They offer young convicts like Crow and Frank what seems like a huge amount of money for a few hours of work. The young guys take nearly all the risk, transporting drugs from one location to another, but they're happy because they can make a couple thousand dollars in an afternoon. The big dogs are happy because they make their money without taking any significant risk. When one of their runners gets caught, they simply hire another one to take the same risk. There are very few snitches in this business, because snitches tend to wind up badly beaten or dead, sometimes along with their friends or even family members.

"Dealers don't play no games," I remember Big Frank saying one day. "They don't play no games at all."

"Tell me you're not going to get involved in some drug deal," I said, after we got our food and found an empty table.

"Like I told you, New," he said, "a man's got to do what a man's got to do."

"Don't you like being out on the streets?" I asked him. "Don't you want to stay out of the fucking joint? Doesn't that matter to you at all?"

"Like I already told you, doing time is just part of the deal," he said.

"To you and Foots, the joint seemed like a big deal. You all had never been in prison before. To Frank and me, it ain't no big thing. It's just part of the deal. You got to play the hand you're dealt. Out here on the streets, you feel free, but I don't. It's like I'm still on lockdown. You understand what I'm saying. Ain't no way they let me play basketball in no Pauley Pavilion unless you get me in. Can you see that? I'm locked out of your world and most of what's in it. Do you understand what I'm saying?"

Neither one of us was happy with the way this conversation was going, so we just shifted to other topics. The Lakers. The Celtics. The Dodgers. Women. Cars. After a while it was time to go.

"Let me give you something for lunch," he said, as we stood up to leave.

"This one's on me, Crow," I said. "I've been thinking about this day for a long time. I was hoping that Big Frank would be here too if he happened to be visiting L.A. Buying lunch is the least I can do to pay you back for what you guys did for me at Lompoc."

"What does that mean?" said Crow. "I didn't do nothing for you. We was just some guys doing time together."

"That's not true," I said. "You, Frank, and Bubba all taught me a lot about doing time. Things to do and things not to do. You kept me out of a lot of trouble I could have gotten into. After Foots and I started to play hoop with the brothers, not a single person, Black, White, or Latino, bothered either one of us. That wasn't my world in there. I was a fish out of water. I didn't know the ropes. Just hanging out with you and Frank and some of the other brothers kept Foots and me out of trouble."

I've always been glad I said that to Crow that day. I'm glad I thanked him for what he and Frank had done for me when I was dropped briefly into a world they understood far better than I did. What I didn't say to him was how frustrated I felt about not being able to reciprocate and provide him some support now that he had been released to the streets. I drove him to a bus stop on Wilshire Boulevard where he could catch a bus that would take him back to south Los Angeles where his mother lived. I offered to drive him to his mother's house, but he turned down the offer.

"You get back to the books, New," he said. "That's your business. I got to take care of my own business now."

§

We agreed to get together to play basketball again in three or four weeks. Fridays or Saturdays were the best days for both of us, but he didn't call for the next four weeks. I didn't think anything of it, because I had my hands full with my own graduate courses and teaching my section of English 1—English Composition for frosh. One Saturday evening the phone rang at a little after midnight.

"Hello," I said, wondering who would call that late.

"New," I heard a voice say. "I'm in trouble. If I don't give them some money in two days, they say they're going to kill me. I need some help."

It was Crow, and I could tell from the tone of his voice that he really was in trouble. He sounded scared. Really scared.

"Who's threatening you?" I asked him.

"Some guys I owe some money to," he said.

"How much do you need?" I asked him. "I'm only working half-time as a teaching assistant right now, but I can get you something." TAs at UCLA in those days were paid about $7,500 per year for teaching three sections of English Composition, one class each quarter. That, and a student loan, enabled me to scrape by.

"I know you don't have much," Crow said. "I could tell that from the pad you're living in, but if you could loan me a hundred dollars, I think I know where I can get the rest."

"How much do you owe them?" I asked. "What's the total?"

"You don't want to know," said Crow.

Even though money was tight for me in those days, I didn't hesitate at all when Crow asked for the hundred dollars. I felt that I owed him more than that much for helping me to stay afloat at Lompoc. I did, however, worry about what might come next. I was pretty sure that whoever Crow owed money to was involved, one way or another, with drugs. I didn't want any drug dealers to know where I lived or to have any contact at all with a young woman I was going out with at the time.

Crow and Big Frank had told me on numerous occasions that "players don't have no real friends" and that "sometimes you just do what you have to do to survive." I also remembered a specific point that Crow made more than once during our conversations out in the yard at Lompoc. "If I'm in your car, New, and I have some drugs with me, say some weed or some heroin, and the cops pull us over for one reason or another, it's *your stuff*, not mine. I'll swear up and down on my mother's life that I never saw that stuff before, that it's your stuff, and that it was in the car when I got into it. Don't you never forget that New. Real players have people they hang out with, but they have very few true friends."

All these thoughts flashed through my mind while I was talking to Crow on the phone. I wanted to help him out of trouble if I could, but I did not want to be connected in any way to the people he was dealing with.

The next day, Crow was waiting for me near the entrance to the Wilshire Branch of Security Pacific Bank. He was wearing the same dark blue warm up suit he wore the day we played ball in Pauley Pavilion. It made me wonder what I'd find if I went to his mother's house where he was staying and checked out the contents of *his* closet. I began to suspect that all his and Bubba's talk about lizard skin shoes and Armani suits was more aspirational than real.

"What's happening, New?" he said as I was getting out of my car. "Thanks for coming. I've got myself into some deep shit."

"No problem," I said. "I'm happy to loan you a hundred. I'm living on a fixed budget right now, but a hundred's not a problem. I wish I had more, but I don't."

"That's cool," he said. "That's really cool. I'll get it back to you in two weeks. Two weeks from today. You can count on that."

I went into the bank and withdrew one hundred dollars in twenty-dollar bills. When I walked back outside, I took a quick look around, just to see if we were being watched or if Crow was being followed by anyone. I didn't see anyone who looked out of place to me, so I handed him the money. Crow took the money from me and quickly put it into his pocket. He looked tired that day, real tired. There were dark circles under his eyes that weren't there the last time I had seen him, and he looked as though he had lost some weight. There was none of the bravado or confidence in his manner that had caused him to stand out at Lompoc.

"This means a lot to me, New," he said. "I can't tell you how much this means to me. I'll get this back to you in two weeks. You can count on that."

We shook hands, the soul shake that was popular in those days. Then he turned and walked down Wilshire toward the bus stop, and I went back to my car and spent the rest of the day in the English Department Reading Room at UCLA.

Two weeks came and went, but I heard nothing from Crow. I thought about the situation long and hard, wondering what I could do to help him out of whatever sort of jam he was in. I decided that if he contacted me to repay the money I had loaned him, I'd try one more time to persuade him to get a job doing something legal so that he could stay out of prison. Staying out of the joint had to be worth something to him. On the other hand, I made a firm decision to "cut him loose" (one of his favorite phrases) if it became clear that he was involved in some way with drugs and drug dealers.

The days turned into weeks, and I heard nothing from Crow. After five weeks passed, it became clear that he was not going to contact me. I wasn't worried about the money. As I said, I felt that I owed him more than a hundred dollars for helping me during a difficult and potentially dangerous time in my life. The fact is, I was feeling guilty and frustrated about not being able to do *more* to help him. He wasn't perfect, but he was an essentially decent human being who appeared to be drowning, and I didn't seem to be able to throw him a lifeline.

I tried to reach him at his mother's house. A woman answered at the other end—Crow's mother, I assumed.

"Could I speak to Richard, please," I asked her. "Richard" was Crow's given name, but no one I knew ever called him that.

"May I ask who is calling?" said the voice at the other end.

"I'm a friend of his," I said. "My name is Eric Newhall. We play basketball together."

"Are you that White boy he played ball with the other day up at UCLA?"

"Yes, that's right," I said. "I'm calling to see if he wants to get together to play some more basketball."

At this point the voice at the other end started to sob uncontrollably. I braced myself for bad news.

"I guess you haven't heard," she said. "Richard is gone. They shot him two weeks ago. They drove by in a car and shot him down while he was taking out the trash. They didn't even stop. Just drove off into the night and left him lying dead in the driveway."

I was shocked when I heard this, but not entirely surprised. "I am so sorry, Mrs. Washington," I said. "I learned a lot from Crow. Will there be some sort of memorial service? I'd like to attend if there is."

"Thank you," she said, "but the funeral was last Friday. No one came but just our family. I guess everyone else was afraid of the drug dealers who shot him. Can't say as I blame them."

"I'm so sorry, Mrs. Washington. I liked your son a lot. He deserved better in this world."

"Thank you for your thoughts, Eric. I appreciate your call. Best of luck to you."

And that was it. Crow was gone. Just like that. His life thrown away, wasted. He had no voice, and he made very little noise when he disappeared. He is the only friend I've ever had who was shot dead in the street. And when I ask myself who or what was responsible for his being incarcerated and for his death, I can't come up with any easy answers.

Some people would say that Crow made a number of bad decisions in his life and got what he deserved for becoming involved with drug dealers. That's too simple. To a great degree, Crow was the victim of a system and circumstances he did not create. For too many of us, it's politically expedient to blame the victim rather than acknowledging that something is terribly wrong with our society's values and priorities. There are literally hundreds of thousands of young Black and Latino men like Crow incarcerated or on parole in the United States today. We are the richest country in the world, yet we incarcerate a higher percentage of our citizens (particularly young Black and Latino men) than any other nation in the world—including South Africa, China, and the former Soviet Union. The numbers are simply staggering, and they suggest that what has come to be called "the school-to-prison pipeline" has replaced the overtly racist system of "Jim Crow" as a means of maintaining the color line without explicitly using race to do so.

§

Foots and I saw each other a few times in Portland after we were both released from McNeil Island late in January 1970. Since then, we've stayed in touch by phone and e-mail. The striking thing about my relationship with Foots is that we can go without talking for months, but when we make contact, it's as though no time has passed at all.

After he was released, Dwight lived in Portland, Oregon, for twenty years, working with his wife, Peggy Ball, to improve wages and working conditions in canning factories. He has remained active in the anti-war movement and the civil rights movement. In his thirties, he went to night school to study computer science. He worked as a computer programmer, then started his own computer consulting business in 1989. In his mid-seventies, Dwight is still working part-time at his computer business.

In many ways, our lives have been quite different, but beneath these superficial differences, Foots and I share several important similarities. Both of us grew up "behind the color line," so to speak, in all–White environments, and both of us recognize today the long-term damage caused by America's persistent de facto segregation of schools and neighborhoods. Our time at Lompoc taught both of us, at an early age, how those in power use race to divide people against each other, blinding us to our common needs and interests. We both know what it feels like to be caged and controlled by those in power, authorities who are indifferent to the well-being of their prisoners. We both took part in the strike at Lompoc and were thrown into the Hole, where we experienced eight days of solidarity that changed both of us forever.

In addition, both of us married smart, strong-willed women of color. Peggy was a member of the Klamath tribe. After she passed away in 2015, Dwight married Elizabeth Woody, an enrolled member of the Warm Spring Tribe, former Poet Laureate of Oregon, and current executive director of the Museum at Warm Springs. Foots and I are part of mixed-race couples and parents of mixed-race children. Both of us have struggled to deal with complicated racial dynamics that many White people never encounter, let alone understand. In a very real way, Du Bois's color line cuts through our lives, damaging everyone on both sides of the line, albeit in different ways.

Dwight Morrill and Elizabeth Woody at their wedding on the Warm Springs Indian Reservation, North-Central Oregon, 2021. *Courtesy Dwight Morrill; used by permission.*

For my part, I've dealt better with the issue of race in my professional life than I have with the racial tensions that have strained relations between Angela and me, and between us and my family of origin, throughout our marriage.

I remember sitting in the yard at Lompoc one warm Saturday afternoon in July, talking with our little group of "hippies" about what we planned to do when we got out of the joint. At the time I really wasn't sure, but when Little John asked me what I planned to do, I remember telling him and the others that most likely I'd go on to graduate school and try to find a job teaching American literature at a college or university. I can still see the look of amazed disbelief on Cohen's face when I said this.

"You've got to be shitting me," he said. "To me that seems like going from one prison to another. Why on earth would you want to go back to school?"

"I don't think schools have to be like prisons," I told Cohen and the others. "I don't think it makes sense to pick up a gun and start shooting people whose political views are different from mine. I don't think the revolution is at hand or even close to being at hand. And I also don't think it makes sense to passively accept things as they are now. Things need to change. The situation seems to call for consciousness raising. Education is simply consciousness raising by another name. We need to reach people who aren't already part of the choir. Schools are a good place to provide young people with a vision of what a democratic society should look like. That's what I want to do when I get out."

It took me from 1971 until 1975 to complete a Ph.D. in American literature at UCLA. My dissertation was entitled *Prisons and Prisoners in the Works of William Faulkner*, a topic that had its roots in my time at Lompoc. While reading Faulkner in prison I noticed how frequently prisoners and prisons appear in his novels. Some of Faulkner's prisoners are literally imprisoned (slaves, convicts, Blacks under Jim Crow), and others are prisoners of civilization and the limiting forces of their imperfect culture. Faulkner loved freedom; he saw humanity as struggling to break free from tethers of different kinds (racial, sexual, economic, historical, the passage of time).

I've taught in the English Department at Occidental College

Eric Newhall in his early years on the faculty at Occidental College, circa 1975. *Photo: Joe Friezer. © Occidental College. Courtesy Special Collections and College Archives, Mary Norton Clapp Library, Occidental College.*

since I finished graduate school—a forty-four-year career teaching modern and contemporary American literature. Reflecting on those forty-four years today, it strikes me that I still owe Crow, Bubba, and Big Frank. Every time I walk onto campus, I remember the promise I made to them at Lompoc to "bring a few brothers and sisters" into any school that hired me. For the last forty-four years, I've tried to repay these debts by working with my faculty colleagues and some supportive administrators to democratize the student body, the faculty, the administration, and the curriculum at Occidental College.

When I was a student at Occidental from 1963 to 1967, there were no Blacks or Latinos on the faculty. None. There was one Asian professor, who taught Asian Philosophy and Religion, but that was it for faculty of color. As an English major, I was never required to read a single work by an author of color, and I was assigned only five or six titles by women: Emily Dickinson, Edith Wharton, Emily and Charlotte Brontë, a few others. The curriculum was very traditional, canonical in its coverage of Western Civilization but utterly indifferent to the cultural contributions of Africa, Latin America, and all of Asia. The student body was homogenous, overwhelmingly White with a sprinkling of Black and Asian students. The Latinos in my graduating class (400 students) in 1967 could be counted on the fingers of two hands.

Eric Newhall lecturing at Occidental College, 1978. *Photo: Joe Friezer.* © *Occidental College. Courtesy Special Collections and College Archives, Mary Norton Clapp Library, Occidental College.*

Anti-apartheid rally calling for Occidental College to divest from all South African investments, February 18, 1981. Students listen to anti-apartheid activist and exiled South African Tim Ngubeni speaking outside the Arthur J. Coons Administration Building, where the Board of Trustees was meeting. Barack Obama, then a student at Oxy, spoke briefly at this rally. *Photo: Thomas Grauman;* © *Thomas Grauman. Courtesy Thomas Grauman.*

I wish I could take Crow, Bubba, and Big Frank around our campus today and show them how things have changed since I did time with them at Lompoc. I'd like them to see that we've added programs in Asian Studies, Black Studies, and Latino Studies to our curriculum. I'd like to tell them that I was on the selection committee that chose Dr. John Slaughter to become the first African-American president of Occidental College. I'd like to tell them that in 1998 *U.S. News and World Report* ranked Occidental College #1 for Diversity among small, liberal arts colleges in the United States. I'd like to tell them that a group of faculty and enlightened administrators created a summer transition program for underrepresented, first year-students that started in 1987 and is still going strong today.

I'd like to tell them that Julian Bond visited my seminar on the 1960s and talked with my students about the early days of SNCC and that I had the honor of introducing Harry Belafonte on the stage in Thorn Hall where Martin Luther King had spoken thirty years earlier. I'd tell them, too, that the first Black president of the United States attended Occidental for two years at the end of the seventies and the beginning of the eighties before he transferred to Columbia University and that I was the faculty speaker at the anti-apartheid rally when future President Obama made his first public, political address. I'd like to be able to tell Crow, Bubba, and Big Frank all these things and to show them that I tried to keep the promise I made so long ago at Lompoc to "bring a little color," a little equity, into Occidental College, but I can't, because Crow is dead, and I've lost touch with Bubba and Big Frank.

Occidental College President John Slaughter and Eric Newhall shake hands at Newhall's retirement party, June 2019. Newhall's spouse, Jacki Rodriguez (in foreground), looks on. *Photo: Marc Campos.* © *Occidental College; used by permission.*

Epilogue

§

One of the sad ironies of my life is that although in my youth I was able to play a small role in bringing temporary peace and solidarity to a group of racially mixed convicts who disliked and distrusted each other, in recent years I haven't been able to bring together the members of my own family—Angela, Cristin, and my youngest daughter Toni—and my four siblings and their spouses and children.

All of us have been caught up in a complex dynamic involving race, class, and strong individual personalities that no one, myself very much included, has been able to navigate. I've come to believe that my family's struggle to deal with the problem of the color line is essentially a microcosm of America's current struggle. Our failures mirror America's failures. I see our estrangement and unraveling as the result of a collective failure. For the last ten years, Angela and I have been estranged from my siblings and their families. We, like the America we live in, have become a house divided.

Why, you may be wondering, would I sour an uplifting prison story about racial solidarity by discussing racial difficulties and tension within my own relatively progressive family? Why not describe the eight beautiful days of community that developed in the Hole at Lompoc during the strike and conclude my narrative on that uplifting note?

Because that would be too easy, not to mention self-serving, and, most important, simply not true to the tangled intractability of racism in the United States today. My family's current estrangement, painful as it is, needs to be part of this story about resisting the problem of the color line, because it's part of the American story and typical, I think, of the difficulties millions of Americans are struggling with today.

The difficulties Angela and I have encountered with my siblings remind me constantly that racism is more complex, more deeply rooted in our culture, and far more difficult to eliminate than most of us realize. My siblings and I recognize *overt* racism (hate crimes, racial discrimination, racial slurs) when we see it, and we repudiate it. But we have difficulty, along with most White people in the United States, recognizing and acknowledging the destructive power of *systemic* and *covert* racism—and, crucially, the way they've shaped us, sown the seeds of unconscious bias.

§

It's difficult to point to a single key incident or explosive moment when things began to go downhill for my family—when estrangement began to set in. What I remember instead is a long series of awkward encounters and uneasy conversations—"micro-incidents"—that took place over a period of about fifteen years—multiple moments and situations when "the pieces just didn't quite fit."

One incident does stand out, however—a moment that's never stopped reverberating in my mind. The spark that lit the fuse was a question Angela raised on Thanksgiving in 2003, thirteen years into our marriage and three years after my parents had passed away.

Mark and Rebecca had invited the entire family to have Thanksgiving dinner at their house that year. My sister, Sally, was unable to take time off from her job in D.C., but Helen, Matt, Mark, and I were there, along with our families. Mark had done a masterful job of carving the turkey, and everyone was passing dishes of stuffing, mashed potatoes, salad, green beans, and cranberry sauce around the table. The conversation skipped around from topic to topic, covering everything from *Scooby Doo* and *My Little Pony* to immigration reform (Matt is an immigration lawyer) and the second Gulf War.

Eventually, my siblings and I began to reminisce about growing up in southwest Portland. Angela sat silently, listening while Helen, Matt, Mark, and I exchanged fond memories from our youth. After listening for a while, Angela, very quietly, raised a question that cuts, I think, to the heart of the racial issues that our country is struggling to resolve today.

"Why did your parents buy a house in a part of Portland that was virtually all White?" she asked. "Why didn't they look for a more diverse neighborhood?"

"They didn't really choose their house that first year in Portland," I reminded her. "Their first year in Portland they were provided a college-owned house at a below-market rent that was available because another faculty member was on sabbatical leave in France. My parents made good friends that first year in that neighborhood, and so did all their children. In most ways, the neighborhood was a good fit for our family. I don't hold it against my parents that they bought a house that they could afford on one salary in a neighborhood that offered so many good things for their family."

"I get it," Angela said. "As a parent, I can understand your parents' desire to buy a house in a neighborhood they already liked that would not force their children to change schools two times in two years. What I don't understand is how we'll ever be able to integrate our public schools if our neighborhoods remain segregated. How can children of different races learn about each other and learn to get along and work together if they live in segregated neighborhoods and go to segregated schools?" Slowly, Angela looked around the table, her gaze level. "Do any of you see a solution to this problem?"

Conflict-averse by nature, my two brothers, Matt, and Mark, simply retreated into their shells and clammed up. They piled more cranberry dressing onto their turkey and kept their eyes riveted to their plates. My sister, Helen, on the other hand, bristled visibly. I said nothing beyond what I'd already said. I thought the question Angela raised, although uncomfortable, was a legitimate question and deserved a serious answer from my siblings.

Angela's experiences growing up in predominantly Latino East Los Angeles differed significantly from my early years in Portland, Oregon. Her perspective on all-White neighborhoods and what they reflect about American society and by extension, the Newhall family, is illuminating and challenging—and indispensable, if we're going to grope our way forward. I don't fault my siblings for defending a decision our parents made long ago in historical circumstances that were significantly different from today's social landscape. But I do fault them for avoiding her questions rather than responding to them thoughtfully, painful as that might have been. Instead, they tacitly declared the topic she raised off-limits, taboo.

That painful, truncated conversation over Thanksgiving dinner embodies the problem our family continues to struggle with today. Angela is the mother of two mixed-race children, defending her children against racism and potential exclusion from the all-White neighborhoods they may encounter in the future. My siblings, on the other hand, are adult, White children of parents they've always seen as enlightened for their times, defending their parents' honor and the integrity of the Newhall family past.

No one in my family of origin has ever, to the best of my knowledge, been guilty of an act of overt racism. One of my brothers had a Black roommate for his first two years of college and spent his junior year studying abroad in Ghana. In the early 1960s, my mother was a member of the Portland chapter of the Student Non-Violent Coordinating Committee (SNCC) until that organization voted in 1966 to remove all Whites. My father, as I've already mentioned, introduced me to the civil rights movement, took me to my first picket line and gave me my initial understanding of non-violent social change. One of my sisters worked in Washington, D.C., as the head of an organization that supports incipient democratic movements around the world. My other sister moved to Mississippi to take a job with ACORN (The Association of Community Organizations for Reform Now), organizing in predominantly Black neighborhoods; this same sister has had long-term relationships with men of color. One of my brothers had a Black roommate for his first two years of college and spent his junior year studying abroad in Ghana.

Simply put, my siblings and I were not raised in a family that encouraged or even tolerated racist behavior. On the contrary, we were encouraged by our parents to defend marginalized people and to speak out against injustice and bigotry whenever we encountered it.

Nonetheless, we're the products of a time and a place, and of an America riven by the color line. In recent years, I've thought a great deal about the whiteness of the social world of my childhood and youth. It was ubiquitous, blinding, and limiting.

When I was growing up, our neighborhood in Portland seemed like a wonderful neighborhood. Is there something wrong with acknowledging that, even celebrating its positive qualities? Or was there something cancerous about its de facto segregation, not only for American society but also for my family of origin and me personally? If so, what was the nature of that evil? And who was responsible for it? To what extent were my parents, through their decision to live in a Whites-only enclave with nice lawns and white picket fences and no Blacks welcomed, part of the problem, as Angela's question implied? Weren't they just a young faculty couple with very little money trying their best to make a home for themselves and their children? Should they have bought a house in another, more integrated part of Portland? Were we all complicit with something we didn't fully understand or even think about at the time? Are anyone's hands ever entirely clean?

It bothers me when Angela suggests that my parents were complicit with segregation, because I know that segregation is wrong. It bothers me when she looks through my high school yearbooks and comments on the total absence of Black and Latino faces. Two of my siblings have told me they think Angela is "overly sensitive."

What does that even mean? How is it possible to be "too sensitive" to social injustice and systemic racism? What is the right amount of sensitivity? Where should we draw the line? And who is protected—and who harmed—by silence and the failure to raise and discuss difficult questions about racial issues? Times were different when my siblings and I were growing up in the suburbs of Portland. The U.S. was Whiter then than it is today. Relatively few Whites had close relationships with people of color. Our ability to empathize with people of different backgrounds was limited by our insulated cultural experiences.

I can't ask my parents if they ever considered buying a house in another, more diverse part of Portland, because they're gone. I don't think it's disrespectful or wrong to raise serious questions about our tendency to wage costly wars abroad and our disinclination to wage a war on poverty and racism here at home. More to the point, I understand why Angela feels compelled to raise such questions. In fact, her willingness to do just that is one of the things I respect most about her.

Epilogue

§

In his *Autobiography*, Malcolm X describes a young White co-ed who is so inspired by one of his speeches that she follows him from her college in New England to New York and approaches him in a restaurant. She asks him what she can do to improve relations between the races in the United States. Malcolm answers her question succinctly: "nothing." Later, he reflects on his response and says that if he had it to do over again, he would give her a different answer. He should have told her, he concludes, to go home and work in her own community. "That's where the racial problem in America resides," he tells us. "Not in the Black community, but in the White community."

What the United States needs today is more cultural understanding and empathy, particularly on the part of White people who continue to have most of the power, money, and influence. Malcolm X was right: the root of the problem lies in White families and in White communities. If we are ever to solve the problem of the color line, White families (like mine) and communities must be willing to recognize that the primary burden for creating change is theirs.

On several different occasions over the years, over breakfast, lunch, or coffee, Angela and I have tried to talk with my siblings about this problem that is tearing our family apart, but my siblings resist the subject. After they leave, Angela tells me that "Race is the elephant in the room. It's the color line, and they are too uneasy to talk about it. Their white privilege allows them to disengage when they feel uncomfortable. I'm a Chicana every day. I can't ever disengage."

§

I don't want to make it sound as if I'm immune to the unconscious biases and cultural blind spots I see in my siblings. I was conditioned and socialized by the same parents, neighborhood, schools, teachers, peers, media, and dominant culture. We are all the products, even the victims, of our social conditioning.

As a result, I've been complicit in accepting and rationalizing my own White privilege, the same privilege I now recognize in my siblings' behavior. I was slow to recognize the residual White privilege they are unconsciously clinging to because much of my early social conditioning was the same as theirs. Much of this conditioning was, in fact, profoundly positive—my mother's commitment to public schools, my father's civil rights and anti-war activism—but some of it was subtly, unconsciously, biased in that it still assumed a central and privileged position for Whites in our extended family structures.

In my family of origin, unconscious bias (a softer name for White privilege) generally takes two related forms: first, White family members feel free to disengage from conversations about race that cause them to feel threatened or uncomfortable, and second, White family members feel free to declare certain questions or topics—especially those that cut too close to the bone of our role, as White people, in the perpetuation of racism and racial injustice—to be off limits or taboo.

This is a difficult and painful discovery for a man to make relatively late in his life. My siblings feel that I have turned my back on them and my parents. Conversely, I now see that my inability to recognize the "unconscious bias" in my siblings *and* myself left Angela feeling at least partially isolated and less than fully supported for over fifteen years of our marriage.

I see no villains in this narrative, just an American family struggling to come to terms with what William Faulkner called "the complex truths of the human heart in conflict with itself." No one should feel ashamed of having unconscious biases; given the level of racism and misogyny present in the United States today, it would be difficult if not impossible to come of age without absorbing some level of racial and gender bias from the culture around us. The question we must confront as individuals and as a society is what to *do* about our biases once we discover that we have them.

§

I was born in 1945, the year World War II ended. Today, I can see that I've lived my entire life in the middle of an ongoing struggle between two large groups of people. One group wishes to transform our country into the real democracy promised by our Constitution; the other group wishes to defer real democracy for as long as possible—ideally, in their view, forever.

In whatever time I have left, I plan to support efforts to achieve real democracy—political, social, economic—in the United States. If we can't integrate our neighborhoods and schools, we will never be able to attain the ease and familiarity required to collaborate with people of different races and cultures in our country and around the globe to save our planet from climate change. The stakes are higher today than they were when I was young. Today, if we cannot learn to work cooperatively with people from cultures and races other than our own, it is not clear that our planet will survive.

How can our country move beyond our current division to some better and more united future? One thing I know with certainty: the first step must be to face our dysfunction directly and talk about it honestly. We've never had that uncomfortable conversation; we've been avoiding it for years.

When I have the words and the time is right, that's what I'm going to say to my brothers and sisters. We need to confront the color line. Our parents were great parents in most ways, but they weren't perfect. Our neighborhood was an excellent neighborhood in most respects, but it wasn't perfect; its homogeneity offered very little opportunity for children to develop the cultural dexterity they need to create a flourishing, egalitarian, multiracial democracy. To come together as a family and as a nation, we must be able to confront and discuss the imperfections of those we love—and ourselves. Even as I say this, I remember James Baldwin's wisdom—and warning—in a 1962 essay he wrote for *The New York Times*: "Not everything that is faced can be changed, but nothing can be changed until it is faced."

§

These days I consider myself to be a "hopeful pessimist." Perhaps the pain my family of origin and Angela and I have felt for years is not simply needless or meaningless suffering. Perhaps our estrangement has been a step in some larger historical process of which we are all a part. "If there is no struggle, there is no progress," Frederick Douglass tells us in *Narrative of the Life of Frederick Douglass, an American Slave*. "Power concedes nothing without demand. It never did and never will." I've read those words to my students at Occidental College for the last forty-four years, and they are as true today as they were when Frederick Douglass wrote them in 1845.

In the summer of George Floyd's murder, millions rose up. Once again, protestors thronged the streets of the United States, calling for an end to systemic racism, police violence, mass incarceration, and White silence, shouting, "I can't breathe," "Get your knee off my neck," and "Black Lives Matter."

Angela and I joined one of the protests; we wanted to support the efforts of some local high school students who had organized the event. I was glad that she and I were in the street together, protesting racial violence. We were aligned. Her placard said, "Justice Now"; mine said, "End white Silence." It was a powerful moment of solidarity for us as a couple, and I began to feel that perhaps we were moving on to some "next phase" in our marriage.

The slogans people were shouting were different from what they

Eric Newhall moderates a panel, "Is Our Democracy in Danger?," during Occidental's annual Alumni Weekend. Held on October 23, 2021, the discussion included former California State Assemblyman (and Oxy alumnus) Hector De La Torre and L.A. mayoral candidate Karen Bass (who went on to win the election, becoming the second Black person—and the first woman—to hold that office). *Photo: Marc Campos. © Occidental College; used by permission.*

were in the 1960s, I noticed, but the goal of the protest was essentially the same—real democracy—the democracy that has been deferred my entire life. At one point, I caught a faint whiff of tear gas that the wind had blown in our direction from somewhere near the front of the demonstration. Instantly, the smell of the gas transported me back to the Hole at Lompoc, fifty years ago. Somehow, I had come full circle. What I began to suspect all those years ago I now know to be true: If you want a just society, you're going to have to fight for it; no one is going to hand it to you. If you want justice, your life will be a permanent struggle. This is not a particularly comforting conclusion, but it's the truth, and it will have to do—for now.

Suggestions for Further Reading

Alexander, Michelle. *The New Jim Crow: Mass Incarceration in the Age of Color Blindness.* New York: The New Press, 2010.
Branch, Taylor. *The King Years: Historic Moments in the Civil Rights Movement.* New York: Simon & Schuster, 2013.
DiAngelo, Robin. *White Fragility: Why It's So Hard for White People to Talk About Racism.* Boston: Beacon Press, 2018.
Douglass, Frederick. *Narrative of the Life of Frederick Douglass, an American Slave.* Boston, 1845.
Ehrhart, W.D. *Passing Time: Memoir of a Vietnam Veteran Against the War.* Jefferson, N.C.: McFarland, 1986.
Ehrhart, W.D. *What We Can and Can't Afford: Essays on Vietnam, Patriotism and American Life.* Jefferson, N.C.: McFarland, 2023.
Ellison, Ralph. *Invisible Man.* New York: Random House, 1952.
Faulkner, William. *Go Down, Moses.* New York: Random House, 1942.
Faulkner, William. *Intruder in the Dust.* New York: Random House, 1948.
Isserman, Maurice, and Michael Kazin. *America Divided: The Civil War of the 1960s.* New York and London: Oxford University Press, 2020.
Kendi, Ibram X. *How to Be an Antiracist.* New York: One World, 2019.
King, Martin Luther, Jr. *A Testament of Hope: The Essential Writings and Speeches.* San Francisco: Harper/San Francisco, 1991.
Lauter, Paul. *Our Sixties: An Activist's History.* Rochester: University of Rochester Press, 2020.
Malcolm X. *The Autobiography of Malcolm X: As Told to Alex Haley.* New York: Grove Press, 1965.
Marable, Manning. *Malcolm X: A Life of Reinvention.* New York: Penguin Books, 2011.
Morgan, Edward. *The 60's Experience: Hard Lessons About Modern America.* Philadelphia: Temple University Press, 1992.
Morrison, Toni. *Beloved.* New York: Random House, 1987.
Morrison, Toni. *Song of Solomon.* New York: Random House, 1977.
Nguyen, Viet Thanh. *The Sympathizer.* New York: Grove/Atlantic, 2015.
O'Brien, Tim. *The Things They Carried.* Boston: Houghton Mifflin, 1990.
Rampersad, Arnold. *Ralph Ellison: A Biography.* New York: Knopf, 2007.
Young, Marilyn Blatt. *The Vietnam Wars, 1945–1990.* New York: HarperCollins, 1991.

Index

Numbers in **_bold italics_** refer to illustrations

Abdul-Jabbar, Kareem **_193_**
abuse, domestic 43–44
ACORN 207
Adams 56–57, 60, 106; on inmate strike 62–63, 79, 135; on mail 56, 94; recruitment by 66; on slogan 95
Admission and Orientation (A & O) 48–50, 55–56, 59–60, 67–68
the *agora* 61
Alexander, Michelle 68
Ali, Muhammad 15, **_193_**
Alinsky, Saul 133–134
the American Dream 117, 120
Angela 117, 144, **_204_**; isolation 210; on segregation 206–207, 208; on White privilege 209; youth 207
Anzaldua, Gloria 50
apartheid, movement against **_203_**, 204
Art 98, 101, 108–109, 115
The Autobiography of Malcolm X 124–126, **_125_**, 129, 132–133

Baker, George L. **_6_**
Baldwin, James 211
Ball, Peggy 199
Barber, Tom 66, 68–71, 122, 158
basketball: in Eric's youth 7, 11; professional 80–81; race and 54–55, 71–72, 81–85
basketball games, interracial 82–85, 87–88, 90–92, 99, 109–110; fouls in 83–84, 90, 101; guards ending 84–85, 92–93; Native players joining 110–113; spectators 83, 85, 91–93, 99–100, 111, 112; tension in 130
Bass, Karen **_212_**
Belafonte, Harry 204
Belloni, Judge 30–31, 33–34, 181
"Beyond Vietnam: A Time to Break Silence" (King speech) 16–17
Big Frank 99–101, 110–112, 186; attempts to recruit 108, 126–127, 130; on drug dealing 194; on Dwight and Eric 144; in the Hole 174–176, 184; returning to prison 190–191; striking 145

"Bigfoot" *see* Morrill, Dwight
Billy Budd (Melville) 177
Black inmates: anger 61, 63; caseworker's warning about 87–88; demands shared with 144; guards frisking 131; helping Eric 117–118, 195; low riders assaulting 130; on police 93; recruiting 63, 66, 80, 108; returning to prison 118–120, 190–191, 194
Black Lives Matter 211–212
Blue 99–100
Bond, Julian 204
books *see* literature
"borderlands" 50
Bradford, Boss 121, 134, 136, 137–138
Breintnall 77, 145
Brittenden, Lewis 58, 79
Brown, Billy 49–50, 52, 105–106, 108
Bubba 96, 98; attempts to recruit 108, 126, 129; in basketball games 81–85, 88–94, 100, 109–113; and books 122–123, 133; demands circulated by 144; in E-Unit 115–120, 124; on the future 118–120; Native players and 110–113; on snitches 141; during strike 140, 141, 143–145, 176
bureaucratic policy 86–87

The Caine Mutiny 76
card games 38, 40, 41
Cash, Johnny 154, 169
Catch-22 (Heller) 158, 162, **_162_**, 165, 172
Celtics 8, 80–81, 116
Chuy 96–99, 101–102, 104–105, 184; attempts to recruit 108–109, 115, 129–130; on inmate strike 138–140; singing in the Hole 168
cigarettes 135, 138, 142, 144, 149, 189
civil disobedience 31
Civil Rights Act 16
civil rights movement 8–9, 10–11, 16, 199; and anti-war movement 17, 19; Eric's parents and 7–9, 207, 209; Faulkner on 136–137; *see also* King, Martin Luther, Jr.
climate change 210
Cohen 56–57, 70, 106; on education 201;

215

on inmate strike 134–135, 138, 145, 147; on organizing inmates 77–79, 95, 108; recruitment by 63–64, 66
colonialism 13, 15–16, 17
color line: breaking 83, 85; gaining knowledge of 117; in mixed-race families 199, 207, 209; White Americans facing 209; *see also* basketball games, interracial; racism
the Commissary 42
A Connecticut Yankee in King Arthur's Court (Twain) 69
conscientious objectors 20, 21
count time 53
crime partners 166
"crime workshop" 163
Crow 80–85, 88–92, 186; advice from 94; attempts to recruit 108, 126, 129; and Big Frank 99–101; on books 122–123, 124–126; and Chuy 98–99; demands circulated by 144, 145; on drug-dealing 194–195; Dwight given shoes by 90; in E-Unit 115–120; and Eric, re-connecting 190–195; Eric teased by 116, 183, 192; on the future 118–120; on guards' control 93; in the Hole 174–176; Native players and 110–113; during strike 140, 141, 143–145; on Surratt being detained 141; trash talking other players 100–101; in trouble 196–199
Curly 99, 101, 109–111, 113
Cutler, Big Mama 105–106, 150–152
Cyclops 92–93

David and Goliath 181
Dawkins 79
A Death in the Family (Agee) 69–70, **70**
De La Torre, Hector **212**
demands, list of 77–79, 141–142, 144, 145
democracy 114–115, 210–211
Democracy in America (de Tocqueville) 114
Denham 56–57, 60, 66, 69, 78, 145
de Tocqueville, Alexis 114
Dog 158–159, 169–170, 171–173, 177; attempt to recruit 77; on Eric and Dwight 183; on Harleys 72; as singer 154, 178; solidarity 184, 185; transfer 182–183; on work assignments 74–75
Dostoevsky, Fyodor 99
Douglass, Frederick 211
the draft 14, 16–17, 21–25
draft resisters: family responses 27–28; famous 15, **193**; mutual support 27; in prison 56, 59, 64, 67, 167–168; prison psychiatrist meeting 74; sentences of, shortened 181–182; and vets, solidarity between 166–168; *see also* hippies
drug dealing 194, 196, 198
Dusty 72, 79, 81, 145–147, 151–152

E-Unit 98, 107–109, 114–115; calls for strike 138–140, 145–147; conversations 115–118, 122–123, 124; as free space 114–115
easy time (good time) 63, 66–68, 76, 139–140, 160
education: as consciousness-raising 201; in prison 58, 86–87; purpose 17–18; vocational 79, 128, 177
eggs 97–98, 101–105, 111
Eisenhower, Dwight 33
EJ 82–84, 90–92
Ellison, Ralph 38, 52, 65, 122

Fall, Bernard B. 13
Faulkner, William 122, 124, 136–137, **137**, 201, 210
FBI interview 25–26
the fish tank 48
Florsheim Wingtips 116–117
Floyd, George 211
food: Hartman and 39, 44, 49–51, 78, 88, 106, 156; at Lompoc, generally 49, 50–51; and Operation Protein 97–98, 101–105
"Foots" *see* Morrill, Dwight
free spaces 114–115
freedom 156
furniture factory 134–135, 151

Gandhi, Mahatma 31
gang rape 74
Garcia, Boss 55
general population 48, 68, 187
Gilman, Richard **18**
good time (easy time) 63, 66–68, 76, 139–140, 160
"The Green, Green Grass of Home" 164
Gridley, Boss 46–47, 48
guards: coercive power 78, 93, 151–152; Eric conversing with 128; inmates taunting 158–159; isolation aiding 114; mail read 56, 57–58; Napoleon complex 103; on race riot 107, 126; racial distrust stoked by 96; serving dinner 158–159; tension among 130–131
Gulf of Tonkin Resolution 14

Harley Davidsons 71–72
Hartman, Dale 39–41, 42–43, 45, 73; aspirations 106; on Billy Brown 105–106; early life 43–44; on easy time 40–41, 75, 104, 136, 139, 151; and food 39, 44, 49–51, 78, 88, 106, 156; as "hippie" 51–52; life of, after prison 189–190; and Operation Protein 102–103, 104–105; on prison humiliations 46–47; on solidarity 61, 63, 95, 136, 139; striking 150–152, 155, 166, 177–178; transfer 182–183; and Winters, tension between 47, 51; work assignment 74, 105–106, 115
Hawk, Tommy 30–31
Heller, Joseph 158, 162, 165
Hell's Angels 183, 184

Index

hippies 51–52, 54, 56–57, 60–61; and low riders 71–72, 74–75; as "okay White boys" 101

the Hole 63, 153; banter 149–150, 162–163; Dwight and Eric sent to 148; Frank and Crow brought to 174; guards threatening 92–93; Hartman in 150–152, 155, 166, 177–178; meals 152, 156; prisoners released 177–178; solidarity 167–171, 183–185; talent shows 153–155, 163–164, 168–171; tear gas 172–173, 212

Humphreys, Lester W. 6

I-Block *see* the Hole
injustice, systemic 127–128, 205, 208
inmate strike 61–63, 77–78, 93–94, 107; demands for 77–79, 141–142, 144, 145; end 176–180; in furniture factory 135–136, 138–140, 145, 150–151, 155, 177, 184; leaders of, separated 178; lessons 155–156; meals 142–143, 144–145; organizing for 61–65, 71, 77–80, 120, 126, 130; over cigarettes 135, 138; people changed by 180–181; prison response 138, 144, 157–159, 171–172; *vs.* race riot 60–61; and racial tension 205; reporting 177; sit down tactics 175; slogan 95, 97, 103, 143; in sports 85; spreading 145; transcending race 143–144, 169–171, 183–185, 205; violence and 146–147; *see also* solidarity; Surratt, John

inmates: as expendable 113; illness feigned 102; institutionalization 118; returning to prison 118–120, 131, 152, 190–191; in the late sixties 1; solidarity among 60–64, 167–171, 183–185; vocational training 79, 128, 177; *see also* Black inmates; hippies; Latino inmates; low riders; Native inmates

Intruder in the Dust (Faulkner) 136–137, *137*
Invisible Man (Ellison) 38, 41, 52, *53*, 65, 69, 122

Jackson, Boss 84–85, 90, 100
Jenkins, L.V. *6*
Johnson, Lyndon 14, 16, 19
Joplin, Janis 156
jury summons 160
justice: peace and 19; and struggle 211–212; *vs.* systemic injustice 127–128, 205, 208

Keimer, Warden 129, 137–138, 146, 177, 180
Keith, William 138, 141, 177, 180; correctional philosophy 60; Dwight and Eric detained by 146–148
Kennedy, John 12, 14, 15
King, Martin Luther, Jr. *10*, 10–11, 31; assassination 22, *23*, 61, 63; Occidental visit 16, 17, *18*, 18–19, 204; on poverty 16, 17, 19, 33; Riverside Church speech 16–17; on Vietnam War 16–17, 168
Korean War 160–161
Ku Klux Klan *6*

labor struggles 133
Lakers 80, 85
Latino inmates 63, 81, 96; attempts to recruit 63, 66, 80, 104, 108–109; as Chicanos 97; guards frisking 131
leadership 101
levitation 169–171
liberation 26
literature: Eric teaching 52, 65, 123, 133, 177, 195–196, 201–202; in prison 66, 68–69, 78, 86–88, 122–123, 124–126, 128–129; and social change 79, 157, 163
Little Joe 158–159, 169–170, 184
Little John *see* Surratt, John
lockdown 144, 156, 174–176
Locksley 156–158
Lompoc Federal Correction Institution *45*, 59; arrival 45–48; beatings 173, 176; books 66, 68–69, 78, 86–88, 122–123, 124–126, 128–129; correctional philosophy 60; farm 121–122, 123; food 49, 50–51; levitating 169–171; parents visiting 95, 109; transfer 42–45; work 41, 66–67, 74–76, 98
Low Rider (inmate) 71–72, 77, 81
low riders 51, 54, 67, 154; basketball games 71–72, 81; as basketball observers 92–93; Black inmates assaulted by 130; honorary 183; race riot started by 57; recruiting 63, 66, 80

M-Unit 73, 98, 114
MacArthur, Douglas 161
mail: guards reading 56, 57–58; in M-Unit 94–95; rules 58–59, 78–79, 131
Malcolm X 124–126, *125*, 129, 143, 145, 209
March on Washington 11
marijuana 52, 62, 67, 165, 190–191
Martinez, Boss 140–141, 145, 146
mass movements 11; *see also* civil rights movement
medical care 59, 79, 177, 181
Melville, Herman 177
mess hall: Eric cleaning 75–76, 101–102; food 50–51; integrating 143–145; and Operation Protein 97–98, 101–105; racial segregation of 50
Mexicans *see* Latino inmates
Montgomery bus boycott 10–11, 17
Moore, John T. *6*
Morgan, Boss 69
Morrill, Dwight *27*, *200*; arrival of, at Lompoc 59; as basketball player 72, 83–84, 91–92, 99–101, 109; as "Bigfoot" 84, 90–91; as draft resister 30–31, *32*, 33–34, 36–37; Eric meeting 26–27; gregariousness 38; in the Hole 150–152, 168, 170, 178, 183–184, 186; inmate strike 63–64, 77, 79, 95, 108, 140–146; in later life 199; levitating Lompoc 170; recruitment attempts 77, 127; reduced sentence 181–182; singing in talent show 154, 168; on slogan 95; Warden Keith

Index

and 146–148, 152–153; work assignment 74
Morrison, Toni 143
Multnomah County Jail *34*
Myers, Hardy 28–30

Native Americans 113, 185
Native inmates: basketball played by 81, 89, 110–113; in the Hole 184; recruiting 63
Native Son (Wright) 123
Newhall, Eric: arraignment 28, 30–33, *32*; as basketball player 11, 72, 82–85, 99–100, 116; childhood picketing experience 7–9; Chuy approaching 96–99; draft refused 24–26; and Dwight, as crime partners 166; as English major 12–13, 15; and farm clerk job 98, 104, 107, 121, 134, 137–138; in graduate school 190, 195–196, 201; on inmate strike 62, 136, 139; journal 187–188; jury summons 160; at marshal's office 35–37; as Occidental student 11–16, 17–20; as organizer 133–134; promise of, to Crow and Bubba 123, 202, 204; reduced sentence 181–182; release 190; self-consciousness 11; sentencing 33–34; shoes 116–117; siblings 205, 206–208, 209–210, 211; statement 31–33; teaching at Occidental 114, 155, 168, *201*, 201–204, *202*, *212*; transfer 186–188; Warden Keith and 146–148, 152–153; work assignments 66–67, 75–76, 97–98, 107–108, 121–122, 123, 134; youth 5–11
Newhall, Eric, father of 5, 61, 158, 207; activism 7–9, 207, 209; books sent 78, 86–87, 88, 129, 131, 132–133; at courthouse 30–31, 34; on Vietnam War 15, 20–21; visits from 42, 95, 109
Newhall, Eric, mother of 5, 36; activism 207, 209; on conscientious objector status 21; at courthouse 30–31, 34; on King 10; visits from 42, 95, 109
Newhall, Eric, wife of *see* Angela
Newhall family: color line 199, 205–209, 210; home *7*, 206–207, 208; moving to Portland 5–6
Ngubeni, Tim *203*

Obama, Barack *203*, 204
O'Brien, Boss 86–88, 98, 107–108, 121, 127–129, 131–132
O'Brien, Tim 162
Occidental College: anti-apartheid rally *203*, 204; Eric teaching 114, 155, 168, *201*, 201–204, *202*, *212*; integration 204; King's visit 16, 17, *18*, 18–19, 204; Whiteness 12–13, 123, 202
Operation Protein 97–98, 101–105
Oregon, history of 5–6
Oregon History Project (website) *6*
Oregon State University *29*

Pauley Pavilion 191, 192, *193*, 194, 195
peace 19, 31, 33, 205
Phenomenal Snuffy 110–113, 175
police racism *6*, 9, 93, 131, 191, 211
political theory 115
Portland, Oregon: culture of, generally 22, 127–128; move to 5; segregation 5–6, 206–208
poverty, war on 16, 17, 19, 33
prejudice *vs.* discrimination 19; *see also* racism
prison: admission of crime in 76–77; dehumanization 68, 103–104, 131, 146, 165; good behavior 67–68; as "house of the dead" 99; lack of privacy 38, 56, 57–59; policies 86–87; returning to 118–120, 131, 152, 190–191; school as 201; segregation 50, 51, 58, 95; slavery 121; units in 73–74; Vietnam vets 164–165; violence 44, 60–61, 74, 130, 134; and war, links between 136; *see also* guards; Lompoc Federal Correction Institution; Rocky Butte Jail
prison psychiatrist 74, 79, 146, 177
prison slang 46, 83, 135, 141
Prisons and Prisoners in the Works of William Faulkner (Newhall) 201
"pruno" 82
Pullen, James 153–155, 163, 168
"punkin'" 83

race: basketball and 54–55, 71–72, 81–85; consciousness 60–61; inmates segregated by 50, 51, 58, 95; solidarity transcending 143–144, 169–171, 183–185, 205
race riot: Bubba and Crow on 126–127; Cohen's experience 63–64; predictions 56–57, 77–78, 106–107, 129–130; solidarity as answer 60–61
racism: in *Invisible Man* 65; legislation's effect 19; in mixed-race families 199, 207, 209; overt *vs.* covert 205, 208; police *6*, 9, 93, 131, 191, 211; restrictions 195; and school-to-prison pipeline 198–199; as White problem 209
Redburn, Boss 51, 75–76, 86, 96, 101–104
rehabilitation 50, 58, 60, 128–129, 165; guards opposed to 130; as talk 46–47, 103, 115, 121, 136, 165
rez ball 110–111
Rocky Butte Jail 37–43; dinner 38–39; Eric's parents visiting 42; lack of privacy 38; length of stay 40–41
Running Wolf, David 110–113, 175, 185
Russell, Bertrand 15

Sartre, Jean-Paul 15
Schwartz, Boss 48–49, 55, 148, 160; and draft resisters 67; in Korea 160–161; mail read by 57–58, 65; working in the Hole 158–160, 170
segregation: neighborhood 5–6, 199, 206–208, 211; in prison 50, 51, 58, 95

Selective Service System (SSS) *see* the draft
self-respect 189–190
sex club 105–106, 150–151
sexual violence 74, 105–106
Slaughter, John 204, **204**
slogan 95, 97, 103, 143
smack talk 116, 183, 192
snitches 141, 153, 166, 176
Snuffy 110–113, 175
social change: leadership 121; literature's role 79, 157, 163; and "long-distance runners" 130
social engagement 114
Socrates 20
solidarity: abstract *vs.* real 80, 147, 155; beyond prison 117–118, 190–195; formation 103; in the Hole 167–171, 183–185; isolation threatening 114; in mess hall 143, 144–145; and move to E-Unit 108; *see also* inmate strike
Sonny *see* Stark, Sonny
Spike 53–54
Spock, Benjamin 32–33
sports 85
Stark, Sonny 161–162, 163–164, 178; Eric and 165–168, 178–179; on tear gas 173; war service of 164–165, 166–168, 178–179
Stevens, Wallace 106
Stockton, Boss 55, 57–59
Stride Toward Freedom (King) **10**, 10–11
strike *see* inmate strike
Student Non-Violent Coordinating Committee (SNCC) 204, 207
Students for a Democratic Society (SDS) 62
Surratt, John 51–52, 54, 55–57, 81; background 62, 115, 157; and Boss Keith 60, 141, 150, 153; on Eric's reduced sentence 182; on furniture factory workers 134–136, 138; on guards "winning" 180; on history 161; in the Hole 150–153, 155, 156–157, 159–161, 169, 171, 178; information gathered by 51, 60, 107; on inmates striking 61–64, 95–96, 120–121, 126–127, 131, 138, 140; as Little John 155; on Malcolm X 125–126; pessimism 89; on race riot 60–62, 77, 106–107, 126–127, 129–130; as singer 155, 169, 178; on solidarity 60–64, 77–80, 95–96, 98; transfer 186
Sweet Pool (James Pullen) 153–155, 163
systemic injustice 127–128, 205, 208

taboos, prison 49–50
talent shows 153–155, 163–164, 168–171
tear gas 172–173, 175–176, 212
television, impact of 9

The Things They Carried (O'Brien) 162
Thompson, Boss 148
Thompson, Fred 103
"throwaway people" 143
Tim 82–84, 91–92, 99–101
Treadwell, Boss 154, 156
Truman, Harry 161

UCLA 20, 22
Unitarian Church 26
United States: division in 162, 205, 209, 210–212; foreign and domestic policy 16–17, 19, 33; imperialism 13–14, 15–16, 17, 33; violence 17

Vandenberg Air Force Base 56, 57, 78, 149
verbal harassment 48
Vietnam Moratorium Day **29**
Vietnam War: and the draft 14–15; historical context 13–14, 161; King on 16–17, 168; prison and, links between 136; and "tunnel rats" 179; veterans 164–165, 166–168
Vietnam War opposition 15–17, 19, 20–21; Eric's statement 31–33; Unitarian Church supporting 26; *see also* draft resisters
violence: domestic 43–44; government purveying 17; and pacifism 21; police 9, 93, 211–212; prison 44, 60–61, 74, 130, 134; *see also* race riot
vocational training 79, 128, 177
Voting Rights Act 16

Washington, D.C., riots **23**
Watts Uprising 17–18
weightlifting, protein for 97–98, 101–102, 104
"The White Cliffs of Dover" 153–154, 163, 168
White people: avoiding discussion of racism 205–208, 209, 210–211; distrust 108–109, 143, 185; fighting racism 209, 211
White privilege 209–210
Williams, Boss 151
Winters, Martin 42, 45, 47, 48, 142; anger 49, 52, 64, 67; attempted recruitment 64; and Hartman, tension between 47, 51; as "low rider" 54; and Spike 53–54
Woody, Elizabeth 199, **200**
Woolworth's sit-in 8–9
Wright, Richard 123

the yard 54–55; as *agora* 61; guards' control 84–85, 92–93; interracial conversation 101; *see also* basketball games, interracial
youth 155–156